Digital Governance and Digital Politics in South Asia

Digital Governance and Digital Politics in South Asia

Editors
Dipankar Sinha
Samir Sharma

BLOOMSBURY
NEW DELHI • LONDON • OXFORD • NEW YORK • SYDNEY

BLOOMSBURY INDIA
Bloomsbury Publishing India Pvt. Ltd
Second Floor, LSC Building No. 4, DDA Complex, Pocket C – 6 & 7,
Vasant Kunj, New Delhi, 110070

BLOOMSBURY, BLOOMSBURY ACADEMIC INDIA and the Diana logo are trademarks of Bloomsbury Publishing Plc

First published in India 2025
This export edition published 2025

Bloomsbury Academic India
An imprint of Bloomsbury Publishing Plc

ISBN: HB: 978-93-56409-37-8; eBook: 978-93-56407-87-9
2 4 6 8 10 9 7 5 3 1

Typeset by Manipal Technologies Limited
Printed & bound in India

Contents

Acknowledgements

From its inception as a 'concept note' for an International Conference at the Department of Political Science, St Joseph's College (North Point) in Darjeeling, India, in mid-September 2022 to its transformation into a published volume by Bloomsbury, this journey has indeed been memorable. Due to various reasons, not every chapter articulated within the confines of that conference has found a place within these pages. However, the remaining gaps have been enriched through the commissioning of individual chapters for the volume. Each contribution is a window to the different aspects of the 'digital' in South Asia; nonetheless, in the pursuit of this exploration, certain South Asian countries, notably Bhutan and Afghanistan, have remained elusive, serving as reminders of the challenges inherent in unifying South Asia as an analytical whole. At a different level, this has unfortunately remained entrenched in the historical narrative and the present complexities of the region.

A defining attribute of this volume lies in its reliance upon emerging scholarship to understand the intricate theme of the 'digital' in South Asia. Here, the editors extend their heartfelt gratitude to the contributors of the individual chapters, whose cooperation throughout the review and publication phases has been effectual in further grasping the concept of the digital in South Asia. Anonymous reviewers, through their invaluable comments and suggestions, have been immensely helpful in enriching the volume. Of course, no word is final in the realm of the social sciences, and through this volume, our intent has only been to inaugurate dialogues concerning the 'digital' in South Asia, harbouring hope for their perpetuation, with an ever-expanding scope.

`In this regard, special recognition is owed by the editors to Mr R. Chandra Sekhar and the entire editorial team at Bloomsbury, whose support has propelled this volume to fruition. Mr Chandra Sekhar's openness and accommodation of our requirements are greatly appreciated. The editors wish to thank Fr Dr Donatus Kujur SJ, the Principal of St Joseph's College (North Point), Darjeeling, for his great enthusiasm for the publication of this volume. Fr Kujur's encouragement and the provision of a generous platform through the college's Department of Political Science have certainly facilitated the realisation of this volume.

On his part, Dipankar wishes to dedicate this volume to the people of the Darjeeling hills, with the hope that one day, they will be able to reap the real benefits of digital governance, shorn of rhetorical excess, in their everyday lives. Words are not sufficient to thank his family (along with four pets) for the continuous display of tolerance. A heartfelt acknowledgement is also reserved by Samir for his partner and wife, Pritaya, for her love and friendship, and to Kashvii, his daughter, for all the blissful distractions. Samir dedicates this volume to his late mother, Renuka Devi Sharma—*Ama*—who, without a doubt, would have been delighted to hold it in her hands.

Dipankar Sinha and Samir Sharma

Figures

Annexure

Tables

Abbreviations

CAGR	Compound Annual Growth Rate
DBT	Direct Benefits Transfer
DFS	Digital Financial Services
GoI	Government of India
GST	Goods and Services Tax
IBEF	India Brand Equity Foundation
IMPS	Immediate Payment Service
MeitY	Ministry of Electronics and Information Technology
mSTAR	Mobile Solutions Technical Assistance and Research
NACH	National Automated Clearing House
NDA	National Democratic Alliance
NEFT	National Electronic Fund Transfer
NPCI	National Payments Corporation of India
PoS	Point of Sale
PMGDISHA	Pradhan Mantri Gramin Digital Saksharta Abhiyan
PMJDY	Pradhan Mantri Jan Dhan Yojana
QR	Quick Response
RBI	Reserve Bank of India
RTGS	Real Time Gross Settlement
SEWA	Self-Employed Women's Association
USD	US Dollars
TRAI	Telecom Regulatory Authority of India
UPI	Unified Payments Interface
USAID	United States Agency for International Development

Introduction

Dipankar Sinha and Samir Sharma

At the very outset, let us clarify that in addressing the exceedingly complex if not outrightly ambiguous theme this volume seeks to adopt the worm's view, organically tied to the reality down below. This view, context-sensitive and bottom-up, is distinct from its alternative, the aerial orientation of a bird's-eye view. Admittedly, no amount of work can be comprehensive enough to embrace all the existing and emerging issues embedded in the process of digitalisation of South Asia. This volume is no exception in this regard. Still, the value of the analyses made here by the contributors hailing from different corners of South Asia lies in raising and reconsidering some of the most vital concerns associated with the concept and practise of governance and the politics of the digital, much of which, to add, are emergent issues.

Two key concepts—digital governance and digital politics—guide the writings in this volume. The common thread of the contributions here lies in contesting the techno-solutionist approaches which, as part of promoting over-simplified solutions to highly complex problems, valourises digital technology as the gold standard. In such endeavours of ours, South Asia is the specific locale. Digital governance (which incorporates 'digital government' but goes much beyond in both depth and spread) and digital politics are not exactly synonymous, but they are closely linked concepts. The inevitable but somewhat fledgling and problematic linkage of the two key concepts constitutes the mainstay of this volume. Digital politics critically investigates the emergence and installation of digital technologies and the roles they play in contemporary times. In order to do so, such politics, through a host of actions and processes at the base, realises and utilises potential power emanating from the combination of data, information, communication, knowledge, sociality and identities. It is positioned to enrich a critical understanding of how new technologies are designed, circulated, regulated and consumed. Here, with the understanding that the whole process has a great impact on the construction and generation of the knowledge system we intend to go deeper into, the purpose is to scrutinise the kind of politics promoted by the zealous promoters of 'governance', in which the ruling establishment acts as the vanguard of a set of rules, norms, mechanisms, sentiments, conducts, behaviours and practices by 'steering' the state, market and civil society in a given direction. We assert that when it comes to governing the digital in a strategised way, technology is steadfastly presented as 'autonomous', which in turn induces us to believe, in a totally superficial manner, that when it comes to exploring 'digital governance', politics is unnecessary and/or redundant, if not outright illegitimate. It may well be described as the 'politics of depoliticisation'. The basic logic that guides such a dictum is that both 'digital' and 'governance' are refined, standardised, nuance-free, decontextualised and made-to-order concepts 'above politics'. With a narrow view of 'governance' bereft of its inherently ethical–moral and equity dimensions, the emerging sociability, which is both the cause and consequence of the digitalisation process, is sought to be made 'apolitical' by way of such false and misleading propositions. The major motive behind such a black-boxing act is to transform the polity into a technopoly in which, despite the tall claim of predictive accuracy, the issues of large-scale asymmetry, inequality and marginalisation remain hidden. Dramatic as it may sound, the bottom line of the design being referred to here is 'adjust or die'.

The attempt comes with a mix of coercive and persuasive power generation; it seeks to erase the diversity, aberrations, tensions and frictions down the line as they are found to be disturbing the 'friction-free' implementation of pre-fixed, readymade public policies. The attempt is undemocratic to the core as it evades public evaluation and matters of opinion and consent. This is exactly why deliberations in an organic counter-perspective, hinted above, assume prime importance. Such a perspective makes us aware of the two major ways by which the mechanistic and technocratic imposition of digitalisation is countered: first, by the limitations and constraints existing at the grassroots level, which often assume a nagging character; second, by way of innovative endeavours, including some subversive acts, which take advantage of the power of the digital to create and disseminate new ideas and new practices. Both the ways incidentally reinforce the claim that where there is power there is counterpower, a point to which we will revert in the subsequent discussion.

Concerning South Asia, it is well known that while the region is marked by historical, cultural and social commonalities and ties, there are many divergences as well. Leaving aside the ancient and medieval times, if we only consider 'modern' South Asia and the prospects of integration of the region, the scenario has remained perpetually problematic. Shared understanding and the perceived sense of 'being together' are often buttressed by mutual suspicion and in some cases by outright hostility. The reference to regional integration is important because there is a consensus that the potential of digitalisation, or for that matter digital governance, can be harnessed better with regional cooperation, rather than in isolation.

The benefits of regional cooperation in developing digital public infrastructure, data protection and cybersecurity, to mention just a few items, are particularly mentioned in the global vision of multilateral digital cooperation. In another part of the world, the European Union (EU) is doing it seriously. To make a brief reference to the EU endeavour in this context, its existing digital regulatory framework has recently been further firmed up by the Digital Security Act (DSA), formally known as the Regulation on a Single Market for Digital Services, 2022. For the member states, the DSA has the goal of creating a safe, predictable, and trustworthy online environment, and protecting the digital space against the spread of illegal content, online disinformation and other societal risks (Digital Services Act, 2022). The EU member states are mandated to adjust their respective digital governance policies in accordance with the EU regulatory framework.

In yet another part of the world, the ASEAN (Association of South East Asian Nations) has the projected ambition of becoming a leading digital community and economic bloc—powered by secure and transformative digital services, technologies and ecosystems—which is expected to be matured through the Digital Master Plan, 2025. The Plan asserts that 'achieving such a vision is a great prize which will require governments, regulators and market players to work together in complementary ways' (Digital Master Plan 2025).

It is clear that when it comes to South Asia, the SAARC (South Asian Association for Regional Cooperation) has not been able to be as proactive as either the EU or the ASEAN, or for that matter, even the SADC (Southern African Development Community). To a certain extent, because of the perceived and real power asymmetry vis-à-vis other states of the region, India has not been able to play the proactive role played by Germany in the case of the EU and South Africa in the SADC. Amidst periodic calls for inter-regional connectivity and technological cooperation, too many political and security issues have come in the way of forming a minimal consensus which could act as the foundation of multilateral cooperation. Even economic cooperation, which is widely considered to be the best starter in initiating and intensifying regional cooperation, remains quite elusive in the region. If this is the case with a tried and tested path like economic cooperation, it is not surprising that the synergised digital initiative in South Asia will continue to remain underdeveloped.

Then again, more fundamentally, the prospect and effectiveness of multilateral cooperation in digital governance depends on the respective capabilities of each state of the region. To develop such capabilities there has to be a judicious mix of material resources and human development. Material resources are a necessary but not a sufficient condition for (digital) development. Human-centric capabilities play a vital role as they inscribe, with a normative impulse, human agency and choice as essential components of subjective well-being. On this count, we put forth a provocative question—governance for whom? This question in turn gives rise to a metaphor-laced ancillary question: are the states in South Asia suffering from the 'cart before the horse' syndrome insofar as prioritising digital governance over human development is concerned? The questions can be addressed to a great extent if South Asia is problematised as a zone of 'transition and tension' vis-à-vis the process of digitalisation. In some cases, the transition is even found in the reverse gear, as in the case of Afghanistan. The main reason for not having an essay on the contemporary digital governance ecosystem in Afghanistan in the volume is that with the Taliban recapturing power on 15 August 2021, there has been a dramatic decline in the way digital governance was being promoted in that country four years after the end of the Taliban 1.0 regime. Among other ways, around the year 2005, the Ministry of Communication and Information Technology of the Government of Afghanistan started utilising the funds provided liberally by the Afghanistan Reconstruction Trust Fund as part of the wider initiative on capacity building vis-à-vis e-governance. But as far as the present scenario is concerned, the digital, at least the way it is being conceptualised here, has no place at all in the Taliban 2.0 agenda of governance and politics.

However, in the kingdom of Bhutan, Information and Communications Technology (ICT) is a core concern for 'governance' as well as for the achievement of the Millennium Development Goals. Along with this, the role of ICT is envisioned as one that would enhance the realisation of its Gross National Happiness (GNH). During its formative years, the digital policy in Bhutan was marked by a disjuncture between the 'objectives/expectations' and 'human/institutional' capacity (World Bank, 2010), but contemporary examples show that Bhutan has been experimenting with a 'do-it-yourself approach to digital government' where the bureaucracy is both a participant and the creator of digital services (UNCTAD 2023). This is expected to enable Bhutan to customise the requirements as per the needs of the country. These developments have also made possible the realisation of a new digital identity system (National Digital Identity) that combines five components or levels. It is too early to fully gauge the implications of the above, but it is clear that while Bhutan was cautious in its adoption of modernisation, in the case of digitalisation, the response is rather forthcoming. Nevertheless, this points towards the need for a greater understanding of the predicaments posed by a bureaucracy-led ICT policy given our concern with a worm-eye view of the digital realities of South Asia.

* * *

If the aforementioned contentions sound very 'political', it is what it is, something which we will subsequently explain. To put the matter straight, digital technologies are not natural formations. They are the innovative products of human endeavour. It does not require any special effort to understand that a great leap forward in digital development is important, but it has to be accompanied by substantial attention to the human factor. This is a serious issue because, in the ultimate analysis, effective development has to have technology in the service of the people. If it is the other way around, it becomes an issue which the researchers, especially from the Global South, are bound to address. Despite some instances of research, especially regarding accessibility and affordability amidst the digital divide, there always remains scope to sneak into the lanes and by-lanes of the information superhighway and come up with pragmatic narratives keeping South Asia in mind. Such a genre of research is to avoid a monochromatic approach by acknowledging the great potential of digital technology but not uncritically promoting it. Let us add in this context that the contributions in this volumetry are to avoid the linearity and neatness of the 'container approach' to the (digital) technology-governance interface and resort to a pragmatic orientation.

Technology has been an ever-growing concern of social science thinking for a considerably long time. However, a profound focus on 'digital' has become a major concern in social science literature, especially since the late twentieth century. It is obvious that the studies of the digital coincide with its emergence and development in society. Such studies are regularly witnessing several epistemic and methodological streams. To cut a long story short, the sociological and political-economic analyses have been gradually complemented by a steep cultural turn. At such a turning point, the sophisticated theoretical expositions of representational and interpretive practices and meaning-making strategies are constructed to understand the complex relations of human experience and the production of knowledge. Against such a backdrop, since the advent of the twenty-first century, a niche has been crafted by viewing digital cultures as overwhelmingly performative. Subsequent efforts are being made to explain how they condition and are themselves shaped by multi-layered techno-social processes and agencies, and what kind of new possibilities they offer in terms of performative practices and interventions (for instance, Leeker, Schipper and Beyes 2017). This volume, however, has a more open-ended political orientation. Our goal here is not only to explore but to foreground, reinforce and recontextualise politics in the interest of the public by injecting and sustaining criticality vis-à-vis the phenomenon of digital governance. For a better understanding of what this 'politics' is all about, the argument put forth by David Berry in *The Critical Theory of the Digital* (2014) may be noted. On developing a critical theory as an antidote to the 'authoritarian computational epistemology', Berry provides a useful insight (2014: 12). With a dual focus on thinking and practice, he notes that humanities and social sciences need to understand and critique the computational as a ubiquitous social phenomenon. Berry puts simultaneous stress on the act of questioning the digital (he also uses the term 'computational') and on creating the possibility of thinking in an age when thinking is increasingly being delegated to machines. He adds that as our societies are increasingly becoming computational, along with the tendency of computational systems to reify all aspects of everyday life, it is crucial that we attend to the mechanisation of reification and the dangers of these processes being crystallised into systems, institutions and consciousness itself. Berry expresses concern that this reified world, while being 'smart' and digital, is being increasingly colonised by computationally enhanced networks, objects and subjects. In the ensuing discussion, we gradually unravel digital politics in terms of two major registers: first, in terms of the dialectic of physical 'connections' and digital 'connectivity', with the assertion that effectively, physical interactions remain important in the era of the progress of virtual connectivity; and second, in terms of the complex and highly dynamic state–market relations, which have become the major force in contemporary development.

The coming of the digital offers unprecedented promises and opportunities, but it also has its quota of constraints and risks. Concerning both digital governance and digital politics, there is thus an impending need to examine the existing frameworks, institutional mechanisms, and regulatory policies and norms, many of which are in a transitional phase. In this process, *networking* becomes a core issue as development policies, programmes and projects are more and more being determined by the informational mode and its constitutive networks as *space of flow*. In this transition the act of governance is supposed to acquire inward flexibility to a considerable extent.

Such flexibility is rationalised on the grounds that the networking-in-governance mechanism requires interrelated organisational transformation as the most viable way to integrate differentiated actor systems and adjust to problems that cannot be tackled by existing formal institutional configurations. But the fact of the matter is that if in the zeal for initiating such 'redemptive' flexibility, the networks themselves turn out to be exclusionary in nature, as they often do, the projected benefits will not only take a fairly long time to percolate to the grassroots level, they will also pose certain risks for those surviving at the bottom of the social and economic strata. Most important, it will subvert the spirit of redistributive justice without which the act of governing loses its soul and becomes hollow.

There is little doubt that digital governance via networking is an exceedingly dicey affair. Even Manuel Castells, who relentlessly emphasises the inevitability of the 'morphological transformation' through the advent of the network society, provides a clear note of warning about the 'potentially exclusionary' networks if they are not adequately managed and regulated. As Castells explains, networks being sets of interconnected nodes with hierarchy, the relationships between nodes are asymmetrical. To quote him:

> A network is simply a set of interconnected nodes. It may have a hierarchy, but it has no centre. Relationships between nodes are asymmetrical, but they are all necessary for the functioning of the network for the circulation of money, information, technology, images, goods, services, or people throughout the network. The most critical distinction in this organizational logic is not stability, but inclusion or exclusion. Networks change relentlessly: they move along, form and reform, in endless variation. Those who remain inside have the opportunity to share and, over time, to increase their chances. Those who drop out, or become switched off, will see their chances vanish. (1999: IV)

The most critical point in this organisational logic, as he points out, is 'to be or not to be' in the network. However, in a later article, Castells (2011: 773–787) seems to be more open to the possibility of 'counterpower'. Thus, even while acknowledging the hegemonic construction of network society, Castells takes care to refer to the mechanisms of resistance to conclude that at the end of the day, the power associated with the 'multidimensional' digital network is 'counterpower' (773). In effect, in what may be described as a paradox, when it comes to digital technologies the policy initiative is packaged with the promise of societal transformation for the welfare of the ordinary people, but it is often followed by the aggravation of inequalities, sourced from the steep digital divide in the tech ecosystem. Such a divide is political as it incorporates in itself a very high concentration of power, which, amidst numerous institutions, organisations and agencies, can be traced back to the oligopolistic ownership and control of the market by the Big Tech corporations. The 'new superpowers' often usurp the power of even the most powerful states of the world and transgress democratic space by private capital. Yet, in another paradox, which is no less political, people continue to devise ways to come to terms with the new technology, not just by indifference or adjustments, but even in some instances by creating counter-hegemonic spaces. In the specific context of South Asia, we find that adequate network management and regulations are both delicate and tricky, and there is hardly a clear and credible roadmap to follow. To make the networks accessible and inclusionary, regulatory mechanisms have to be put in place, not only for efficient and effective governance but also for the democratisation of power relations between the ruler and the ruled. Otherwise, the day-to-day deployment of engineered technology in the region will remain truncated, messy, chaotic and, to repeat, utterly exclusionary.

The coming of the digital also calls for a thorough scrutiny of the institutions to understand what the digital is all about in practice. In this context, Fernando Filgueiras and Virgilio Almeida (2020) offer a set of relevant questions while analysing why governing the digital world requires specific thinking about how institutions are built and how they can be effective in governing a complex world in which the 'die of the digital world' is cast by power relations involving governments, technological companies, civil society and international organisations. The questions raised by them are as follows: 1) How do these actors fit into the governance process of the digital world? 2) How is the governance of the digital world designed? 3) What institutions are needed in the digital world to constitute governance that results in the greatest benefit for society and that is resilient to face the different turbulent contexts that technological change carries?

* * *

The moot question is whether the promotion of digital governance in South Asian countries is keeping in mind the need for expanding the baseline of human development. The imagery of the 'cart before the horse', mentioned earlier, is important. A paper on '(De)Politicizing Information Technology: Towards an Inclusionary Perspective' (Sinha 2010: 2) has cited several instances from South Asia to arrive at the following observation:

> Information Technology (IT) in/for development has become both a catch-all term and an attractive political slogan. In effect IT is hyped as a sort of 'magic wand', at times on the basis of abstract models, that is supposed to eradicate social deprivation and economic disparity almost instantaneously… IT has a key role in the construction of a better economy, society and empowerment of ordinary people in developing countries. However, its uncritical promotion in communication about policy and political discourse—without taking into account the social reality that exists in developing countries… enforces certain closures… severely undermining diversity of opinions, the space for dissent and the need for democratic scrutiny, all of which are supposed to provide legitimacy for any public policy claiming to have problem-solving strategies.

The governance–politics linkage has always been important, but in the digital era it acquires new twists and turns which are much different from the analogue era. Social science research has to negotiate the 'new reality' that confronts us. Today we are increasingly pushed into the whirlwind of datafication which is taking over our own experiential reality. We are being subtly dictated to, without having much knowledge of them, by up-end technologies like algorithms, artificial intelligence, robotics and machine learning and innovative formats like metadata. Even the much-publicised Web 2.0 platforms are supposedly revolutionising the dynamics of contemporary information and communication order by user-generated/-driven content (such as blogs, tagging, comments and likes–dislikes ratings). But while they are found to be long on participatory potential at least up until now they are yet to show substantive and sustained citizen engagement and participation (Merchant 2012: 263–281). All these agencies and mechanisms have a common thread, taking in our private opinions, self-expressions and preferences under surveillance and scattering them, only to unilaterally determine the contours and spirit of public policies. It is true that the proliferation of social media and social networking sites, in converting the users into 'prosumers' (combined roles of producers and consumers), has resulted in major sources of information creation, gathering and circulation. It has also put the hitherto dominant print and electronic media under severe strain, and some even in survival crises. But to what extent the still 'individualised' social media remains an agency with 'noise value' and to what degree it is able to co-create and reshape the dominant architecture of information and communication are subjects and issues that need further watch and intense scrutiny. Few would doubt that the emergence and transgression of new technology, wryly called immersive or transgressive technology, in our everyday life is a major mediating factor in creating the difference between the two periods—analogue and digital. At the same time, it is important to keep in mind that behind this transition lies the invincible power of the global high-tech giants which are bent on controlling thought and action, a process which is being critiqued as emergent digital (neo) colonialism.

In the arena of public policy formulation and implementation, it is only obvious that the governance–politics linkage will be very much at play. It is because public policies are the means to achieve a proclaimed end—development as social transformation for the benefit of all. The twenty-first century has revealed how policy discourse spills over public discourse in promoting 'good governance' in terms of 'inclusive technology'. 'Information' in such designed discourse moves far ahead of land, labour and capital as a foundational resource, and it continues to be steadily nurtured by digital networks. There is no problem as such with the promotion of information till the information loop and trope become more and more technocratic, and information loses its organic character. In such cases, to reiterate a point stated earlier, the human-sourced 'connections' continue to be sacrificed at the pedestal of technology-propelled 'connectivity'. This is exactly where our concern lies.

* * *

The generation and intervention of appropriate politics become very important as they make us aware that contrary to the dominant claim, technology is not neutral. As a classic observation goes, technology is neutral insofar as no one knows what technology is used for and so far it has never been used. Technology, even in the much-vaunted 'cutting edge' category, lacks its own consciousness and will. At the same time, technology's fate in terms of its diffusion depends overwhelmingly on those who run governance. Beyond its purely physical form, the unequal patterns of privilege and exclusivity emerge when technology is embedded with knowledge of what it is used for and how it works, which incidentally is a major concern of governance. Nor can governance be mechanically neutral. For the developing states of South Asia, which are struggling to provide basic amenities to the majority of people, governance must adopt an inclusionary bias to serve the underprivileged, marginalised segments of the population. Digital technology cannot be out of this ambit simply by showcasing its potential and power.

'Governance' in the contemporary sense entails collective action based on certain 'rational' parameters. Proponents of governance are relentlessly advocating open, transparent, responsible, accountable and predictable policymaking through economic deregulation and political decentralisation. The act (rather business) of governance, along with its derivatives like 'good governance' and 'democratic governance', engraves power play and governance structures, combining political and organisational forms, and exudes power through a set of rules for managing a collective enterprise. Decision-making lies at the heart of governance, but who makes decisions with what degree of accountability and transparency have become cardinal issues in understanding the nature of governance. For any country, including those in South Asia, the questions that come to the fore are the following: 1) Is governance being appropriately distributed in an inequitable society? 2) Is there any significant change in policy formulation and decision-making process beyond the apparent distribution of public policies and programmes?

The questions relate to what we have described as the new dynamics between the state and the market. Also, we are addressing the main theme in a backdrop of power play in which the (welfare) state is in a very awkward position vis-à-vis the market. The market, which is overwhelmingly leveraged by the oligopolistic control of global tech corporations, has an unabashed top-heavy capital-led profit-centrism, with a strong operational logic of its own. The market-nurtured, high-tech-sourced networks bypass many areas and many people, and reforms occur somewhere up above for some exceptionally privileged people. As a result, ordinary people are marginalised and even wasted, which leads to a diminished credibility of governance. Social and political unrest is an unavoidable outcome of such a twisted process, which periodically gives rise to volatile situations. In the context of South Asia, Afghanistan is an extreme case, and Sri Lanka, Pakistan and Bangladesh are the 'notable' ones, at least at this moment. This, however, does not necessarily mean that other countries of South Asia are providing the 'best practices' of governance.

* * *

To situate the problem in a kaleidoscopic landscape, the twin issues of digital access and affordability are integrally linked to the backstage process of democratisation. Democratisation is expected to be on friendly terms with human development, though the relations between the two may at times become tenuous and stressed. But insofar as South Asia is concerned when it comes to democratisation, the process is either absent or at best in a 'hide-and-seek' mode. There is an evident thrust on one-way, unilateral information dissemination by the ruling establishments, which tends to arbitrarily define and decide what people need. In the mainstream discursive regimes, digital technology is considered to be too sophisticated an artefact to be brought under the purview of general public consultation and discussion. Contrary to the culture of transparency constantly publicised by the advocates of network governance, digital technology, 'implanted' from above, runs the risk of being non-interactive insofar as public communication is concerned. This, in turn, gives rise to fear, mystification and false glorification of new technology, none of which is conducive to utilising its potential. The critiques of such a technocratic stance are becoming forceful. For instance, the official Indian approach to digital governance with the flagship programme of Digital India at the centrestage has invited critical observations, such as the following: 'The heady language of Digital India… divides in favour of a discourse that views the digital as a benign force that is autonomous and disembedded from the social, but which has the intrinsic power to transform the country into a modern, digital nation and its millions of people into "digital natives"' (Thomas 2019: 2–3).

There have been calls for the adoption of a pragmatic and bottom-up approach beyond mere expressions of 'good intentions' by the powers that be. Thus, Kenneth Keniston (2003: 14–28) focuses on the potential and predicaments of the Indian digital reality, which, as we see, are equally applicable to South Asia as a whole. The lessons are as follows:

- It should be introduced when (and only when) they constitute the most effective available way of meeting basic human needs and fulfilling fundamental human rights. Information and Communications Technology (ICT) can have a positive role in development, but it is neither a panacea nor necessarily the first line of attack in combating poverty, misery and injustice.
- It has to meet core human needs; the most creative use of ICT in development requires the use of the vast array of computer-based technologies to better meet local needs; local needs are to be defined by local people and not by 'well wishing' government officials, international aid agencies and NGOs who claim to know the grassroots level reality.
- Local language and local content are essential.
- Projects must be (or soon become) economically self-sustaining.
- Economic roots in the user communities are essential—otherwise, the projects vanish without a trace; warning about inflated rhetoric

and grandiose plans as the ratio of rhetoric to achievement is dangerously high.

- There should be no false idea of the trickle-down power of the flourishing sector of ICT as bridging the digital divide; the imperative that the ICT programmes are to reach and benefit the intended beneficiaries is complex and problematic.
- The experience of both success and failure vis-à-vis ICT for development within and between nations ought to be shared.
- The voices and interests of the disadvantaged and the digitally unempowered are to be represented in bodies concerning ICT policy regulation and infrastructure.

The digital governance ecosystem and its embedded politics concern a broad rubric of themes vis-à-vis South Asia: the digital space, sovereignty, cybersecurity, digital literacy, infrastructure and logistics, digital citizenship, identity construction, cyber-activism, subversion, dissent and protest, rhetoric, collective online action, social media and social networking, digital geopolitics and so forth. It is gratifying to note that they have in different degrees found a place in this volume. The essays here deal with diverse locations, experiences, images, understanding and interpretations. With a humanist orientation, they come together with the ambition of providing a little stimulus to the critical debate setting space vis-à-vis South Asia on a theme that affects our thinking and doing in everyday life.

As noted at the outset, through interlocking sub-thematic discourses, the volume seeks to interrogate the critical intersections of politics and governance in South Asia, with a focus on issues such as strategy, policies and standards, infrastructure, services, skills and capacity building, including insights on their performance and measurement. The main themes addressed by the essays are wide and include prospects and challenges of digital citizenship and political participation, social media activism, e-government and governance, ICT policy and digital finance and banking. Against this backdrop, the ensemble of essays attempts to unravel the linkages between digital governance and digital politics and concentrate on the emerging issues, challenges and predicaments of such linkages in South Asia, extending the analysis to include non-state actors and communities. It is time to provide an overview of the ten essays.

* * *

The first essay on 'Digital Finance and Digital Payments Interface in India: A Reality Check' by Bishal Rai examines the development trajectory and trends of Digital Financial Services (DFS) in terms of digital payments, effective since 2014. Digital Financial Services refers to the transition from cash to a digital ecosystem and is sought to be effected by a large volume of digital payments. The specific focus is on the volume and value of payments transacted through various digital platforms to date. Since 2014, India has made considerable progress in the field of financial inclusion by trying to bring as many people as practically possible under the banking system. Financial inclusion overlaps with the evolution of the DFS, and the process can be seen as one of the motivating forces to bring the country under the umbrella of Digital India. Various programmes such as the Pradhan Mantri Jan Dhan Yojna (PMJDY), popularly known as the JAM (Jan Dhan, Aadhaar, Mobile) trinity, demonetisation and the Goods and Services Tax (GST) initiated by the National Democratic Alliance (NDA) government provided an impetus for increasing usage of DFS. The journey of India's digital financial inclusion has been propelled through digital technology usage, high penetration of mobile phones and smartphones supplemented by low data costs and support from institutions such as the United States Agency for International Development (USAID) in partnership with non-profits such as FHI-360, IFMR-LEAD and Intellecap. The essay, however, argues that despite these interventions, India has not been able to take a major leap from the cash to the digital ecosystem as several contentious issues remain to be addressed.

The second essay entitled 'Digitalising the Census in India: Roadway to e-Governance?' by Nisha Tamang locates the 'paradigm shift' from a manual census to the modern data processing system within the framework of e-governance. It highlights the nature of the transition of the Indian census from paper to electronic in the form of self-enumeration. There is a particular focus on the role of GIS

(Geographical Information System) in census mapping. The essay suggests the implementation of a hybrid mode for the next census in 2021, which has been delayed due to the COVID-19 pandemic, arguing that unforeseen events like the pandemic can have a serious bearing on field-based data collection. It concludes that these issues call for a geospatial-based census enumeration which has a highly promising role in a country like India.

The third essay, 'Digital Technologies and Elections: Negotiating Key Challenges' by Tshumila Lama, discusses the use of digital technologies in governance and has a specific focus on elections. It argues that while digitalisation has increased efficiency and made the process easier and faster, the mode is not infallible. The essay examines the prospects of elections and digital technologies with a critical question—is India ready for more digitalisation of the election process? In this context, the essay flags issues of organisational and logistical challenges, alongside the expressed concern about the security of the electoral process and data protection. Assessing the role and transformations through digital technologies in the different stages of the election processes, the essay also critically analyses the major challenges posed by such transformations by taking into account the measures taken by the Election Commission of India (ECI) to tackle them.

The fourth essay by Jigme Yeshe Lama, titled 'Digital Politics of an Exiled State: The Case of the Tibetans in India', investigates the rise of digital politics among the Tibetans in exile. It explains how digital politics in the exiled Tibetan community has increased the 'secular' in a domain in which the 'religious' still holds the ultimate sway. While writings on Tibetan digital activism are in plenty, few have focused on the digital aspects of politics in the exile community. Ever since their exile in India and South Asia in 1950, the Tibetan government in exile, which is the Central Tibetan Administration (CTA), has provided a government for Tibetan refugees. In 2011, the 14th Dalai Lama relinquished his political powers in favour of a directly elected leader, and the consequent electoral politics led to the use of digital media in the exile community. Through the employment of digital mediums, the CTA is seen to be embracing digital governance. Against this backdrop, the essay argues that social media-mediated politics in exile has increased the notion of 'secularisation' in Tibetan society, leading to a rise in non-religious discourses in the exile political narrative. The essay concludes that the trend of embracing digital politics by the Tibetans in exile is also an innovative mode of bringing them closer to 'politics' in exile.

Looking at the larger backdrop of how digital and social media offer important new tools for social movements, activists and critics of the state elsewhere, the fifth essay on 'King of the Jungle': Digital Protest as Normative Disruptions in India's Northeast' by Kaustubh Deka stresses on the peculiarities that digital politics can assume in a securitised 'zone of exception' like India's Northeast. From innovative YouTube channels to radical Instagram pages, India's Northeast, as the essay notes, is undergoing a luminal phase of social restructuring, largely routed through the digital space. In such a space, a section of the youth has started critically interrogating the normative boundaries that have come to construe the region. These digital interventions have created 'frictions' in the social discourse of the region and provoked varied responses from the power structures. Through a few examples, the essay seeks to understand the different ways in which digital forums are providing the youth with innovative and at times disruptive methods of engaging with the existing narratives in the region. It is increasingly seen that from engagements with ecological themes and sharp expositions on issues like racial discrimination to various topics of existential strife, the digital lifeworld in the region has assumed much vibrancy.

The following two essays rest on certain developments in Nepal. The sixth essay, 'Evolution of Nepal's ICT Policies: In the Lens of Document Analysis' by Nischal Regmi and Shailesh B. Pandey, critically examines the evolution of Nepal's Information and Communication Technology (ICT) policies by interrogating some plans, policies, by-laws and acts published over a time span of more than three decades. Using document analysis techniques such as n-gram and topic modelling to characterise the policy focus in the selected time period, the contributors observe that Nepal's policies are largely informed by the global narratives of dominant digital technology. The focal point of the policy documents, as the argument goes, are umbrella terms such as 'information technology', 'information and communication technologies' and 'internet of things'. The inference is that the policy vision swings between the erection of new infrastructure and increasing access to the technology bundle. The essay notes an inherent bias whereby the rapid growth in infrastructure and its perceived access is seen as 'adequate' to derive benefit from new technologies. This, the argument follows, is evident from a lack of understanding of the ICT users and their needs, with very few discussions on digital inequality, and overlooking the role of prerequisite infrastructures for a properly functioning ICT infrastructure. Since the focus of the newer policy documents has made a terminological shift towards the 'internet of things', 'Big Data' and 'Digital Transformation', an evident trend is found in the technology bias of the policymakers. The contributors argue that these state-of-the-art terms along with their associated narratives are going to 'uncritically' shape the forthcoming ICT policies of Nepal. They conclude that the overall focus of the policies has been fixated on building physical infrastructure, and very little attention is paid to addressing the significant issues of digital inequality and the possible ill effects of ICT.

Shifting the analytical lens to the issue of identity in a digital age, in the seventh essay on 'Digital Re-fashioning of Identity: Insights from the Nepal Picture Library', Rahul Ganguly seeks to grapple with the questions of the 'digital' as a 'space' and its potential to re-imagine the nation in ways that challenge and go beyond the mainstream statist notions. This essay locates and interrogates the digital vis-à-vis the debates on the democratisation of historical imaginations, also identifying limits of the same. Taking up a strand of the democratisation argument, the effort is to understand the ways in which the digital operates and creates spaces for the (re)construction and performance of identities which may potentially challenge the hegemonic forms of constructions. Focusing on the Nepal Picture Library (NPL), the essay situates the discussions on the development of Nepal as a Hindu monarchy until 2008. Simultaneously, pointing out that the *Mulki Ain*, one of the foundational legal texts, effectively made Nepal an 'upper-caste Hindu country', the essay reveals how it led to the structural marginalisation of various ethnic groups and so-called lower-caste groups, and no less important, their 'erasure' from the public imagination of what it means to be a 'Nepali'. Analysing the NPL, an online photo archive, as a digital site for (re)fashioning the Nepali identity, the essay not only notes the importance of the archive as an agency to establish and expand the visual archive of Nepali social and cultural history, but it also interrogates the same to understand to what extent such an archive provides a route to (re)inscribing the previously eroded identities in the Nepali public consciousness.

Bangladesh occupies the centre stage of the eighth essay, 'Digital Politics in Bangladesh: Interactive Dynamics Between Practices, Public and Policy of the internet' by Ratan Kumar Roy and Preeksha Malhotra, which maps the digital culture and traces its role in giving birth to digital politics. While exploring such processes, the flagship campaign 'Digital Bangladesh', becomes the major focus. Here, the impact of the ambitious campaign is measured through its major visible outcomes and critical concerns—that too with a dual emphasis on media and politics. In light of the campaign, this essay examines the interface of technology and society—the interrelationship of certain practices, public and policy domains in governing the digital. The essay also takes into account the triangulation of these three factors in light of the political trajectory of 'digital Bangladesh'. The contributors also scrutinise the policies and legislative recourses like the amendments to the Information and Communication Technology (ICT) Act, 2006, the Digital Security Act, 2018 and the more recent Digital Data Protection Bill, 2022, to name a few, and discuss how they are perceived by the major stakeholders, especially the public.

The ninth essay, 'Hashtagification of Political Slogans: Catalysing Propagation of Political Narratives' by Rizvan Saeed, examines the case of Pakistan with regard to digital activism and the use of Twitter hashtags, which propagate or counter the political narratives by the two prominent political parties—Pakistan Tehreek-e-Insaf and Pakistan Muslim League. The analysis of Twitter hashtags, run by the political parties in very recent times, reveals the use of emotional appeals, internet memetics and networked support as vital tools to push political agendas in the digital sphere. Technological and social affordances of the platform, namely, digital anonymity, decentralisation, low transaction cost, easy reproducibility of the content and social accessibility facilitated the hashtagification process. The essay puts forth the argument that the process transforms political slogans into news stories and vice-versa, and visuals like memes are disseminated through organised online networks. These networks on their part amplify the propagation of hashtags on Twitter. The analysis also reveals that the digital engagement of political activists earns them privileged positions in 'information networks', also indicating some sort of enhancement of social capital. It is also argued that gradually Twitter users became a crowd-sourced political elite, the 'Networked Gatekeepers'. New political Twitter activists conform to the line of the 'gatekeepers' to propagate new political narratives and make their way upwards in the digital sphere.

The 10th and final essay, 'E-Governance and Cybercrime in Sri Lanka: A Study of Legislations' by Vishaka Suriyabandara, Vinsuka Kannangara and Sathya Gunawardana, based on an empirical study in Sri Lanka, identifies the factors behind the rising cyber crimes affecting the ICT sector. The survey makes use of questionnaires delivered to the employees in the ICT departments of several government organisations. Utilising this method, appropriate variables are measured and assessed on how they affect the IT sector. As there is no such study or research done related to cybercrimes and cybersecurity in Sri Lanka, the essay makes a significant contribution and will be of relevance to the policymakers in the government and the private IT and ICT sectors. Additionally, the study also looks at the cybercrime and cybersecurity architecture of Sri Lanka with special reference to the specific legislations which include the Electronic Transactions Act No. 19 of 2006, Computer Crimes Act No. 24 of 2007, Payment and Settlement Systems Act No. 28 of 2005, Payment Devices Frauds Act No. 30 of 2006 and the recently enacted Personal Data Protection Act No. 9 of 2022. The critical analysis followed by specific policy recommendations is done in the global and South Asian backdrops.

Conclusion

The discussion above and the essays that follow make it amply clear that digital governance is not a smooth outcome of some whimsical or random mix of digital technologies. One cannot just add an 'e' as a prefix to governance and remain complacent about an impending 'revolutionary' change. Enunciation of digital governance involves an indispensable, inscrutable and sensitive issue—to adapt the 'digital' in governance in order to generate the circulation and sustenance of 'systemic trust' in emerging technologies. It can be done by expanding opportunities for people at the ground level, including but going beyond strategic and economic interests. If there is at all a thumb rule for researchers working on the theme, it is this: rather than constructing a utopian state of digital technology governing people, the focus is to be made on the ways and means of governing such technologies in the public interest, for which governance is supposed to exist in the first place.

The editors have a modest hope that this volume will ensure in its own little way setting an agenda for future research and theorisation on its central theme.

References

D.M. Berry. 2014. *Critical Theory of the Digital*. New York: Bloomsbury.

M. Castells. 1999. 'Information Technology, Globalization and Social Development', UNRISD Discussion Paper No. 114, Geneva.

——. 2011. 'A Network Theory of Power'. *International Journal of Communication* 5, 773–787. Available at: https://ijoc.org/index.php/ijoc/article/view/1136/553 (accessed 15 December 2023).

Digital Master Services Plan. 2025. Available at: https://asean.org/wp-content/uploads/2021/08/ASEAN-Digital-Masterplan-2025.pdf (accessed 3 January 2024).

Digital Services Act. 2022. Available at:https://ec.europa.eu/commission/presscorner/detail/en/ip_22_2545 (accessed 1 January 2024).

F. Filgueiras and V. Almeida. 2021. *Governing for Digital World: Neither More State nor More Market*. Cham: Palgrave Macmillan.

K. Keniston. 2003. 'Introduction'. In *The Four Digital Divides*, edited by Kenneth Keniston and Deepak Kumar, 1–34. Delhi: Sage Publications. Available at: http://web.mit.edu/~kken/Public/PAPERS/Intro_Sage.html (accessed 3 January 2023).

M. Leeker, I. Schipper and T. Beyes, ed. 2017. *Performing the Digital: Performativity and Performance Studies in Digital Cultures*. Bielefeld: Transcript Verlag.

P. Merchant. 2012. 'An Illustrated Framework for the Analysis of Web 2.0 Interactivity'. *Contemporary Social Science*, 7(3): 263–281.

D. Sinha. 2010. '(De)Politicizing Information Technology: Towards an Inclusionary Perspective', Media@LSE Electronic Working Paper #19, Department of Media and Communications, London: London School of Economics. Available at: https://www.lse.ac.uk/media-and communications/assets/documents/research/working-paper-series/EWP19.pdf (accessed 19 February 2023).

P.N. Thomas. 2019. *Media Dynamics in South Asia: The Politics of Digital India*. New Delhi: Oxford University Press.

UNCTAD. 2023. 'How Bhutan's Civil Servants Are Building a Digital Government System'. Available at: https://unctad.org/news/how-bhutans-civil-servants-are-building-digital-government-system (accessed 25 January 2024).

World Bank. 2010. 'Strategic Assessment of Bhutan's E-Governance Program'. Available at: https://elibrary.worldbank.org/action/showCitFormats?doi=10.1596%2F27599 (accessed 3 January 2024).

Section 1

INDIA

1

Digital Finance and Digital Payments Interface in India

A Reality Check

Bishal Rai

Introduction

Digital finance (payments) is spurred by the idea of 'financial inclusion'—a notion that is considered to be a priority agenda for the Government of India (GoI) for 'inclusive growth'. Financial inclusion is also recognised as the key factor for the purpose of poverty alleviation. At the micro level, access to basic financial services and their usage is observed by scholars to reduce poverty, increase resilience and ameliorate the lives of the poor in general, and women in particular (Demirgüç-Kunt et al. 2022: 1). Also, studies by Burgess and Pande (2005), Beck et al. (2007), Bruhn and Love (2014), Suri and Jack (2016), Maripally and Bridwell (2017), Gautam et al. (2021) and Das and Chatterjee (2021) show that access to finance and financial services can contribute significantly to poverty alleviation. This dimension of financial inclusion, that is, reaching the excluded groups such as people with low income or the poorest of the poor is a special and unique dimension of financial inclusion (Sriram 2018: 32). Further, it is held that

> access to formal finance can boost job creation, reduce vulnerability to economic shocks and increase investments in human capital. Without adequate access to formal financial services, individuals and firms need to rely on their own limited resources or on costly informal sources of finance to meet their financial needs and pursue growth

> opportunities... (National Strategy for Financial Inclusion 2019–24, RBI, 2020: 1)

In this context, India, since 2014, has witnessed considerable progress in the case of financial inclusion where between 2011 and 2017, the adult share in account more than doubled to reach 80 per cent (Demirgüç-Kunt et al. 2018: 19). The notion of financial inclusion coincides with the evolution of Digital Financial Services (DFS) in India, which can be seen as a component of the 'Digital India' initiative. DFS refers to technology-driven services which make use of digital infrastructures such as mobiles, computers and the internet. DFS attempts to negate the reliance on traditional banking and the associated usage of cash. Provided that digital infrastructure is strengthened, DFS potentially permits individuals and businesses to make seamless transactions across regions and parties (Kumar et al. 2019: 6). The potential of financial inclusion infused with financial technology to eradicate poverty is sought to be realised not only by India but also by other countries across the globe and therefore has special appeal for developing and underdeveloped economies.

Developing economies, such as Kenya in the last decade, have shown rapid progress in financial inclusion to eliminate poverty. Starting from April 2007 onwards, utilising phones through the launching of M-PESA, Kenya has been able to lift two per cent of households out of poverty (Gautam et al. 2021: 1; Suri and Jack 2016: 1288). Any asymmetric information relating to financial matters poses high costs and can have adverse effects mostly on the groups with lower income. In this direction, financial inclusion facilitates payments, reducing asymmetric information, thereby helping households to climb up the economic ladder. Financial inclusion along with mobile penetration is observed to reduce the incidence of poverty while increasing per capita household consumption of both food and non-food items (Abor et al. 2018: 2–3). In this context, India under the National Democratic Alliance (NDA) government accelerated financial inclusion when its prime minister announced the Pradhan Mantri Jan Dhan Yojana (PMJDY)[1] on 15 August 2014, which provided free accounts or zero balance accounts. The motive behind launching PMJDY was the National

Mission for Financial Inclusion, which aims to cover all households in the country with both banking facilities and the provision for having a bank account for each household. Since its inception, more than 430 million beneficiaries amounting to approximately US dollars (USD) 19.71 billion were banked under PMJDY. On the successful completion of seven years of PMJDY in 2021, India's Finance Minister stated that:

> The journey of PMJDY led interventions undertaken over a short span of 7 years has in effect, produced both transformational as well as directional change thereby making the emerging Financial Inclusion ecosystem capable of delivering financial services to the last person of the society—the poorest of the poor… (Ministry of Finance, GoI 2021)

The government thus intends to implement a clear vision of reaching the section of people who were untouched and therefore remained outside the periphery of the formal financial services. However, the impact of India's digital finance push sees limitations despite the massive growth in the opening of accounts. This is due to inoperative accounts or account dormancy along with low levels of usage. According to the US-funded Mobile Solutions Technical Assistance and Research (mSTAR)[2] report, account dormancy is more among lower-income and rural populations due to lower access to technology. To address this issue, there is a need for digital push through the 'viability of agent networks, (digital) financial literacy, the preference for cash as a means of payment and jewellery and livestock as tools of savings' (mSTAR 2019: 2). Nevertheless, according to the Ministry of Finance, in August 2021, out of 430 million total PMJDY accounts, 368.6 million or 86 per cent were operative and only 8.2 per cent of PMJDY accounts were zero balance accounts. The operative accounts in 2017 accounted for 76 per cent (Ministry of Finance GoI 2021). Thus, the percentage of operative (dormancy) accounts has increased (declined) over time but gaps persist between operative and inoperative accounts. The data by the Reserve Bank of India (RBI) in its Payments Vision 2025 reflects that mobile banking and internet banking users increased by 99 per cent and 18 per cent respectively between March 2019 and September 2021. Further, the total digital payments increased by 216 per cent and 10 per cent in volume and value respectively, for March 2022 when compared to March 2019 (Reserve Bank of India 2022: 6). The increased usage of digital payments was seen post the launch of the Goods and Services Tax (GST) rather than demonetisation, where people used digital payments for the first time due to cash restrictions. However, it could not translate into long-term use of digital payments.

The growth in such digital payments (finance), which is an indication of growth in financial inclusion, has been supplemented by the rate at which smartphones or mobiles with low-cost (though not free) internet has penetrated populations who previously remained outside the boundaries of the digital economy. People now just pay the subscription fees for their monthly usage of mobile phone services which comes with the benefits of an unlimited package that in turn facilitates digital finance (payments). At the end of 2017, India had 446 million internet users, 95 per cent of whom accessed the internet through mobile. The number of such internet users increased to over 825 million as of 31 March 2021; 97 per cent of them accessed the internet through mobile (Telecom Regulatory Authority of India 2021). Also, as of June 2018, Paytm[3] claimed to have its services being used in over 300,000 villages, facilitating cashless transactions through its smartphone app and QR code solutions (*The Economic Times* 2018). While over 130 million rural Indians used the internet or 15 internet subscriptions per 100 rural people in 2017–2018, it increased to over 322 million rural Indians who used the internet or 36 internet subscriptions per 100 rural people in 2020–2021 (Telecom Regulatory Authority of India 2018; 2021). This growth in digital inclusion due to low data costs has made it possible for the poorer and less urban population to access the digital economy, thereby extending the digital frontiers to a new horizon. However, much remains to be accomplished so as to include the rural populations in a formal banking process. Until this is achieved, the usage of digital financial services will be limited.

According to the Global Findex Database (2021) by Demirgüç-Kunt et al. (2022: 21), 78 per cent of men and 74 per cent of women throughout the world have an account, thereby creating a gender gap of 4 per cent in terms of account ownership. In 2021, while 74 per cent of men had an account, only 68 per cent of women had an account in developing economies. This reflects that in developing economies, the average gap is wider, which comes to 6 per cent showing that any notion of financial inclusion has to address gender inequalities. This is possible only when women have control over their earnings and are in a position to undertake both personal and productive expenditures. Such control is in turn contingent upon (more) women entering the formal banking system, allowing them to not only access bank accounts but also have savings mechanisms and other related financial services (Ashraf et al. 2010; Alam 2012; Islam et al. 2014; as cited in Gammage et al. 2017: 4; Suri and Jack 2016: 1292).

Hence, though untapped opportunities exist to expand the usage of financial services by the poor in general and women in particular, much progress has occurred lately when compared to the previous decade. In this direction, India also has shown progress in reducing the gender gap in account ownership, from nearly 20 per cent in 2014 to 6 per cent in 2017 (Demirgüç-Kunt et al. 2018: 25). However, in 2021, it was also reported that almost 67 per cent of urban women transacted payments through digital modes on a general basis and 64 per cent or 6 out of 10 women on a regular basis (*Financial Express* 2021). As far as women in rural India are concerned, the Self-Employed Women's Association (SEWA), a trade union, imparted training to 400,000 women in operating and using mobile-based digital payments (World Economic Forum 2022).

Despite the absence of opportunities in the case of digital financial inclusion or for that matter in the case of digital payments, much progress has been made in India. As noted before, the journey of India's digital financial inclusion has been initiated through technology usage and support from institutions such as the United States Agency for International Development (USAID) in partnership with non-profits such as FHI-360, IFMR-LEAD and Intellecap (mSTAR 2019: 2). In 2021, India recorded real-time transactions of 48 billion, the largest number of transactions worldwide (*The Times of India* 2022). This has, however, been possible due to initiatives taken by the government along with the involvement of various institutions and organisations. These institutions or organisations not only keep track of digital payments through various means but also regulate, monitor and work on strengthening the digital payment infrastructure. Along with these initiatives, they are also involved in creating awareness through promotions of digital payments with all the stakeholders and citizens to digitally empower them in the creation of a digital and knowledgeable society. Some of these institutions and organisations are the Reserve Bank of India (RBI), the Telecom Regulatory Authority of India (TRAI), the National Payments Corporation of India (NPCI), the Ministry of Electronics and Information Technology (MeitY as mentioned in the list of abbreviations) and fintechs along with the Ministry of Finance. While the DigiDhan Mission[4] is one among such initiatives taken by the GoI under MeitY to promote a cashless or digital payment ecosystem in India, the Pradhan Mantri Gramin Digital Saksharta Abhiyan (PMGDISHA) is another initiative to usher in digital literacy in rural India by covering 60 million rural households or one person per household by 31 March 2023.[5]

Objectives of the Study

Given the discussions made in the previous section, the objectives of the study are threefold: first, to examine the trajectory and trends of DFS in terms of digital payments in India since 2014 and trace its progress; second, to examine the bulk of payments transacted through various digital platforms to date; and third, to identify various institutions/organisations involved for the transformation from cash to digital ecosystem in India.

Data and Methodology

Since the study is based on secondary sources, it has made use of the literature available on financial inclusion and digital finance (payments). The study has also relied on government reports and data from various institutions such as the Reserve Bank of India (RBI), the National Payments Corporation of India (NPCI), the Ministry of Information and Technology (MeitY), the Telecom Regulatory Authority of India (TRAI) and the Ministry of Finance. The data collected through secondary sources has been analysed and interpreted with the help of tables, charts and diagrams, ratios and percentages.

Findings of the Study

The Progress and Achievements of PMJDY So Far

Since the motive of the government behind launching PMJDY in 2014 was laid down in the National Mission for Financial Inclusion, it becomes imperative to track its progress. It not only visualised people accessing financial services at affordable costs but over time, it also aimed to make people use technology and mobile phones for the purpose of banking. In this context, evidence clearly suggests that there has been much progress under PMJDY since its inception as a substantial number of people who were unbanked were brought under the banking services. To 'bank the unbanked' is important not only to bring the marginalised and socio-economically neglected section of the population under financial inclusion but also to lead to the usage of other (digital) financial services over the course of time. Table 1.1 shows that the PMJDY accounts (in millions) in August 2015 were 179, which swelled up to 462.5 million in August 2022 out of which 257.1 million or 55.59 per cent of the accounts belonged to women. Also, the majority of the accounts that opened were from rural and semi-urban areas (Ministry of Finance 2022). Furthermore, the deposits in August 2015 were USD 3.50 billion, which increased to USD 21.87 billion in August 2022 (see Table 1.1).

Table 1.1: Table of PMJDY Accounts

Month/Year	PMJDY Accounts (in millions)	Deposits Under PMJDY Accounts (in billions)	PMJDY Operative Accounts (in millions)
Aug-15	179.0	3.50	-
Aug-16	241.0	6.28	-
Aug-17	309.0	10.21	231.5
Aug-18	325.4	11.73	263.4
Aug-19	367.9	14.45	301.6
Aug-20	404.1	17.41	349.0
Aug-21	430.4	19.71	368.6
Aug-22	462.5	21.87	375.7

Source: Compiled by author from the data of the Ministry of Finance, GoI, 2021.

However, inoperative accounts or account dormancy is of utmost importance when considering financial inclusion. Evidence also indicates a gap between operative and inoperative accounts. Out of 309 million PMJDY accounts in August 2017, the operative accounts were 231.5 million, thereby creating a gap of almost 25 per cent between operative and inoperative accounts. The data also reveals that the gap narrowed down and as of August 2021, it was only 14.4 per cent (see Fig. 1.1). However, it increased to 18.8 per cent in August 2022, higher than it was in August 2021. This gap between operative and inoperative accounts needs to be narrowed down if the vision of a cashless economy is to be escalated further.

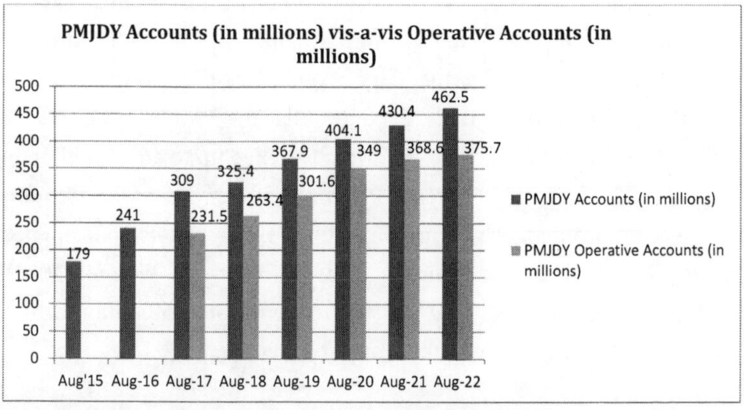

Figure 1.1: PMJDY Accounts vis-à-vis Operative Accounts
Source: Compiled by author from the data of the Ministry of Finance, GoI, 2021.

Digital Payments: Volume and Value

In terms of digital payments which include retail electronic payments comprising credit transactions processed through National Electronic Fund Transfer (NEFT), fast payments such as the Unified Payments Interface (UPI), Immediate Payment Service (IMPS) and direct debits via the National Automated Clearing House (NACH), there has been considerable growth both in volume and value (see Fig. 1.2). According to RBI (2020), digital payments have grown at a compound annual growth rate (CAGR) of 65 per cent and 42 per cent in terms of volume and value respectively over a period of five years, that is, between the financial years (FY) 2014–2015 and 2018–2019. While the volume of all such digital payments in the FY 2014–2015 was only 3,520 million, it increased to 23,390 million in the FY 2018–2019. Further, in the FY 2014–2015, the value of digital payments was USD 13460.11 billion; it increased to USD 23425.8 billion in the FY 2018–2019. This certainly reflects the growth in the process of digitisation in India (see Fig. 1.2). Apart from this, it also reflects the growing confidence and comfort among the masses in the usage of digital platforms for transactions. However, considering the population and geographical spread of the country, there is ample scope for inclusion.

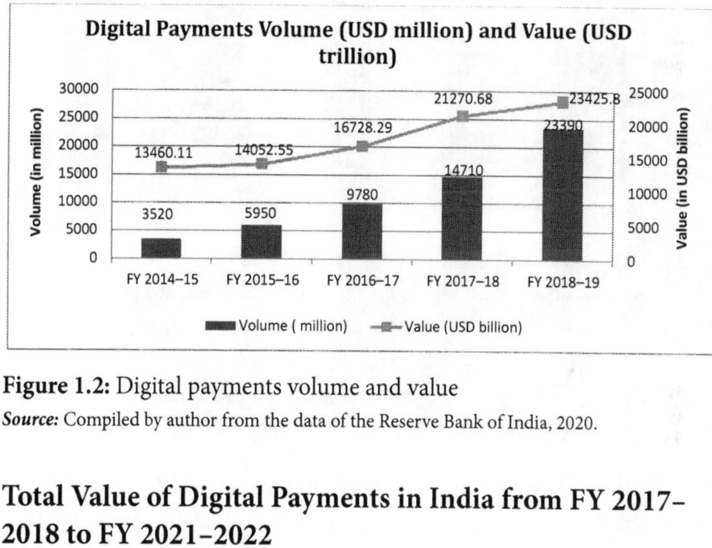

Figure 1.2: Digital payments volume and value

Source: Compiled by author from the data of the Reserve Bank of India, 2020.

Total Value of Digital Payments in India from FY 2017–2018 to FY 2021–2022

The DFS and financial inclusion become meaningful only if digital modes of payment are accessed and utilised. In this context, it was found that the total value of digital payments in India further increased from FY 2017–2018 to FY 2021–2022 with a slight decrease in FY 2020–2021 (see Fig. 1.3). The total value of digital payments across India for the FY 2017–2018 was USD 21.25 trillion while in the FY 2021–2022, it increased to USD 23.59 trillion. The total value of digital payments included large-scale interbank payments, such as Real Time Gross Settlement (RTGS) and NEFT as well as payments used by individuals, such as credit and debit cards or UPI transactions. According to the

India Brand Equity Foundation (IBEF), digital payments in India have witnessed exponential growth over the period FY 2010–2020. It represents a CAGR of 43 per cent in value over the last years, that is, FY 2010–2020 (IBEF 2022: 3). However, the transition to a fully cashless or digital ecosystem is still awaited and is a work in progress. It is only time that will help assess how much progress has been made in this direction.

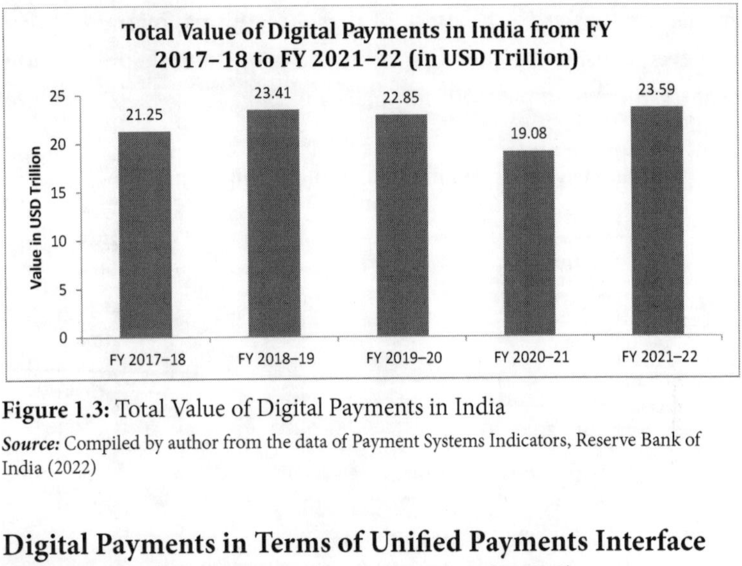

Figure 1.3: Total Value of Digital Payments in India

Source: Compiled by author from the data of Payment Systems Indicators, Reserve Bank of India (2022)

Digital Payments in Terms of Unified Payments Interface (UPI) and Immediate Payment Service (IMPS)

The most convenient way of making use of digital services is through smartphones that are connected to the internet. In this context, the study has made use of the data pertaining to the Unified Payment Interface (UPI) and Immediate Payment Service (IMPS) since these applications are easily installed on smartphones. The data ranges from April 2021 to December 2022 to examine the trend in the use of these digital modes of payment and shows that both modes of payment have increased over time, but the use of UPI as the digital mode of payment has increased rapidly than IMPS over the year. While the value of UPI transactions in April 2021 was USD 66.63 billion, it increased to the tune of USD 155.44 billion by December 2022. As far as IMPS is concerned, the total value of IMPS transactions in billions in April 2021 was USD 40.43; it too increased to the tune of USD 59 billion by December 2022. This points to the fact that the access and usage of UPI as the mode of digital payment has progressed faster in terms of usage than IMPS over the period of time (see Fig. 1.4). According to the RBI report (2022), India transacts over 260 million digital payments every day through different payment systems whereby UPI alone processes more than two-thirds of the payment.

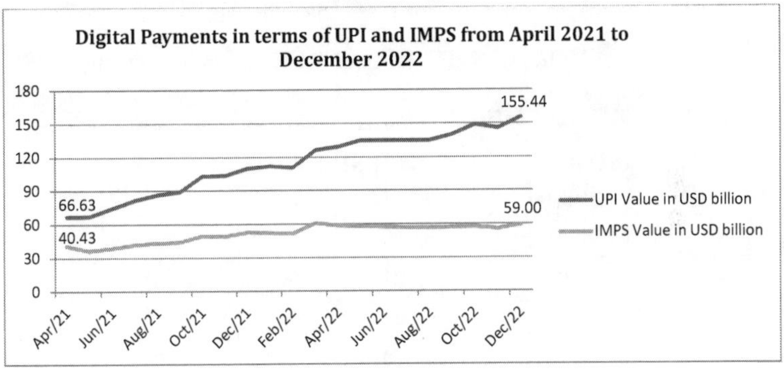

Figure 1.4: Digital Payments in terms of UPI and IMPS

Source: Compiled by author from data of National Payments Corporation of India (NPCI), 2021–2022.

Digital Payments in terms of NEFT, RTGS and Point of Sale (PoS)

The preceding section highlighted the usage of UPI and IMPS as modes of digital payment for the period April 2021 to December 2022. This section discusses other modes of digital payment for the same period, that is, April 2021 to December 2022. The other modes are NEFT, RTGS, NACH and PoS. NEFT and RTGS are also available offline but the data discussed here is only restricted to online transactions. The data pertaining to these modes of payment systems reflects their usage over the period noted at the outset of this subsection. The data reveals that the usage of these payment systems has been increasing with slight fluctuations between the periods. The figures not only reflect the usage of DFS that are available but also depict how consumers have gained the confidence and comfort of using these different payment systems. The value of NEFT (in billions) and RTGS (in billions) was USD 274.85 and USD 1182.40 respectively in April 2021. It increased to USD 361.83 billion and USD 1666.87 billion respectively by December 2022. Also, the value of NACH (in billions) was USD 21.84 in April 2021 which increased to USD 35.66 billion in December 2022. The figures for PoS reflect certain fluctuations over the period noted at the outset of this section. However, the values certainly highlight the increased usage of various digital platforms (see Table 1.2).

Table 1.2: Table of Values of NEFT, RTGS, NACH and PoS from April 2021 to October 2022

Month/Year	NEFT (USD billions)	RTGS (USD billions)	NACH (USD billions)	PoS (USD billions)
Apr-21	274.85	1182.40	21.84	15.41
May-21	248.39	1142.21	26.54	12.95
Jun-21	285.23	1386.48	21.71	15.41
Jul-21	295.77	1441.27	20.07	184.22
Aug-21	297.95	1369.89	22.89	19.16
Sep-21	328.96	1504.92	21.63	19.19
Oct-21	330.57	1352.84	25.83	24.05
Nov-21	310.79	1324.42	22.95	20.92
Dec-21	361.28	1719.16	25.52	21.19
Jan-22	328.08	14034.20	28.55	19.82
Feb-22	330.46	1377.41	24.94	19.03
Mar-22	458.23	1897.01	28.99	10.44
Apr-22	327.96	1456.67	28.28	10.94
May-22	329.50	1446.87	30.16	11.20
Jun-22	348.14	1583.80	28.59	10.30
Jul-22	330.42	1452.71	29.17	10.43
Aug-22	330.74	1466.13	30.21	10.75
Sep-22	364.72	1720.67	29.08	10.41
Oct-22	331.39	1403.83	31.45	12.19
Nov-22	334.61	1506.11	31.97	10.27
Dec-22	361.83	1666.87	35.66	11.09

Source: Compiled by the author from the data of RBI (2021–2022) data and NPCI (2021–2022).

Conclusion

The launch of the National Mission for Financial Inclusion coinciding with the Digital Financial Services in India has shown much progress since 2014. Many who did not have access to formal banking have been brought under the formal banking system. However, a lot remains to be achieved in this direction, particularly in the rural areas. More marginalised and socio-economically weaker sections of the population need to be brought under the different schemes/ platforms of financial inclusion. This is necessary for the people to benefit from various welfare schemes and to reach them directly through Direct Benefits Transfer (DBT) launched by the government. Further, the percentage of inactive accounts in India, which is 35 per cent, and still the highest in the world, needs to be lowered (Demirgüç-Kunt et al. 2022: 119).

In addition to the purpose it serves, financial inclusion is significant for all digital transactions. It also has the potential of generating positive externalities such as increased savings, investment and thereby economic growth (Chakrabarty 2013: 13). Financial inclusion is thus the first step in the direction of digital payments and the transition from a cash ecosystem to a digital ecosystem. In this aspect, progress can be seen since 2014 when the bulk of the payments is now channelled through digital modes of payment with growth in the usage of UPI. Though the usage of digital payments gained momentum during demonetisation (though not very significant), greater usage has been witnessed post the launch of GST and especially after the occurrence of the COVID-19 pandemic. The pandemic led more than 80 million adults in India to make their first digital payments (Demirgüç-Kunt et al. 2022: 3). The data further reveals that the share of digital transactions in the total volume of non-cash retail payments in the year 2020–2021 accounted to 98.8 per cent which increased to 99.3 per cent during 2021–2022 (Reserve Bank of India 2022: 175). The increased use of digital payments has been due to the high penetration of mobile phones/smartphones supplemented by low data costs. However, the digital penetration in the rural areas where a majority of the Indian population resides has not been the same. Cash transactions are still preferred in rural areas when compared to digital payments. There is therefore a need for greater digital literacy and the related expansion of payment infrastructure in the rural areas to break barriers in the direction of a digital ecosystem. Until this is realised, the vision of a truly Digital India will not meet with success.

Notes

1 PMJDY is the Prime Minister People's Fund Programme to bring about comprehensive financial inclusion of all the households in the country. See Pradhan Mantri Jan-Dhan Yojana | Department of Financial Services | Ministry of Finance (pmjdy.gov.in) for more details (accessed 31 January 2023).
2 The Mobile Solutions Technical Assistance and Research or the (mSTAR) project is funded by the US Agency for International Development (USAID), focuses on the adoption and scale-up of financial inclusion, digital finance and development of informatics. See The Mobile Solutions Technical Assistance and Research (mSTAR) | Archive-U.S. Agency for International Development (usaid.gov) for more details (accessed 31 January 2023).
3 Paytm is an Indian digital payments and financial services company.
4 More details at DigiDhan Mission | Ministry of Electronics and Information Technology, Government of India (meity.gov.in) (accessed 31 January 2023).
5 Overview of PMGDISHA—Pradhan Mantri Gramin Digital Saksharta Abhiyan for more details (accessed 31 January 2023).

References

N. Ashraf, D. Karlan and W. Yin. 2010. 'Female Empowerment: Impact of a Commitment Savings Product in the Philippines'. *World Development,* 38 (3): 333–344.

S. Alam. 2012. 'The Effect of Gender-Based Returns to Borrowing on Intra-Household Resource Allocation in Rural Bangladesh'. *World Development,* 40 (6): 1164–1180.

J.Y. Abor, M. Amidu and H. Issahaku. 2018. 'Mobile Telephony, Financial Inclusion and Inclusive Growth'. *Journal of African Business,* 19 (3): 430–453. Available at: https://doi.org/10.1080/15228916.2017.1419332 (accessed 29 August 2022).

R. Burgess and R. Pande. 2005. 'Do Rural Banks Matter? Evidence from the Indian Social Banking Experiment'. *American Economic Review,* 95 (3): 780–795.

T. Beck, D. Kunt and R. Levine. 2007. 'Finance, Inequality and the Poor'. *Journal of Economic Growth*, 12: 27–49.

M. Bruhn and I. Love. 2014. 'The Real Impact of Improved Access to Finance: Evidence from Mexico'. *Journal of Finance*, 69 (3): 1347–1376.

K.C. Chakrabarty. 2013. 'Financial Inclusion in India: Journey So Far and Way Forward', Keynote Address at Finance Inclusion Conclave Organised by CNBC TV, 18, 6 September, New Delhi.

S. Chandha. 2022. 'At 48 Billion, India Accounts for Largest Number of Real-time Transactions in the World'. *The Times of India,* 25 April. Available online: https://timesofindia.indiatimes.com/business/india-business/exclusive-at-48-billion-india-accounts-for-largest-number-of-real-time-transactions-in-the world/articleshow/91070124.cms (accessed 1 September 2022).

Demirgüc-Kunt, A.L. Klapper, D. Singer, S. Ansar and J. Hess. 2018. 'The Global Findex Database 2017: Measuring Financial Inclusion and the Fintech Revolution'. Washington, DC: The World Bank.

Demirgüç-Kunt, A.L. Klapper, D. Singer and S. Ansar. 2022. 'The Global Findex Database 2021: Financial Inclusion, Digital Payments, and Resilience in the Age of COVID-19'. Washington, DC: The World Bank.

S. Das and A. Chatterjee. 2021. 'Role of ICT Dissemination and Digital Finance in Poverty Eradication and Income Inequality Reduction: A Sub-national Level Study from India'. Chennai, India: Madras School of Economics.

S. Gammage, A. Kes, L.Winograd, N. Sultana, S. Hiller and S. Bourgault. 2017. 'Gender and Digital Financial Inclusion: What Do We Know and What Do We Need to Know'. *International Centre for Research on Women (ICRW).* Available at: https://www.icrw.org/wp-content/uploads/2017/11/Gender-and-digital-financial-inclusion.pdf (accessed 27 August 2022).

R.S. Gautam, J. Kanoujiya, V.M. Bhimavarapu and S. Rastogi. 2021. 'Financial Technology and Its Impact on Poverty in India'. *International Journal of Management and Humanities,* 6 (3): 1–10.

M.S. Islam, M.F. Ahmed and M.S. Alam. 2014. 'The Role of Microcredit Program on Women Empowerment: Empirical Evidence from Rural Bangladesh'. *Developing Country Studies*, 4 (5): 90–97.

India Brand Equity Foundation. 2022. 'Digital Payments and Their Impact on the Indian Economy, April 2022. Available online: https://www.ibef.org/research/case-study/digital-payments-and-their-impact-on-the-indian-economy (accessed 15 October 2022).

R. Kumar, V. Mishra and S. Saha. 2019. 'Digital Financial Services in India: An Analysis of Trends in Digital Payment'. *International Journal of Research and Analytical Reviews*, 6 (2): 6–22.

A. Maripally and L. Bridwell. 2017. 'The Future of Financial Inclusion and Its Impact on Poverty Reduction in India'. *Competition Forum*, American Society for Competitiveness. 15 (2): 329–335.

Ministry of Finance. 2021. 'Pradhan Mantri Jan-Dhan Yojana (PMJDY): National Mission for Financial Inclusion, Completes Seven Years of Successful Implementation'. Available at: https://pib.gov.in/PressReleaseIframePage.aspx?PRID=1749749 (accessed 28 August 2022).

———. 2022. 'Pradhan Mantri Jan-Dhan Yojana (PMJDY): National Mission for Financial Inclusion, Completes Eight Years of Successful Implementation'. Available at: https://www.pib.gov.in/PressReleasePage.aspx?PRID=1854909 (accessed 4 September 2022).

Mobile Solutions Technical Assistance and Research. 2019. 'India Digital Financial Inclusion: Journey Map Report'. Available at: https://www.usaid.gov/digital-development/india-digital-financial-inclusion-journey-map-report (accessed 9 August 2022).

National Payments Corporation of India. 2021–2022. 'Monthly Product Statistics'. Available at: https://www.npci.org.in/statistics/monthly-matrix (accessed 24 January 2023).

'Paytm's More Welcome in Rural, Semi-urban Areas', *Economic Times*, 11 June 2018. Available at: https://economictimes.indiatimes.com/small-biz/startups/newsbuzz/paytms-more-welcome-in-rural-semi-urban-areas/articleshow/64535894.cms?from=mdr (accessed 20 August 2022).

Reserve Bank of India. 2020. 'Assessment of the Progress of Digitisation from Cash to Electronic'. Available at: https://rbidocs.rbi.org.in/rdocs/Publications/PDFs/CASHB74203395BD64E2ABC1BD5F68D8AEF13.PDF (accessed 3 September 2022).

———. 2020. 'National Strategy for Financial Inclusion: 2019–2024'. Available at: https://rbidocs.rbi.org.in/rdocs//PublicationReport/Pdfs/NSFIREPORT100119FF91DAA6B73B497A923CC11E0811776D.PDF (accessed 27 August 2022).

———. (2021–2022), 'Bankwise Volumes in NEFT/RTGS/Mobile Transactions/Internet Banking Transactions'. Available at: https://rbi.org.in/Scripts/NEFTView.aspx (accessed on 24 January 2023).

———. 2022. 'Payment and Settlement Systems and Information Technology'. Available at: https://rbidocs.rbi.org.in/rdocs/AnnualReport/PDFs/9PAYMENTANDSETTLEMENT033C9414C22C4370AD16C837C55EDDC9.PDF (accessed 26 August 2022).

———. 2022. 'Payments Vision 2025', Department of Payment and Settlement Systems, Available at: https://rbidocs.rbi.org.in/rdocs//PublicationReport/

Pdfs/PAYMENTSVISION2025844D11300C884DC4ACB8E56B7348F4D4.PDF (accessed 16 January 2023).

———. 2022. 'Annual Report 2021–22'. Available at: https://rbidocs.rbi.org.in/rdocs/AnnualReport/PDFs/0RBIAR2021226AD1119F-F6674A13865C988DF70B4E1A.PDF (accessed 16 January 2023).

———. 2022. 'Payment Systems Indicators'. Available online: https://m.rbi.org.in/scripts/PublicationsView.aspx?Id=21160 (accessed 17 January 2023).

S. Sinha. 2021. 'Two-thirds of Urban Indian Women Use Digital Payment Modes Regularly: Survey', *Financial Express*, 4 March. Available online: https://www.financialexpress.com/money/two-thirds-of-urban-indian-women-use-digital-payment-modes-regularly-survey/2206174/ (accessed 17 August 2022).

M.S. Sriram, ed. 2018. *Talking Financial Inclusion in Liberalised India: Conversations with Governors of the Reserve Bank of India*, 1st edn, London and New York: Routledge.

T. Suri and William Jack. 2016. 'The Long-run Poverty and Gender Impacts of Mobile Money', *Science*, American Association for the Advancement of *Science*, 354 (6317): 1288–1292.

Telecom Regulatory Authority of India. 2018. 'Annual Report 2017–18'. Available at: https://www.trai.gov.in/sites/default/files/Annual_Report_21022019.pdf (accessed 30 August 2022).

———. 2021. 'Annual Report 2020–21'. Available at: https://www.trai.gov.in/sites/default/files/Annual_Report_06042022_0.pdf (accessed 30 August 2022).

World Economic Forum. (2022). 'How digital payments bring new economic opportunities for women in rural India', 5 August. Available at: https://www.weforum.org/agenda/2022/08/digital-payments-economic-opportunities-women-rural-india/ (accessed 26 August 2022).

2

Digitalising the Census in India

Roadway to e-Governance?

Nisha Tamang

Introduction

Ever since the end of the nineteenth century, there have been efforts to take advantage of a succession of newly available technologies to make large and costly statistical enquiries more efficient and effective. Herman Hollerith (1860–1929), a statistician, inventor and businessman, stands out as an early adaptor of modern technology in census work. He borrowed from the ideas of Joseph-Marie Jacquard who had invented punched cards to control looms—'Jacquard looms'. Hollerith saw a way to use such cards in the process of sorting and tabulation. By doing this, he not only expedited the release of the results of the 1890 census in the United States of America but also started an entire industry (Dekker 1994; Dekker 2001: 55).

A population census is the 'total process of collecting, compiling, and publishing demographic, economic, and social data pertaining to a specific time to all persons in a country or delimited part of a country'(UN 1958: 3). Etymologically, the term census has a Latin root *censere* (to assess). In the political context of Europe after Napoleon, the term ripped into two, 'a count of citizens and their asset' became 'census' and 'state official in charge of scrutiny and suppression of citizens' became 'censor' (The India Forum: 2023). In the Roman Republic, the census was a list that kept the records of all adult males who were considered fit to join the military. Censuses were primarily used as a tool for taxation or war purposes and were mostly regarded as suspicious by those being enumerated. However, in the nineteenth century, gradually, the census started to be accepted by the public. In the modern period, the census forms the backbone of the decision-making process in an attempt to answer pressing societal demands.

Politically, the census is viewed as an instrument of state power to enumerate, classify and govern the people. It also demonstrates state power over the people, which exemplifies the legacies of colonial rule in India. In colonial India, religion, caste and race-based enumeration and classification of the population were seen as attempts to 'divide and rule' (Bhagat 2003: 2). In the book *Population and the Political Imagination*, Bhagat notes the gradual transition of population counts in different political regimes as a mere headcount to a more sophisticated, comprehensive and powerful instrument of statecraft. It also stresses the role of the census as a key bio-political strategy in governance. It further relates the census, NPR (National Population Register) and NRC (National Register for Citizens) as instruments of state power to enumerate, classify and govern people. The census department retained by the Ministry of Home Affairs instead of the Ministry of Statistics and Programme Implementation bears testimony to the legacies of governance and politics exercised by the colonial power. The premise that 'the true measure of the power of a state is in its population' (Hacking 1990: 18, cited in Baffour, King and Valente 2013: 408) is a testament to such a view.

Seen as one of the largest administrative exercises, the Indian census is all set to embark on a new digital journey. The Government of India has attempted a mammoth exercise of digitising the 16th census through e-governance of a 'knowledge society' for the governed and 'surveillance society' for the government. The sudden arrival of the COVID-19 pandemic also compelled the government to make a paradigm shift in the matter of governance. The flaw in the unsustainable and traditional pen-paper system has called for a technological boost to revamp the census operations. Thus, strengthening the Information and Technology sector to make way for a consensus is expected to make the census cost-effective and scientific.

India's Census-making at a Glance

The census reflects the socio-economic, demographic and cultural milieu of a society and the nation at large. No doubt it is called the storehouse and warehouse of socio-economic and demographic information. Throughout history, the censuses have served to provide information to governments, that is, to understand the development of the nation and its populace on several fronts, especially for policy formulation (Ashkpour 2019: 15). The earliest references to the census in India can be traced back to the Mauryan period in Kautilya's *Arthashastra* (321–296 BCE) and later during the Mughal period in the writings of Abul Fazl (1595–1596) in the *Ain-e-Akbari*.

The Indian census boasts of being one of the largest administrative exercises uninterruptedly undertaken in the world. However, the latest census, which should have been conducted in 2021, is yet to commence due to the COVID-19 outbreak; it is expected to be completed by 2024 (*Times of India* 2023). India's first census (Census of 1881), as a complete enumeration, can be taken as one of the earliest in the entire Asia-Pacific region, falling under the category of modern censuses. Australia, one of the developed nations in the Asia Pacific region, lists their first national census in 1911, almost 30 years later (ESCAP 2021: 1).

In ancient India, during 800–600 BCE, the earliest literature, the *Rig Veda*, reveals counting the population for various reasons such as collecting tax and as a measure of state policy. Kautilya's celebrated work *Arthasastra*, written around 321–296 CE, also stresses the necessity of a population count. The administrative report of Mughal emperors such as Akbar in the *Ain-e-Akbari* also mentions collecting data on population and industry (Jha 2017: 324). This shows that the administrative skills and formative ideas of governance were well recognised during the pre-British era.

In British India, the Census of 1830 conducted by Henry Walter in Dacca (presently Dhaka, capital of Bangladesh) can be taken as the first complete census. From 1836 to 1837, the second census of Fort St George's Presidency was conducted. The colonial government, by means of their revenue officials, ordered the then local government to conduct the quinquennial population count in 1849, following which a periodic system of counting the population was followed in Madras till the imperial census was taken. Gradually, the quinquennial census of 1866 to 1867, which is credited with actually counting heads in most parts of the country through a uniform schedule, merged with the imperial census of 1871, which was non-synchronous. The first synchronous census in British India, conducted on 17 February 1881 by W.C. Plowden, the Census Commissioner, paved the way for the modern synchronous census. After that, there was no looking back, as the census is undertaken once every 10 years without interruption.

Constrains of Census Data

The census data becomes all the more important in the inter-census year 2011 to 2021 as the country witnessed events like demonetisation in 2016, the introduction of GST (Goods and Services Tax) in 2017 and the COVID-19 lockdown. The delay could trigger a large-scale data loss. Since the socio-economic surveys bank on it, the delay can deviate from the real-time data and compromise the result. It hampers planning, programmes and schemes and misses out on targets as mere estimations and projections yield flawed results. India has recently surpassed China as the world's most populous nation as per analysts' estimates (*The Economic Times* 2023). While India's population was 1.42 billion as of 18 January 2023, China, for the first time, reported a fall of 850,000 since the 1960s and now stands at 1.41 billion (*Down to Earth* 2023). The census is yet to be validated because India has not done a real headcount in more than a decade.

The census data gives an insight into the changing dynamics of demography and is the bedrock for policymaking and welfare schemes. However, the credibility of the quality of the data has always come under a scanner. Though the headcount is portrayed as an apolitical exercise, the quality and quantity of data invariably reflect some colour. The census is regarded as a gigantic exercise of statistical excellence. Nevertheless, it does leave out many people and gives underestimated results. The Post Enumeration Survey estimates the extent and type of under- and over-counting errors. In 2011, India's census missed 27.85

million people, a population roughly the size of the state of Punjab at the time. While the rate of omissions is worse in urban India than in rural areas, it has slightly improved in urban areas, while it has consistently worsened in rural areas, meaning that every decade, the census has missed more and more people in rural areas. The homeless too tend to get left out of electoral rolls. India's voter list, for instance, suffers from a gender bias, with women left out in much larger numbers than men (*Mint* 2020). Hence, special efforts are to be made to sensitise the target groups, such as women, children and physically disabled persons.

The Making of Digital Census via e-Governance

The making of a digital census via e-governance refers to the use of information technologies by government agencies. Such technologies are Wide Area Networks (WAN), internet and mobile computing, which have the ability to transform relations among citizens, businesses and other arms of government. The digital thrust of the census is about 'governance' keeping pace with Information and Communications Technologies (ICT) to facilitate the smooth functioning of policy frameworks. In India, the NeGP (National e-Governance Plan), NKN (National Knowledge Network) and the UIDAI (Unique Identification Authority of India) fall within the ambit of e-governance. Additionally, the Census Web Service is an open standard-based web application that interacts with other web applications for sharing citizen data which is intended to share reliable census data across different e-governance applications with accuracy (Dutta, Devi and Arora 2017: 45).

In this regard, the makings of an e-census are definitely a historical development. The traditional and manual data entry through pen-paper mode and rigorous processing of census data (manually) came to a halt when hand-punching machines were used for converting data into a machine-readable form in the 1961 census. For tabulation and printing of census tables, a 'serial rolling total tabulator cum printer' was used. The electronic computers, mainly IBM-1401s, prepared most of the tables in the 1971 census (Office of the Registrar General of India, 2021). In the 1981 census, for the first time, the data-entry activities were decentralised into 15 data centres including one at the headquarters, that is, the Office of the Registrar General of India, to convert paper-based information into machine-readable for using 'key to disk' machines provided by Google Cloud Storage, the Electronics Corporation of India Limited and ICT. In the 1991 census, the Office of the Registrar General & Census Commissioner of India (ORGI & CCI) installed the Medha-930 main-frame computing facility at the data processing division. However, it was the 2001 census that made a quantum stride in technology. The schedules for the phases were scanned through high-speed scanners and hand-written data from the schedules were converted into a digitised form through Intelligent Character Reading. The Optical Mark Recognition (OMR)/Optical Character Recognition (OCR)/Intelligent Character Recognition (ICR) technologies were evaluated and ICR was found to be acceptable as the viable solution for census data-processing activities.

For the first time in 2002, the ORGI used the 'Census Info' to disseminate census data; users could access the Census Info India Dashboard to get a consolidated report on census results (Census of India 2001). In 2002, a data dissemination unit (DDU) was set up in all the directorates through social media platforms such as Facebook and Twitter. India was also one of the first countries to use the image-based Automatic Form Processing Technology taking the help of high-speed duplex scanners for image capturing. India has also adopted a more developed ICR technology with advanced features while conducting the 2011 census. Further, extensive quality checks and data validation were also undertaken at each stage of data processing and analysis, using the CS Pro Software (Zhimomi 2012). The 16th census is expected to be the first digital census, as has been announced by the Ministry of Home Affairs, Government of India. Moreover, on 1 February 2021, the finance minister announced a budget of INR 37.68 billion (US $ 470 million) for conducting the 2021 census (*India Today* 2021). Though announced, the operation was delayed and caused disruptions to statistical operations. As noted before, in the 150-year history of census in India, only in 1941 was the census disrupted, the reason being the Second World War. At that time, the data tabulation was not completed, but the data had been collected successfully. Even in 1961, during the Chinese aggression or in 1971, when India was involved in the struggle for the liberation of Bangladesh, the census was conducted successfully (*The Print* 2022). However, India is not an exception to the disruptions caused by the COVID-19 Pandemic. The UNSD (United Nations Statistics Division) 2021 survey results indicate that 78 per cent of the 23 respondent countries in Asia and the Pacific region were affected by the COVID-19 outbreak. The affected countries either postponed their censuses (50 per cent) or extended the enumeration period (39 per cent) (ESCAP 2021: 6).

Census and the Digital Domain

The 16th census of India will venture into the digital domain with the hope of facilitating 100 per cent census coverage. In order to ensure the best coverage of the census, an attempt is being made to digitise the built-up area spread across the country to compare with the mobile mapping app data received from the field. Though the data collection from the field across the censuses was 100 per cent, its level of digitisation varied from 5 per cent to 45 per cent for some parameters till 1991. After the advent of sophisticated IT tools like OMR, OCR, ICR, etc., nearly 100 per cent of data has been captured through these IT tools for the last two censuses conducted in 2001 and 2011 (Annual Report 2021–2022, Ministry of Home Affairs: 236).

For the first time, the census exercise will be conducted both in digital mode and through paper schedules (questionnaires/forms) to enhance active participation. A mobile application (installed on the enumerator's phone) for data collection and a census portal for monitoring and managing have been developed. The annual report of the Ministry of Home Affairs 2021 and 2022 notes that the mobile applications developed in-house for the collection of data through smartphones have been rigorously tested and have been further updated and improved. The enumerators can collect data either through smartphones using the mobile applications developed by ORGI or on conventional paper questionnaires and submit the same directly through the mobile application using the smartphone. The responses can be codified by making use of a code directory to speed up the process and release data at the earliest. In case of connectivity issues, paper schedules can also be used for data entry. There is an option of self-enumeration during both phases of the census, that is, house listing, housing census and population enumeration. The data, then, is placed by the system in any one of three data centres of ORGI located at Delhi, Lucknow and Bengaluru. Paper questionnaires are scanned, digitised through ICR at 18 data capture centres of ORGI and then transmitted to any of the three aforementioned data centres.

The CMMS (Management and Monitoring through Census web portal) has been envisioned to manage and monitor the ongoing activities of the census. The ORGI has planned to set up the captive security operation centre (SOC) and security incident event management (SIEM) with suitable HW/SW appliances at all three ORGI data centres to enhance data security. Mostly, government officials and government schoolteachers will be trained as enumerators for the collection of data details through both the online and offline modes. Through a Gazette Notification on 11 March 2022, the Registrar-General of India notified the amended census rules which read as follows: 'A person may fill up, complete and submit the census schedule through self-enumeration'. It added that self-enumeration 'means filling-up, completion and submission of census schedule by respondents themselves' (*The Hindu* 2022).

After the census portal is created for self-enumeration, the respondent can log in using their mobile number to fill out the form for population enumeration in the census portal. It will be multilingual, as the respondents will have a choice of 16 languages from which to respond. Citizens can access the portal from electronic gadgets. To fill out the form, the codes will be displayed on the screen, and an identification number or a reference code will be generated once the formality of self-enumeration is complete. This reference code then can be shared with the enumerators as and when they visit the home of the respondent. The reference number will automatically sync all the data which have been filled online, completing the enumeration from the respondent's end (*Times of India* 2022). New software (e-Swaroop) is also being developed which will act as a platform to link the registration of births and deaths. The birth of a child will be entered into the software, and as soon as the child attains the age of eighteen, the name will get registered in the voter's list, and automatically, the profile will be closed with the death of the individual. The amendment of the Registration of Birth and Death Act of 1969 has also been proposed.

In addition to this, the information of a person shifting his/her/their residence will also be updated accordingly on the portal so that they enjoy voting facilities in the new residence. The details of the population will also be automatically updated in the census software (*Hindustan Times* 2022). Integration of an Online Census Application with the UIDAI database is also proposed for accessing existing information. The enumerator will request the web server for the opening of the census web pages using a browser, after which the web page is displayed on the screen. The twelve-digit UID is sent to the UIDAI web server which then communicates with the UIDAI database to get the data. It sends data in Extensible Markup Language (XML) format and is filled in automatically. After the entry of all information, the data is finally stored in the census database (Dutta, Devi and Arora 2017: 47).

It is interesting to note that the e-census made its debut in the recent caste survey in the state of Bihar. The government launched the survey from 7 January 2023 onwards to compile data on each family digitally through a mobile application from the panchayat to the district level (*Hindustan Times* 2023). The aim was to enhance the socio-economic visibility of unrepresented caste groups, eventually leading to their greater participation in governance and planning. Since the inception of the census in India in 1871, there have been strong views for and against the collection of caste-based data (Maheshwari 1996: 105; Deshpande and Sundar 1998: 2158). The supporters of caste-based census opine that since caste is indispensable to India's socio-cultural milieu, it needs to be reflected in the census. On the other hand, many anticipate that it might create a fissure in the socio-cultural diversity of India. Nevertheless, despite strong anti-caste movements, caste continues to dominate the socio-political scenario of India, and it is believed that people do not 'cast their votes' rather they 'vote their caste' (*Times of India* 2022). This might eventually impact the scenario of the nation with a ripple effect on the structures and processes of governance.

Geospatial Information and Census Mapping

Another quantum leap in census-taking is the growing role of the geographic information system (GIS). The growing use of modern geospatial technologies in census mapping has ushered in rapid improvements in pre-enumeration, enumeration, and post-enumeration phases. A GIS-based census operation helps with planning processes, supports fieldwork, improves the accuracy of the data collected and contributes to capturing, analysing, processing, disseminating and enhancing data quality and coverage. It also integrates statistical and geospatial information for data analysis and evidence-based decision-making for future censuses and surveys (Laaribi and Peters 2019:10). During the pre-enumeration phase, GIS can generate maps of different administrative units of the states, districts, villages, towns and even the wards. It can be used to design, and if necessary, modify the same to minimise time and maximise efficiency. The Global Positioning System (GPS) points and air photos can also work wonders for the creation of maps. During the post-enumeration stage, GIS can help to evaluate the data coverage in different geographical units and enhance their quality. The final stage of data dissemination and communication includes the preparation of thematic maps to help visualise data both for policy formulation and also to augment research. Similarly, GPS is a major tool for direct capture of location information and building GIS databases for the purpose of census operations. Geo-coding and assigning geographic coordinates (latitude, longitude) to specific locations like streets and buildings also helps in preparing and modifying maps.

The 2021 census utilises the latest census-mapping techniques, namely standardisation of GIS spatial database design, geo-referencing of administrative units, the latest mobile-mapping application (Arc GIS Quick Capture) for field operations and built-up area digitisation work (Jain and Kaur 2021: 540). The preparation of web-based interactive maps for the dissemination of census results is also being considered. However, there are some challenges in opting for a full digital census-mapping approach. The GIS-based census should be planned and developed at an early stage of census planning to allow sufficient time to produce full national coverage maps. Since the use of these technologies has crucial impacts on the different stages of the census exercise, it should be implemented in a consistent and timely manner before field execution (Laaribi and Peters 2019: 12).

Census: A Potent Tool for e-governance

E-governance is increasingly seen as an all-inclusive process to achieve participation and preparedness for governance. Census is one such exercise that endeavours to take e-services to the masses. The census as a comprehensive database attempts to reflect the socio-economic and demographic characteristics as well as the levels of development and under-development of a geographical unit. The census data also attempts to capture lopsided development and seeks to reflect transformations in demographic history. It also highlights the areas and regions that remain outside the developmental process, needing immediate policy interventions. The changes that occur on the socio-cultural, economic, demographic and linguistic fronts are specifically mirrored in the census, which is why it is a dynamic exercise. The results of the census are ultimately expected to help formulate policy plans and welfare schemes for those who are in need.

In India the *Beti Bachao, Beti Padhao* scheme for 'empowering the girl child' was launched on 22 January 2015 to address the poor crude sex ratio in some states as reflected by the 2011 census. Another vital scheme named the Pradhan Mantra Ujjwala Yojana (PMUY) was a flagship scheme launched on 1 May 2016 to make Liquid Petroleum Gas available to deprived rural households based on the outcome of the 2011 census. The government also planned 22 welfare schemes based on the result of the 2011 census focusing mainly on providing electricity and gas to every home, giving impetus to road connectivity, building houses for the poor, constructing toilets, providing clean drinking water and opening bank branches in the rural areas (*The Hindu* 2022). The census also reflects the stages of development of different states in the education and economic sectors, health infrastructure, employment planning and urban and rural area policy planning; it prioritises the backward states to bridge the developmental gap. The 2011 census took the lead in collecting information of households headed by a person from the transgender community, throwing light on the changing social milieu of the country. Looking at the current demographic dividend as reflected by the 2011 census, the issue of 'brain drain' also acquires relevance. India's five-year plans and other development plans depend heavily on census data which gives an impetus for formulating policies. The digital census system can be incorporated with other departments like health, food supply, education, youth and social welfare, whereby the information generated can then be linked with the social and economic information of citizens like bank accounts, vehicles and property (Dutta, Devi and Arora 2019: 473).

Challenges Ahead

The benefits of a census can only be reaped by maximising accessibility to the remotest corner of India, but questions arise on the preparedness of the people for e-participation. A digital transition phase from a paper census to an e-census needs a revamp of the methodological aspects, which, if not addressed prudently, is sure to incur erroneous results. Census 2011 shows that only 15.54 million households (6.3% of the total population) have computers/laptops, with 7.6 million households having internet connectivity and another 14.50 million having broadband subscriptions. The biggest challenge is to bridge this digital divide. It is generally observed that a relatively high literacy rate, easy access to mobile devices and computers and a considerable amount of computer literacy are the prerequisites of a digital census (*Times Now* 2022). The challenges are manifold and country-specific and addressing them depends on improving the baseline of human development of the society. Sometimes, a quantum leap, especially of an abrupt kind, into such initiatives does not yield encouraging results. Some developed nations are still struggling to conduct a 100 per cent paperless census. The census planners should work hard on the failure stories and evaluate all the pros and cons to mitigate the adverse effects. In other words, there are ample opportunities to learn from cross-country comparisons.

Some of the prerequisites for facilitating e-governance through digital census are mentioned below.

1. Proper planning at the inception and model building;
2. Conducting a pilot census for testing the entire processes of data collection;
3. Generating mass awareness on the importance and necessity of digital census at the grassroots level to combat low response;
4. Building trust, confidence and above all, focusing on citizen acceptance in e-governance;
5. Bridging barriers between respondents and enumerators, which is a serious deterrent in traditional collection modes;
6. Preparing digitally empowered respondents by facilitating internet connectivity, making mobile devices accessible and affordable;
7. Reaching out to every household for address canvassing;
8. Familiarising the enumerators and respondents with the technicalities of data collection;
9. Meeting the costs of high initial investment;
10. Addressing issues of data piracy, hacking and data security.

Meeting the 'challenges' is certainly a challenge in itself. The sudden shift from the pen-paper mode to the paperless and online mode will definitely create some confusion among the masses, which highlights the need for physical assistance booths. In this regard, UN statistics indicate that more than 30 countries have switched to a hybrid paper-based and internet-based self-enumeration model to address the issues. Some are making the transition now or have done so for 15 years or more (*Times Now* 2022). In the Indian scenario, considering the present challenges of a digital transition, a model that suits its hybrid populace needs to be prudently chosen. In order to create an ITC-enabled populace, the Government of India has already embarked on a journey of digital literacy to ensure active participation in the digital domain through 'The Digital Saksharta Abhiyan' (DISHA) or 'National Digital Literacy Mission' (NDLM).

A mixed-mode collection procedure combining the latest technology for the digitally ready respondents and the traditional methods of face-to-face interview (pen-paper mode or electronic questionnaire on handheld electronic devices) will ensure a wider audience. A follow-up attempt could be made in case of non-response with computer-assisted telephone interviewing (CATI) when a telephone number is available. In case of refusal from the respondent, the address may be selected for computer-assisted personal interviewing (CAPI). In either case, the technology should be perfectly tailored to suit the needs of the grassroots-level respondents. This point has many implications for the vision of Digital India, which includes 'governance and services on demand' and 'digitally empowering citizens'—visions which are expected to pave the way for holistic inclusion (ASSOCHAM 2015: 16). However, it remains to be seen in what manner these new initiatives will transform the governance processes at large.

Conclusion

The census is the backbone of any statistical inquiry for states. In the case of India, it is seen as a reliable and accurate source of data. While there are numerous issues with regard to census data, for the formulation of national plans, public policies, administrative measures and various welfare schemes, the Government of India and the governments of the states rely heavily on the authenticity of census data. The gamut of electronic records and information can be used to formulate socio-economic and administrative policies and aid the planners, policymakers and researchers at the local and national levels. The evolving technologies coupled with the extensive use of satellite imagery in the making of the census are certainly growing. The latest ones relate to the inclusion of artificial intelligence, robotics and machine learning in the domain of census and e-governance. However, given the constraints and the limitations, it would be too early to say that the traditional mode of census will fade into oblivion.

References

Ashkpour. 2019. 'Theory and Practice of Historical Census Data Harmonization', MA diss., Geboren Te Tehran, Iran Erasmus, University of Rotterdam.

ASSOCHAM INDIA. 2015. 'E-governance and Digital India Empowering Indian Citizens through Technology'. Available at: https://www2.deloitte.com/content/dam/Deloitte/in/Documents/technology-media-telecommunications/in-tmt-empowering-indian-citizens-through-technology-noexp (accessed 6 December 2022).

Annual Report 2021–2022. Ministry of Home Affairs, Government of India.

Bernard Baffour, Tom King and Paolo Valente. 2013. 'The Modern Census: Evolution, Examples and Evaluation'. International Statistical Review, 81 (3): 407–425.

R.B. Bhagat. 2003. 'Role of Census in Racial and Ethnic Construction: US, British and Indian Census'. Economic and Political Weekly, 22 (February): 686–691.

———. 2022. *Population and the Political Imagination—Census, Register and Citizenship in India*. London and New York: Routledge.

D. Bhati. 2022. 'Digital-census-in-India-know-the-process phases-and-provision-for-self-enumeration'. Jagran[TV]. Available at: https://www.jagrantv.com/en-show/digital-census-in-india-know-the-process-phases-and-provision-for-self-enumeration-watch-video-rc1030967 (accessed 14 December 2022).

Bloomberg. 18 January 2023. 'India's population has already overtaken China's, Analysts Estimate', *The Economic Times*. Available online: https://economictimes.indiatimes.com/news/india/indias-population-has-already-overtaken-chinas-analysts-estimate/articleshow/97079163.cms?from=mdr (accessed 8 February 2023).

Census of India. 2001 data-online. National Portal of India. Available at: https://www.india.gov.in/census-2001-data-online (accessed 3 November 2022).

Dekker. 1994. 'Computer Methods in Population Census Data Processing'. *International Statistical Review*, 62 (1): 55–70.

———. 2001. 'Adapting new technologies to Census Operations', Symposium on Global Review of 2000 Round of Population and Housing Censuses: Mid-Decade Assessment and Future Prospects Statistics Division Department of Economic and Social Affairs United Nations Secretariat New York'. Available at: https://unstats.un.org/unsd/demographic/docs/symposium_06.htm (accessed 27 December 2021).

S. Deshpande and N. Sundar. 1998. 'Caste and the Census'. *Economic and Political Weekly*, 33(32) (accessed on 10 January 2022).

G.N. Devy. 2023. 'Census of India: Gone with the Wind'. *The India Forum*. Available at: https://www.theindiaforum.in/article/census-india-gone-wind (accessed 14 December 2022).

Down to Earth. 2023. 'India surpasses China to become most populous country in the world'[video]. Available at: https://www.downtoearth.org.in/video/governance/india-surpasses-china-to-become-most-populous-country-in-the-world-87257 (assessed 4 February 2023).

Dutta, S.M. Devi and M. Arora. 2017. 'Online Census-based Information Sharing for Delivery of e-Governance Services'. Research Gate Conference Paper, 2017. Available at: https://www.researchgate.net/publication/316838619_Online_Census-based_Information_Sharing_for_Delivery_of_e-Governance_Services (accessed 23 December 2022).

———. 2019. 'Design of UID based Online Census System for Electronic Governance Applications'. *Journal of Emerging Technologies and Innovative Research*, 6 (5): 472–483.

ESCAP.2021. 'Are population censuses in Asia and the Pacific evolving?' Statistics Division, United Nations, 30, 1–7. Available at: https://www.unescap.org/kp/2021/are-population-censuses-asia-and-pacific-evolving(accessed 4 December 2022).

I.M. Hacking. 1990. *The Taming of Chance*. Cambridge, UK: Cambridge University Press.

D. Hazra. 10 May 2022. 'Amit Shah promises e-census: How will an electronic census work?', *Times Now*. Available online: https://www.timesnownews.com/technology-science/amit-shah-promises-e-census-how-will-an-electronic-census-work-article-91467657 (accessed 14 December 2022).

HT Editorial. 9 January 2023. 'Bihar Caste Census Must be Foolproof'. *The Hindustan Times*, 9 January. Available at: https://www.hindustantimes.com/editorials/bihar-caste-census-must-be-foolproof-101673186654704.html (accessed 22 January 2023).

A. Jain and V. Kaur. 2021. 'Census Mapping in India and Role of GIS: A Look Ahead at Census 2021'. *Sage Publications*, 67 (4): 540–558.

M.K. Jha. 2017. 'History of Indian Census and its Features'. *Inspira-Journal of Commerce, Economics & Computer Science*, 3 (3): 323–330.

A. Laaribi and L. Peters. 2019. *GIS and the 2020 Census: Modernizing Official Statistics*. California: Esri Press.

S. Maheshwari. 1996. The Census Administration under the Raj and After, 1st ed. New Delhi: Concept Publishing House. Office of the Registrar General of India. 2021. Information Technology Division. Ministry of Home Affairs, Government of India. Available at: https://censusindia.gov.in/census.website/node/168 (accessed 23 October 2023).

D. Mandal. 2022. 'Decade without data—Why India is delaying Census when US, UK, China went ahead during Covid'. *The Print*, 13 May. Available at:

https://theprint.in/opinion/decade-without-data-why-india-is-delaying-census-when-us-uk-china-went-ahead-during-covid/954383/ (accessed 26 October 2022).

U. Parashar. 2022. 'New census software that will address many tasks under 1 platform by 2024'. *Hindustan Times*, 9 May. Available at: https://www.hindustantimes.com/india-news/new-census-software-that-will-address-many-tasks-under-1-platform-by-2024-amit-shah-101652108604239.html(accessed 11September 2022).

Press Trust of India. 2021. 'Budget 2021: Census to go digital for the first time with Rs 3,768 Crore Allocation'. *India Today*, 1 February. Available at: https://www.indiatoday.in/business/budget-2021/story/budget-2021-census-to-go-digital-for-the-first-time-with-rs-3768-crore-allocation-nirmala-sitharaman-1764702-2021-02-01 (accessed 18 October 2021).

S. Rukmini. 2020. 'Census misses many people, so will NPR'. *Live Mint*, 26 February. Available at: https://www.livemint.com/news/india/census-misses-many-people-so-will-npr-11582632237507.html (accessed 5 October 2022).

S. Raghuraman. 2023. 'If US, UK, Brazil Could Conduct Census, Why Can't India?' *Times of India*, 21 January. Available at: https://timesofindia.indiatimes.com/india/why-the-census-matters-let-us-count-the-ways/articleshow/97204679.cms (accessed 22 January 2023).

Special Correspondent. 2022. 'Census rules amended to allow self-enumeration, digital data collection'. *The Hindu*, 13 March. Available at: https://www.thehindu.com/news/national/census-rules-amended-to-allow-self-enumeration-digital-data-collection/article65217776.ece (accessed 12 September 2022).

United Nations. 1958. Principles and Recommendations for National Population Censuses. United Nations: New York.

H.V. Zhimomi. 2012. Use of Technology for Census Data Analysis and Dissemination with Special Reference to the Census Info Dashboard. Nagaland: Director, Census Operations.

3

Digital Technologies and Elections in India

Negotiating Key Challenges

Tshumila Lama

Introduction

Nearly all the countries of the world use digital technologies in their election process for greater efficiency, and India is no exception. Digital technologies are used in different stages of the election process—from the registration of voters, election campaigns, identity verification, vote casting, counting, and finally the declarations of the results. Although the use of digital technologies in elections has increased efficiency and has made the election process easier and faster, the mode is not infallible. While some (Callen et al. 2016; Debnath et al. 2017; Stockemer 2018) agree that the use of digital technologies increases electoral efficiency and transparency, there are others (Yard 2010; Cheeseman 2018; Russell and Zamfir 2018; Garnett and James 2020; Maurer 2020) who are concerned about the organisational and logistical challenges that new digital technologies generate. Besides, in the age of information and cyber warfare, the security of the electoral process and data is a concern.

In India, the introduction of Electronic Voting Machines (EVMs) has made elections free and fair in a relative sense, reducing the scope of electoral fraud. However, there is no guarantee that the EVMs cannot be tampered with and be subject to external cyber-attacks. In the present times, the proliferation of internet connectivity and the use of smartphones, along with digital and social media, have opened new avenues for election campaigns. For instance, the 2014 general election was dubbed by Neyazi et al. (2016: 412) as the first 'internet election' when political parties like the Bhartiya Janata Party (BJP), the Indian National Congress (INC), the Communist Party of India (Marxist) (CPIM) and the Aam Aadmi Party (AAP) made extensive use of digital and social media in their campaigns.

The 2019 general election saw the parties relying more on digital campaigns than in 2014. Although the campaigns certainly have advantages using platforms like Google, Facebook (now Meta), Twitter, WhatsApp, YouTube and ShareChat, there are also several issues such as bribery and corruption, paid news and political advertising, including manipulation and disinformation. A large volume of content is posted online, which has made it difficult for the voters to differentiate between the 'real' and the 'fake'. In order to regulate online content, several measures have been taken by the Election Commission of India (ECI) and companies like Google, Facebook, Twitter and WhatsApp. The question of I-voting (internet voting) is another critical issue that is under scrutiny. In India, many rural and peripheral areas still have a dearth of infrastructure and connectivity. Additionally, illiteracy rates and lack of digital awareness or literacy are still very high among the voters. These factors put a big question mark regarding digital initiatives such as I-voting.

Against such a backdrop, this chapter assesses the role and transformations of the different stages of the election process through the use of digital technologies. The study would also analyse the challenges posed by such changes and discuss measures taken by ECI to tackle them. Further, an attempt is made to discuss the prospects with a critical question—whether India is ready for more digitalisation of the election process or not.

How Do Digital Technologies Matter?

India follows the 'first-past-the-post'[1] electoral system and the principle of universal adult franchise where every citizen above 18 has the right to vote. The ECI, an autonomous constitutional body, is responsible for conducting free and fair elections. Article 324 of the Constitution of India provides that the general elections, state legislature elections, and elections for the President and the Vice President are under the superintendence, direction and control of the ECI.[2] The ECI is also responsible for the delimitation of constituencies, preparation of electoral rolls, recognition of political parties and allotment of party symbols. The Supreme Court of India, in the Mohinder Singh Gill vs Chief Election Commissioner Case AIR 851 (1978), ruled that where existing laws and provisions are silent, the ECI has the authority to fill the gaps. As noted before, the use of digital technologies has become an integral part of the election process, and their role in the entire process can be divided into two major themes: first, the use of digital technologies in the number of electoral activities from casting to the counting of votes; and second, the use of digital and social media for campaigning.

Electronic Voting Machines (EVMs)

The introduction of EVMs replacing the paper ballot system for voting was a significant step taken by the ECI towards the digitalisation of the election process. The objective was to strengthen the electoral process, reduce electoral fraud, and reduce the costs of conducting elections. The EVMs were first used on an experimental basis in 1982 in the Paravur Assembly by-election in Kerala. However, because of the absence of any specific law prescribed for using voting machines, the Supreme Court, in an Election Appeal (A.C. Jose vs. Sivan Pillay and others, AIR 1984 SC 921) arising out of a petition related to the use of the machine in the Paravur Assembly constituency, ruled that the EVMs could not be used without a necessary provision. The Representation of the People Act, 1951, was amended in December 1988 with the insertion of a new section 61A, empowering the Commission to use the EVMs in such constituencies as it may deem necessary (Bhalla 1998: 230–232). Finally, in 1998, the EVMs were used in 25 Legislative Assembly constituencies spread across three states: Madhya Pradesh, Rajasthan and Delhi. Its use was further expanded in 1999 to 45 parliamentary constituencies, and later, in February 2000, to 45 assembly constituencies of the Haryana assembly elections. In the 2001 assembly elections of Tamil Nadu, Kerala, Puducherry and West Bengal, the EVMs were used in all the assembly constituencies. It was finally in the 2004 general elections that the EVMs were used in all 543 parliamentary constituencies in the country. Since then, EVMs have been used in every election (Election Commission of India, n.d.). According to Debnath, Kapoor and Ravi (2017: 7), the use of voting machines simplified the voting procedure and quickened the process of ascertaining results. It also reduced the cost of conducting elections as the ECI could avoid printing millions of ballots. It was seen that improper and multiple stamps on paper ballots, making the voter's choice unclear, inevitably lead to the dismissal of her/his/their vote. Since EVMs could record only one response, the possibility of rejected votes was virtually eliminated.

Web and Mobile Applications

The ECI has also developed a number of web and mobile applications to conduct the activities of the election process with greater convenience and transparency. There is an official ECI website that provides overall information about the election process, political parties and candidates.[3] It also has detailed information about the elections from 1952 onwards and is updated regularly. There is a Voter Portal which provides the facility of searching for names in the electoral roll by using the electronic photo identity card (EPIC) number or personal details, along with facilities such as registration of new voters, correction of particulars and migration cases inside (or outside) the assembly constituency. A mobile application called Voter Helpline also allows the voters to verify their name, the polling station and other details on the voter card and the election schedule. This mobile application can also submit forms for voter registration, migration and correction. The candidates can also file their nomination online through the Candidate Nomination Application by digitising their affidavit and depositing the security amount through online payment. Additionally, political parties can also track their application for registration online through the Political Party Registration Tracking Online portal.

The PWD Application was also launched to ensure a wider participation of Persons with Disabilities (PWD). Through an app called cVIGIL, citizens can report violations of the model code of conduct by capturing and submitting live photos or videos, and the election machinery is expected to spring into action immediately as they receive evidentiary proof of violation from citizens. A Voter Turnout App launched in April 2019 provides the approximate voter turnout percentage of each assembly constituency or parliamentary constituency to the larger public. An application called ENCORE Counting (Enabling Communications on Real-Time Environment) was launched in March 2019 for the counting of votes, monitoring of end-to-end processes and declaration of results, which are published online through the ECI Results Portal, Voter Helpline App and Election Trends TV (Election Commission of India, n.d.).

Electronically Transmitted Postal Ballot System

The Representation of the People Act, 1950, permits the 'service voters'[4] to register in the electoral rolls of a constituency where they are ordinarily residing. The postal ballot paper to the service voters is sent by the Returning Officer after printing the ballot for each and every service voter of the constituency. They are then put in an envelope inscribed with the address of the Record Office for each service voter. Since the electoral roll was not updated, the Record Officer faced a challenge in identifying the present place of posting of the service voter, thus causing issues of timely delivery, which led to a low turnout of the service voters of only about three to four per cent in the general election to the Lok Sabha in 2014.

Taking this into consideration, the ECI introduced the Electronically Transmitted Postal Ballot System (ETPBS) in October 2016. It is a one-way electronic transmission of postal ballots to the service voters where they cast their vote and send it to the respective returning officer via post. The complete process is secured through multiple checks and protocols to ensure safe transmission. Upon receipt of the postal ballot at the counting centres, the returning officer validates the receipt by a series of QR codes with that of the transmitted system. As a result, in the 2019 Lok Sabha election, 1,084,266 e-postal ballots were received through electronic transmission, indicating 60.14 per cent turnout, which was a significant improvement compared to the 2014 Lok Sabha election (Election Commission of India 2020).

Electoral Campaigns through Digital and Social Media

The proliferation of internet connectivity and the use of smartphones, along with digital and social media, have opened up new avenues for election campaigns. The internet offers the potential 'to revolutionize political activity far more profoundly than the telephone or television ever did, for unlike them, it offers the possibility of direct two-way interaction between the citizens and politicians' (Ferdinand 2000: 1). It is true that the cost, volume, directionality, speed, targeting and convergence, theoretically speaking, have made the internet a democratising tool (Stromer-Galley 2000: 41).

It was the 2014 general election that marked a change in the electoral campaigning strategy in India. Traditionally, candidates relied on local and cultivated knowledge and used techniques such as opinion polls, voter banks, door-to-door campaigning, booth-wise caste and religious profiling and communication from key community leaders and volunteers to focus on groups of voters (Sharma 2018). In contrast, in the 2014 elections, the use of data, technology and digital platforms played a central role in the way the campaigns were designed, structured, targeted, implemented and communicated (Hickok 2018: 4). Major political parties like the BJP, INC, CPI(M), AAP, Bahujan Samaj Party (BSP) and Nationalist Congress Party (NCP), used digital and social media such as Twitter, Google, Facebook, WhatsApp, Instagram, YouTube and others for campaigning in 2014. These online platforms served as a primary channel of communication and information between the party members. Also, they opened a direct communication channel between the party candidates and the general public. Through these platforms, the political parties and their candidates interacted with the public about their campaigns, rallies, meetings and interviews and encouraged the public to engage with the elections.

While AAP, INC and BJP each utilised digital tools, the general perception was that the BJP's digital campaign was the most robust, engaging and strategic of the three parties (Price 2015: 102–110). The Narendra Modi campaign of the BJP comprised several components, such as a social media analytics division, an Information Technology Cell and Mission 272+, which leveraged data to inform campaign messages, methods and focus. The campaigning strategy of the BJP that leveraged technology includes initiatives such as Chai Pe Charcha,[5] 3D Hologram Rallies,[6] Modi Aane Wale Hai,[7] NaMo Number,[8] Mere Sapno Ka Bharat,[9] Bharat Vijay Rallies,[10] Vijay Sankalp Diwas,[11] Modi for PM Fund[12] and The Indian Republic[13] (Hickok 2018: 5). The BJP was very articulate on social media and its posts were very concise yet comprehensive, crisp, neat, focused and self-explanatory; thus, they were able to successfully attract the attention of the voter (Kanungo 2015: 218).

Despite extensive use of digital media for electoral campaigns in 2014, scholars like Kanungo (2015: 227) concluded that social media was not a game changer in the 16th Lok Sabha elections as only a tiny elite section had access to digital technology and internet connections while the vast population remained unaffected by it. However, he stressed that social media has been significantly used by political parties to attract voters, particularly young and first-time voters. Parties used this medium to raise funds, connect with the electorate and mobilise or recruit volunteers. Apart from interacting, parties also used social media to raise issues, attack their opponents and promote their own leadership. Social media has undoubtedly made a considerable impact and will continue to make inroads into the election campaign in the future.

The launch of the Digital India Campaign[14] by the Government of India (GoI) in 2015 and the rise of cheap rates on mass mobile telephony have made the idea of the digital divide less relevant in India. According to the Telecom Regulatory Authority of India (TRAI)[15] between 2014 and 2019, the number of internet users went up by eight times. In May 2014, it was 65.3 million, and in May 2019, it reached 581.51 million. By May 2019, roughly one-third of Indians had access to Facebook (up from 9 per cent in 2014), WhatsApp and YouTube (CSDS Lokniti 2019). This increase in the number of internet users was also facilitated by the launch of the private Jio phone networks in September 2016, which initially provided cheap data rates.[16]

The 2019 general election in India, which was the first post-Jio general election, relied more heavily on digital electoral campaigns when compared to 2014. Although the BJP had an advantage in its early use of digital tools, by 2019, the INC had equally used smartphones, which had become widely available by then. It also created a Data Analytics Department headed by Praveen Chakravarty, a former investment banker. However, the BJP vastly outspent the INC on social media. Still, besides money, this advantage is mainly seen as an outcome of good organisational skills, with the BJP's small central team in Delhi able to engage millions of 'social media volunteers' around the country (Sardesai 2020: 226–227, 232–233). Political parties spent huge amounts on advertising in the 2019 general election. Between February and May 2019, Google and Facebook declared cumulative political online advertising of US$ 7.10 million. Google declared 12,276 political advertisements worth US$ 3.55 million (Mehta 2019). In its India Ad Library, Facebook declared a total of 132,419 advertisements worth US$ 3.54 million. The BJP dominated digital political spending on both platforms. On Google, it accounted for 41.4 per cent (US$1.47 million) of political advertising, with Tamil Nadu's Dravida Munneta Kazhagam (DMK) a distant second with 13.6 per cent (US$ 484.6 thousand) and the Congress third with 10 per cent (US$ 363.4 thousand). The BJP also dominated Facebook, accounting for 14.7 per cent (US$ 520.9 thousand) of political advertising, with the INC coming in a distant second with 6.1 per cent (US$ 218 thousand) of political advertising (*The Times of India* 2019).

In 2019, although there were many factors, digital campaigning was certainly one of the factors that contributed to the electoral success of the BJP. In the words of Neyazi and Schroeder (2021: 88), the use of digital media 'translated into visibility in traditional media, plus as a tool for on-the-ground mobilization both among active supporters and in terms of getting out the vote, were certainly necessary conditions for Modi's overwhelming electoral success'. Thus, according to Mehta (2019: 1), 'what happens on digital platforms is no longer an externality or an adjunct to offline politics—it is constitutive of it and inseparable from larger political mobilisation'.

Challenges of Digitalisation of the Election Process

Digital technology has indeed made the election process efficient, but there are also many challenges. Let me enumerate some such issues.

Hacking and External Attacks

Although the use of EVMs has reduced electoral fraud, it does not mean that the EVMs cannot be tampered with. Electronic voting systems are vulnerable to hacking and attacks, both internal and external. In 2010, a Hyderabad-based engineer, in collaboration with an American computer scientist and a Dutch Hacker, demonstrated two different methods of tampering with the machines to manipulate the results. According to them, the EVM could be, one, physically tampered with to favour a particular candidate, and two, the candidate's vote could also be stolen from the machine (Sircar 2019). In 2014, a US-based Indian cyber expert appeared at a news conference through Skype and claimed that 200 seats in the 2014 elections that INC would have won had been rigged in favour of the BJP by 'manipulating' data transmission through 'military-grade modulators' installed in various parts of the country. The ECI however rejected the allegations, which nevertheless have created profound mistrust among the parties and voters regarding the Electronic Voting System (Sonwalkar 2019). With increased dependence on digital technology, Indian elections are potential targets of external hacking and cyber-attacks, leading to trust issues and questions about the credibility of the system.

Regulation of data

The digitalisation of elections and campaigns has also changed the nature of electoral data and information. The electoral data, which once was non-digitised and could be accessed only by competent authorities, is now accessible to everyone with (il)legitimate motives. The data can also be accessed by external actors and manipulated. A large amount of data about the elections, campaigns, voters' personalities and political preferences is also available on digital and social media platforms. Such data, held by corporations such as Google and other social media companies, are helpful for parties and candidates for micro-targeting. Due to this, there has been commodification and commercialisation of electoral and voter data. Multinational companies purchase localised registers to create new centralised datasets, which are then used to generate profit (James and Bernal 2020: 24–27). Companies such as Cambridge Analytica have been known to harvest personal information and data from millions of Facebook users without their consent in order to advise campaigning and consultancy teams for monetary gains (*The Guardian* 2018a; 2018b). This has raised serious concerns regarding a breach of privacy, misuse of data and the ability to manipulate elections.

Disinformation

There is a growing concern in India over the (dis)information to sway public opinion and/or political behaviour, which is facilitated by the rapid flow of information and data through digital and social media. A large volume of online content makes it difficult for voters to differentiate between real and fake information. The Reuters Institute India Digital News Report published just before the Lok Sabha election 2019 showed that 57 per cent of the respondents were worried about whether the online news on their social media feed was credible (Aneez et al. 2019: 8). In 2018, a fake survey report claiming that BJP would win 135 seats in the Karnataka state elections had been doing the rounds on WhatsApp with a British Broadcasting Corporation (BBC) link provided for legitimacy. In view of this, the BBC had to issue a clarification that it had not commissioned any pre-poll survey in Karnataka (Dalmia 2018). The Oxford Internet Institute's (OII) study also found that WhatsApp messaging was used widely by all political parties to spread (dis)information (Campbell-Smith & Bradshaw 2019: 4). In India, a specific area of concern is WhatsApp, which has often been called a 'blackhole of disinformation' (Ponniah 2019). (Dis)information in the form of messages shared by WhatsApp and Facebook has led to a series of troubling incidents in India and is one of the critical challenges posed by the extensive use of digital platforms.

Measures Taken by the ECI

In view of the challenges noted above, the ECI adopted several measures and reforms in the electoral laws. Some of the important measures can be discussed briefly under the following heads:

Voter Verification Paper Audit-Trial (VVPAT)

To prevent EVM tampering and increase electoral transparency, the ECI has introduced the Voter Verification Paper Audit-Trial (VVPAT). It is a sophisticated machine that enables the voter to see whether her/his/their vote recorded in the EVM is the same as they have cast through the automatic generation of a printed paper slip, which is then automatically dropped in a sealed box. This system provides a backup in case of loss of votes in the EVMs and also helps to tally the results to test whether the total votes in the machine have been correctly counted. The VVPAT was first used in 2013 in the Noksen Assembly constituency (Nagaland) and was used in all the 543 parliamentary constituencies in the 2019 General Election. In 2019, a number of political leaders approached the Supreme Court to direct the ECI to match at least 50 per cent of VVPAT paper slips with the total vote count recorded by the EVMs. The Supreme Court bench led by the Chief Justice of India, however, did not accept the opposition parties' arguments to have 33 per cent to 50 per cent votes verified. Nevertheless, the Supreme Court on 8 April 2019 ordered the ECI to increase the VVPAT slips from one EVM per Assembly constituency to five, which was to be randomly selected. Following the Court order, votes cast in about 20,625 EVMs across the country were verified through the paper trail in the 2019 general election (Mathur 2019).

Instructions on the Use of Social Media

In October 2013, the ECI issued the 'Instructions of the Commission with respect to use of Social Media in Election Campaigning' to the political parties on the use of social media in election campaigns by their candidates. Candidates are required to submit an affidavit with their social media accounts and contact details, obtain pre-certification of all advertisements on electronic media, including those on social media, provide a report on expenditure incurred on campaigning through the internet, including social media websites and on companies/consultancies engaged for creative development of content with the stipulation of adherence to the model code of content on the internet and social media.[17]

Media Certification and Monitoring Committee

Since 2013, the ECI has also established a district-level Media Certification and Monitoring Committee to monitor cable TV and satellite channels, radio broadcasts and FM transmissions, and print media and social media for paid news and political advertising.

Transparency and Accountability in Funding

In 2013, in an attempt to bring transparency to campaign funding, a legal framework was established to allow private firms to donate any amount of funding to political parties as long as the amount is disclosed. Accordingly, the Electoral Trust Scheme 2013 was designed to bring in more transparency in the funds provided by corporate entities to the political parties for their election-related expenses. The ECI has circulated guidelines for the submission of contribution reports of electoral trusts through an annual report. In 2014, the ECI also issued guidelines[18] to all political parties, listing ways to increase transparency and accountability in funding and election expenditure.

Seeding of Aadhar

For better identity and verification of voters, in 2018, the ECI filed a plea with the Supreme Court to make seeding of Aadhaar cards with EPIC necessary to redress electoral fraud (Financial Express 2018).

Voluntary Code of Ethics

To regulate online content, major social media companies agreed to a 'voluntary code of ethics' submitted by the Internet & Mobile Association of India (IAMAI) to ECI on 20 March 2019. It entailed that the companies would voluntarily agree to four key initiatives: first, they will conduct education and communication campaigns building awareness on elections. Second, they will create a high-priority dedicated grievance redressal channel to take action on objectionable posts reported to the ECI under various electoral laws like Section 126 of the Representation of the People Act, 1951. More importantly, this included commitments by tech companies to act within three hours for reported violations during the mandatory 48-hour no-campaigning-and-silence period for candidates before voting. Third, they will ensure pre-certification of all political advertisements published on their platforms from the government's media certification and monitoring committees, as mandated by the Supreme Court. Fourth, they are to transparently report paid political advertisements and label and disclose them as such (ECI 2019).[19] The ECI later reported that 909 posts were eventually taken down during the election period by tech platforms through the grievance redressal mechanism (ECI 2019). In view of the above, Facebook removed 650 posts, Twitter deleted 220 tweets and ShareChat removed 31 posts from their platforms. YouTube also removed five videos, and three WhatsApp service users were disabled after being flagged by the ECI for violation of the code (*NDTV* 2019).

Future Prospects: Possibilities of I-voting

The ECI is currently exploring the possibilities of implementing I-voting (also sometimes called e-voting or online voting) through high-end technologies such as blockchain. I-voting would allow the voters to cast their votes remotely. In 2020, the ECI conducted several discussions and demonstrations with state governments, policy think tanks and private industry stakeholders to explore the idea of a nationwide remote blockchain election system. In February 2020, it collaborated with the Indian Institute of Technology, Madras (IIT-M), to develop a new technology allowing remote voting via a blockchain system (Rajkotwala 2021). In October 2021, the state government of Telangana developed the first smartphone app for I-voting called TSEC (Telangana State Election Commission) voting app and conducted a mock I-voting experiment at Khammam Municipality. The State Commission believed that such an app would help people who face challenges in voting physically, for example, persons with disabilities, senior citizens and military personnel. There are certainly some advantages of I-voting. For instance, it reduces geographical barriers and can increase voter turnout.

However, it is subject to high-security risks as hackers tend to attack the servers of electoral authorities or voter devices to manipulate the results. The risks are so high that cyber security experts in 2014 recommended Estonia, then the only country in the world using I-voting, to discontinue I-voting (Russell and Zamfir 2018: 9). Many Western countries like Holland, Germany and Ireland have reverted to the paper ballot system to avoid security risks.

In India, apart from security risks, there are other issues as well that need to be taken into serious consideration. In recent years, though there has been a substantial increase in the number of internet users,[20] there are issues of connectivity. In many parts of the country, the illiteracy[21] rate and level of ignorance are still very high among the voters, and a vast section of the population finds it extremely difficult to understand the digital process. Given such conditions, the implementation of I-voting would make the scenario even more complex. It would require substantial technological advancement and electoral management skills to deal with the problems that would come along with implementing such a system. Given India's constraints, the country does not seem to be ready for that. Therefore, when India is struggling to deal with the existing challenges of the digitalisation of the election process, the idea of implementing the system of I-voting requires more intense discussions and debates with all stakeholders.

Conclusion

Digital technology lays bare the nagging contention between the issue of (electoral) efficiency and that of (electoral) transparency. Efficiency is certainly welcome, but not at the cost of transparency. The conduct of free, fair and impartial elections is integral to the success of democracy, but the challenges that digitalisation of the election process has raised are significant. Additional issues, such as the security of data and (dis) information, remain to be addressed seriously. India, the world's largest democracy, in trying to deal with these challenges, requires extensive revision of the existing electoral laws and policies, development and advancement of appropriate technical resources and robust cybersecurity laws to ensure digitalisation of the election process without compromising the credibility and integrity of the entire electoral process.

Notes

1 Also called the simple majority system where the candidate with the highest number of votes in a constituency wins.
2 For the elections to local bodies such as panchayats and municipalities in the states, there is a separate State Election Commission.
3 See https://eci.gov.in/ (accessed 3 August 2022).
4 Persons working in the Central Forces under the Arms Act and government officials deployed in embassies outside the country.
5 Digital programme for public outreach and communication focusing on governance, women and agrarian crisis that leveraged satellite, DTH and internet and mobile technology to facilitate 'conversations over tea' with individuals within and outside of India.
6 3D hologram technology was used to hold 1,350 3D rallies across India at the state and constituency levels.
7 GPS-enabled video trucks went to villages in the state of Uttar Pradesh to ensure outreach in remote areas.
8 Strategy to gain more supporters through gamification where individuals are incentivised to collect contacts which are represented by a voter ID and phone number.
9 Citizens were given the opportunity to record short videos on their vision for India. Individuals could submit through email, SMS, WhatsApp or voice message. Chosen videos would be published on the 'India 272' campaign portal.
10 It leveraged social media to ensure outreach and engagement on the ground reports prior to the event so as to inform each rally speech with local context.
11 It leveraged technology to engage with booth-level workers for the BJP across the country.
12 Placed ads on Facebook and on the Modi website for monetary contributions.
13 Online news portal that sought to engage with the public via internet and mobile platforms.
14 Campaign launched on 1 July 2015 by the GoI with a vision to transform India into a digitally empowered society and knowledge economy with 'Power to Empower' as its motto.
15 Telecom Regulatory Authority of India (TRAI) is a regulatory body set up in 1997 by the Government of India and is the regulator of the telecommunications sector in India.
16 Reliance Jio Infocomm Limited (Jio) is an Indian Telecommunications Company. On 5 September 2016, the company launched its 4G services offering free data and voice services until 31 December 2016.
17 See https://www.eci.gov.in/files/file/6629-instructions-of-the-commission-with-respect-to-use-of-social-media-in-election-campaigning/ (accessed 25 August 2022).

18 See https://eci.gov.in/files/file/5036-guidelines-on-transparency-and-accountability-in-party-funds-and-election-expenditure-matter-regardingdated-29082014/ (accessed 30 August 2022).

19 See https://www.eci.gov.in/files/file/9468-voluntary-code-of-ethics-by-the-social-media-platforms-for-the-general-election-2019/ (accessed 25 August 2022).

20 According to the Digital 2022 Report in India, the internet penetration rate in India stood at 47.0 per cent of the total population at the start of 2022.

21 As per the 2011 Census Report of GoI, the literacy rate in the country is 74.04 per cent.

References

'Aadhaar linking news update: Election Commission appeals for mandatory seeding of 12-digit UID with Voter-ID'. 2018. *Financial Express*, 11 March. Available at: https://www.financialexpress.com/aadhaar-card/aadhaar-linking-news-update-election-commission-appeals-for-mandatory-seeding-of-12-digit-uid-with-voter-id/1094332/ (accessed 9 September 2022).

'"Cash-Strapped" Congress Spent Rs 820 Crore on 2019 Lok Sabha Polls'. 2019. *The Times of India*, 8 November. Available at: https://timesofindia.indiatimes.com/india/cash-strapped-congress-spent-rs-820-crore-on-2019-lok-sabha-polls/articleshow/71963145.cms (accessed 4 September 2022).

'Digital 2022: India'. 2022. *Datareportal*, 15 February. Available at: https://datareportal.com/reports/digital-2022-india (accessed 17 August 2022).

'ETPBS'. 2020. *Election Commission of India*, 18 February. Available at: https://eci.gov.in/it-applications/web-applications/etpbs-r7/ (accessed 24 January 2023).

'From Electors to Elections from Voter to Voting and from Candidates to Counting: ICT Apps Create a Perfect Ecosystem'. n.d. *Election Commission of India*. Available at: https://eci.gov.in/divisions-of-eci/ict-apps/ (accessed 22 August 2022).

'History of EVM'. n.d. *Election Commission of India*. Available at: https://eci.gov.in/voter/history-of-evm/ (accessed 22 August 2022).

'How Cambridge Analytica turned Facebook 'likes' into a lucrative political tool'. 2018. *The Guardian*, 17 March. Available at: https://www.theguardian.com/technology/2018/mar/17/facebook-cambridge-analytica-kogan-data-algorithm (accessed on 2 September 2022).

'Over 900 Posts Taken Down from Social Media Platforms During 2019 Polls'. 2019. *NDTV*, 19 May. Available at: https://www.ndtv.com/india-news/lok-sabha-election-2019-over-900-posts-taken-down-from-social-media-platforms-during-national-polls-2039866 (accessed 4 September 2022).

'Revealed: 50 million Facebook Profiles Harvested for Cambridge Analytica in Major Data Breach'. 2018b. *The Guardian*, 17 March. Available at: https://www.theguardian.com/news/2018/mar/17/cambridge-analytica-facebook-influence-us-election (accessed 2 September 2022).

'Social Media and Political Behaviour'. 2019. *CSDS Lokniti*. Available at: https://www.csds.in/uploads/custom_files/Report-SMPB.pdf (accessed 5 September 2022).

Z. Aneez, T.A. Neyazi, A. Kalogeropoulous and R.K. Nielsen. 2019. 'Reuters Institute India Digital News Report'. *Reuters Institute for the Study of Journalism*. Available at: https://reutersinstitute.politics.ox.ac.uk/sites/default/files/2019-03/India_DNR_FINAL.pdf (accessed 27 August 2022).

R.P. Bhalla. 1998. *Elections in India: Legacy and Vision*. New Delhi: S. Chand and Company.

M. Callen, C.C. Gibson, D.F. Jung and J.D. Long. 2016. 'Improving electoral integrity with information and communications technology'. *Journal of Experimental Political Science*, 3(1): 4–17.

U. Campbell-Smith and S. Bradshaw. 2019. 'Global cyber troops country profile: India'. *Oxford Internet Institute*, University of Oxford. Available at: https://www.readkong.com/page/global-cyber-troops-country-profile-india-8977519 (accessed 4 September 2022).

N. Cheeseman, G. Lynch and J. Willis. 2018. 'Digital dilemmas: The Unintended Consequences of Election Technology'. *Democratization*, 25 (8): 1397–1418.

V. Dalmia. 2018. 'Tackling the Digital Threat to Elections in India', *Mint*, 9 May. Available at: https://www.livemint.com/Opinion/94bediK20HQ8JPRBg6UUcN/Tackling-the-digital-threat-to-elections-in-India.html (accessed 1 September 2022).

S. Debnath, M. Kapoor and S. Ravi. 2017. 'The Impact of Electronic Voting Machines on Electoral Frauds, Democracy and Development'. *Brookings Institution*, 16 March. Available Online: https://www.brookings.edu/wp-content/uploads/2016/10/evm_march2017.pdf (accessed 20 August 2022).

P. Ferdinand. 2000. 'The Internet, Democracy and Democratization', *Democratization*, 7(1): 1–17.

A.H. Garnett and T.S. James. 2020. 'Cyber Elections in the Digital Age: Threats and Opportunities of Technology for Electoral Integrity'. *Election Law Journal*, 19 (2): 111–126.

E. Hickok. 2018. 'Digital Platforms, Technologies, and Data Use in the General Elections in India', in partnership with Tactical Technology Collective's Our Data Our Selves project.

T.S. James and P. Bernal. 2020. *Is It Time for Automatic Voter Registration in the UK?* York: Joseph Rowntree Reform Trust.

N.T. Kanungo. 2015. 'India's Digital Poll Battle: Political Parties and Social Media in the 16th Lok Sabha Elections'. *Studies in Indian Politics,* 3(2): 212–228.

A. Mathur. 2019. 'Supreme Court orders EC to increase VVPAT verification from one EVM to five', *India Today*, 8 April. Available at: https://www.indiatoday.in/elections/lok-sabha-2019/story/supreme-court-election-commission-increase-vvpat-verification-evm-1496819-2019-04-08 (accessed 24 January 2023).

A.D. Maurer. 2020. *Digital Technologies in Elections: Questions, Lessons learned and Perspectives.* Council of Europe Publishing.

N. Mehta. 2019. 'Digital Politics in India's 2019 General Elections'. *Economic and Political Weekly*, 54 (51).

T.A. Neyazi and R. Schroeder. 2021. 'Was the 2019 Indian Election Won by Digital Media?' *The Communication Review*, 24 (2): 87–106.

T.A. Neyazi, A. Kumar and H.A. Semetko. 2016. 'Campaigns, Digital Media and Mobilization in India', *The International Journal of Press/Politics*, 21 (3): 398–416.

K. Ponniah. 2019. 'WhatsApp: The 'Black Hole' of Fake News in India's Election', *BBC News*, 6 April. Available at: https://www.bbc.com/news/world-asia-india-47797151 (accessed 12 September 2022).

L. Price. 2015. *The Modi Effect: inside Narendra Modi's Campaign to Transform India.* London: Hachette UK.

M. Rajkotwala. 2021. 'E-voting to become reality soon? Here's what Election Commission should do before going for blockchain polls', *FirstPost*, 9 October. Available at: https://www.firstpost.com/india/e-voting-to-become-reality-soon-heres-what-election-commission-should-do-before-going-for-blockchain-polls-10038021.html (accessed 8 August 2022).

M. Russell and L. Zamfir. 2018. 'Digital Technology in Elections: Efficiency versus Credibility?' *European Parliamentary Research Service.*

R. Sardesai. 2020. *2019: How Modi Won India?* Noida, India: Harper Collins.

S.N. Sharma. 2018. 'Why India has Nothing to Fear from Rightful Use of Big Data', *The Economic Times*, 1 April. Available at: https://economictimes.indiatimes.com/news/politics-and-nation/why-india-has-nothing-to-fear-from-rightful-use-of-big-data/articleshow/63560703.cms?from=mdr (accessed 14 August 2022).

S. Sircar. 2019. '"EVM Hack Still Possible": Engineer Who Demonstrated It in 2010', *The Quint*, 25 January. Available at: https://www.thequint.com/

news/india/evm-hack-still-possible-hari-prasad-who-demonstrated-it-in-2010#read-more (accessed 28 August 2022).

P. Sonwalkar. 2019. 'EVMs hacked in 2014, claims US-based Indian "cyber expert", EC rejects allegations', *Hindustan Times*, 21 January. Available at: https://www.hindustantimes.com/world-news/evms-hacked-in-2014-claims-us-based-indian-cyber-expert-ec-rejects-allegations/story-hz113fWFOXp6DpDe5DO5LI.html# (accessed 28 August 2022).

J. Stromer-Galley. 2000. 'Democratizing Democracy: Strong Democracy, US Political Campaigns and the Internet'. *Democratization,* 7 (1): 36–58.

M. Yard, ed. 2010. *Direct Democracy: Progress and Pitfalls of Election Technology*. Washington, DC: International Foundation for Electoral Systems.

4

Digital Politics of an Exiled State

The Case of the Tibetans in India

Jigme Yeshe Lama

Introduction

While writings on Tibetan digital activism are growing, very few have delved into the digital aspects of politics in the exiled community. This chapter attempts to fill this gap through a critical focus on the dynamism of the digital politics of the Tibetans in exile. It is important to note here that India has emerged as the prime locale for the enactment of such politics.

Since the 1960s, the Tibetan government in exile, also known as the Central Tibetan Administration (CTA), has provided a government for the Tibetan refugees. The CTA was established by the 14th Dalai Lama in the aftermath of the Chinese invasion of Tibet in 1950. As a fully functional government, the CTA consists of an executive, a legislature and a judiciary that is aided by an efficient bureaucracy. In 2011, due to various factors, the 14th Dalai Lama relinquished his political powers in favour of a directly elected leader. Electoral politics led to the use and rise of digital media, especially social media platforms. The candidates contesting for the posts of the *sikyong* (President of CTA) and Tibetan parliament employed social media to campaign for votes. Both the supporters and detractors have utilised social media platforms, furthering the relevance of digital politics. It is seen that politics mediated through social media in exile has increased the notion of 'secularisation' in Tibetan society. The embracing of digital politics by Tibetans in exile is also a mode of bringing Tibetans closer to 'politics' in exile. This is observed with

Tibet TV, the CTA's WebTV station that was launched in 2006 where the official narrative regarding the initiation of WebTV was to provide political information to exiled Tibetans.

In 2011, a 43-year-old senior fellow of Harvard Law School, Lobsang Sangay, was elected as the *kalon tripa* (Prime Minister) of the Tibetan Government in Exile or CTA. He won 27,051 votes (55 per cent) in the final round of polling held on 20 March 2011. The other two candidates were former ministers of CTA, Tenzin Namgyal Tethong and Tashi Wangdi (Staff Reporter 2011). Since 2001, the Tibetans have directly elected their *kalon tripa*, thus accelerating the process of democratisation in the exiled community. In this context, the issues of democratic politics, including the role of the Dalai Lama and the CTA, will be elaborated on later in the chapter. Here, it is important to note that the 2011 elections of the Tibetan Prime Minister in exile can be dubbed as a 'paradigm shift' as the new *kalon tripa*, Lobsang Sangay, was a layperson who hailed from a somewhat common background. It was observed that the *kalon tripa*s, prior to 2001, were appointed by the Dalai Lama and belonged mostly to elite backgrounds. They were former aristocrats or religious personages, which also included the first directly elected Prime Minister, Samdhong Rinpoche. He is a recognised reincarnated monk, the fifth of his line, belonging to the great monastic university of Drepung in Lhasa. Since the early days of exile, the Dalai Lama, who acted as the spiritual and earlier political leader of the Tibetans, in order to democratise the exiled community, had voluntarily given up political power in a step-by-step manner, through his own initiative and without any pressure from below (Phuntso 2004: 126). Following these developments, democratisation among Tibetans in exile reached a crescendo with the election of Lobsang Sangay and the consequent relinquishing of political power by the Dalai Lama in 2011.

Furthermore, the foundations of Tibetan democracy were strengthened in the 2011 elections for choosing the *kalon tripa* and other members of the Tibetan parliament in exile, as the candidates themselves campaigned through digital and social media. With exiled Tibetan communities spread across 46 Tibetan settlements in India, Nepal and Bhutan, political campaigning through the digital mode for the seats of the executive and legislature of the CTA became necessary (Norbu 2004: 126). Presently, digital politics assumes relevance as the number of Tibetans in the West has increased and a significant proportion of Tibetan youth in India reside in cities that are located far away from their settlement camps. Through the digital, Tibetan politicians have tried to communicate with them in an attempt to strengthen ideas of democracy. While digital platforms, especially social networking apps and sites, have provided exiled politicians with access to the exiled population, they also grant a space for the latter to voice their myriad opinions regarding politics and the politicians. For instance, in the run-up to the 2011 *kalon tripa* elections, a public debate was organised by the popular online news portal Phayul.com on 9 September 2010 (Lobsang Tsering 2012). The debate is modelled on the lines of the US Presidential debates, where the candidates make their opening statements after which the floor is opened to questions from the public. It was uploaded on social media and even shared in 2018 by Facebook users. Thus, Tibetans with access to social media have participated by sharing and commenting on these debates, leading to a growth in democratic practices in the exiled Tibetan community. However, the quality of these kinds of democratic practices is debatable and will be analysed further in the chapter.

Tibetan Government in Exile: An Outline

Before delving into the various aspects of digital politics in the exiled Tibetan community, an outline of the Tibetan government in exile or the CTA is necessary. The CTA remains the core of Tibetan politics as it fashions the ruling discourses in the exiled community. The CTA was established by the Dalai Lama on 29 April 1960 in the north Indian town of Dharamshala (McConnell 2016: 4). A government in exile had to be established as the 14th Dalai Lama along with tens of thousands of Tibetans had to escape their homeland in Tibet and seek refuge in India. It was in the aftermath of a failed uprising against the Chinese in 1959 that the Tibetan hierarch along with his followers took flight to the neighbouring countries in South Asia. The newly formed People's Republic of China (PRC) under the leadership of Mao Zedong and the Communist Party of China (CPC) invaded Tibet in 1950. From 1950–1959, the Chinese Communists tried to co-opt the traditional Tibetan government, which ended in failure leading to the revolt of 1959 that terminated the traditional setup headed by the Dalai Lama. The pre-1950 traditional government, known as the *Ganden Phodrang* government, needs greater interrogation because the CTA dubs itself as a continuation of the same. It draws legitimation out of a direct succession of the central Tibetan government in Lhasa (Roemer 2009: 6).

Georges Dreyfus (1995) informs us that the *Ganden Phodrang* government is based on the union of the religious and the political known as *chos sri dzungdrel* whereby the political system in Tibet was informed by Buddhist principles, which provide its main sources of legitimacy. The union of the religious and the political went beyond legitimisation and it provided a social framework that makes sense of some of the most particular characteristics of Tibetan culture (the institution of the reincarnated lama and the political dominance of religious groups throughout most of Tibetan history). Buddhism is seen to have shaped the process of the formation of political institutions in Tibet. It also contributed to the unifying of Tibet as Buddhism brought a standardisation of writing. More importantly, the introduction of Buddhism also promoted the development of legal codes, basic to more centralised forms of political authority (Dreyfus 1995: 118–120).

The *chos sri dzungdrel* is illustrated in pre-1950 Tibet by the physical and conceptual location of the Lhasa government in relation to the outlying provinces and by the centrality of the Dalai Lama in that Tibetan cultural universe. The path to Lhasa was both secular and religious. It was frequented by pilgrims who thronged the sacred sites in Lhasa to see the Dalai Lama, but the path was also for the seekers of legal justice, complaints and appeals. All these paths theoretically converged towards one centre, which was the Dalai Lama (Dreyfus 1995: 122). It was the fifth Dalai Lama, Ngawang Lobsang Gyatso, who established the *Ganden Phodrang* government, after receiving military support from Gushri Khan, the leader of the Qosot Mongols who entered into a priest-patron relationship with the Dalai Lama (Lopes 2015: 53). The Dalai Lamas are a line of reincarnated monks belonging to the Geluk or Yellow Hat school of Tibetan Buddhism and are seen as emanations of Avalokiteshwara (the Bodhisattva of Compassion). Thus, they are spiritual masters, who are primarily simple monks or lamas. This understanding of the Dalai Lama helps us to comprehend the construction of the status of monks, especially Geluk monks, which constituted the foundation on which the Tibetan state was established (Lopes 2015: 74). Monks were now a part of the Tibetan state and served as officials and this practice has continued in exile (post-1959) with monks being elected to the Tibetan parliament. Additionally, a few monks have also served as ministers in past cabinets of the CTA.

While the Dalai Lama was at the apex of the Tibetan political system, there was the presence of a bureaucracy and an administrative system which governed the country. The government was administered by both lay and monk officials whereby the former was recruited from estate-holding, hereditary, lay aristocracy, consisting of about 150–200 families. Each aristocratic family had to provide one male member to serve as a government official. It was the fifth Dalai Lama who created the 16 positions in the government to be filled by monks. In the later years, the number of monk officials increased, and before the Chinese invasion of Tibet, several hundred monk officials controlled religious and monastic affairs playing important roles in the administration of secular affairs. During the minor period of the Dalai Lama, the administration was under a regent, who was an incarnate lama selected to rule by the National Assembly. In many cases, as is seen in the context of the Reting-Traktra controversy in the early twentieth century, the regents were often involved in misgovernance and corruption. The government was headed by a *lonchen* or *silon*, often translated as 'prime minister', which was not really an equivalent title as this was a titular position, and their powers were greatly diminished over time (Goldstein 2007: 8–12). Beneath the Dalai Lama and the *lonchen* were the offices of the Tibetan government, which had varied composition and functions, each being headed by a fixed number of officials and a fixed ratio of a monk to lay officials, if they included both the categories (Roemer 2009: 17).

The highest government office beneath the regent and *lonchen* was the *kashag* which is equivalent to the cabinet and is present in the CTA.

Pre-1950 Tibet's cabinet had three lay officials and a monk official appointed by the ruler, and all decision-making was done through a consensus. The *kashag* was the administrative centre of the Tibetan government. It ultimately received all secular information—requests, telegrams and the like—and sorted them, and then sent each item to the appropriate office (or an official) for examination. No secular matter could reach the ruler without going through the *kashag*, and the *kashag's* seal was required for most formal orders of the government. In addition, it initiated surveys, investigations, developed new policies and submitted recommendations for promotions and demotions of lay officials to the ruler. According to Goldstein (2007: 13–15), the power of the *kashag* emanated from the fact that they had direct contact with the ruler and could block the transmission of requests, petitions or recommendations.

Independent Tibet also had a National Assembly that was created during the 1860s to resolve an internal crisis. Known as the *tshongdu*, the assembly selected the regents and came to play an important role in national affairs. From 1913–1951, there were three types of assemblies, all of which met irregularly at the request of the *kashag* to consider and give opinions on specific questions supplied to it by the *kashag*. The smallest of the assemblies was a standing committee consisting of the four heads of the *yigtsang* (the four *trunyichenmo*) and the four heads of the *yigtsang* office (the four *tsipons*). Called the eight *trunyichenmo* and *tsipon*s, it was usually convened by the *kashag* to widen the base of support for a proposal to be presented to the ruler. The larger of the other two assemblies is called the Full National Assembly (*Tshongdu Gyentsom*). Its members consisted of the abbots and ex-abbots of the three major Gelukpa monasteries, Ganden, Sera and Drepung, Trungtsigye, and all the lay and monk officials present in Lhasa at the time. Representatives from a number of incarnations and monasteries such as Reting, Kundeling, Tsomoling, Tsecholing, Ditru, Tashilhunpo, the Ganden Tri Rinpoche and Sakya were present. Also, the captains and lieutenants of the army who were stationed in Lhasa, the 20 minor officials who were in charge of collecting house taxes and arranging corvee taxes in Lhasa and about 30 clerks were present (Goldstein 2007: 19–20). The *Ganden Phodrang* government under the Dalai Lamas formulated and implemented laws in Tibet. For instance, the traditional government used to implement laws regarding wildlife conservation, through the Mountain Valley Edict which generally dealt with wildlife conservation, preventing the killing of certain animals, birds and aquatic creatures during certain periods of the year (Norbu 2009).

Pre-1951 Tibet had diplomatic relations with neighbouring countries, including China, Nepal, Bhutan, Mongolia and British India. The Simla Agreement of 1914 which drew the borders between Tibet and the Northeast Frontier Agency (NEFA), comprising modern-day Arunachal Pradesh in India, was signed between the British and the Lhasa government. Lhasa also had tribute relations with several polities, including the Lopchak mission, whereby the rulers of Ladakh sent an official mission to Lhasa with gifts to the *Ganden Phodrang* government as well as leading lamas and monasteries in Central Tibet (Bray 2012: 44). However, the Tibetan government did not have full territorial control of ethnically Tibetan areas. By the 1950s, the Lhasa administration still did not control eastern Kham and most of Amdo (northeastern Tibet). These regions were ruled by a handful of chieftains, monasteries and kingdoms. The Lhasa government did have a series of engagements with these polities. Yet, the lack of defined borders and 'the fact that the central government did not exercise day-to-day control over the whole population' does not necessarily imply that Tibet did not exist as a state. Rather, it simply means that the nature of the Tibetan system cannot be neatly pigeonholed into a Euro-American political framework (McConnell 2016: 50).

Thus in 1950, when the People's Liberation Army (PLA) invaded Tibet, they encountered a fully functional state. While the Chinese Communists dub this invasion as the liberation of Tibet and Tibetans, it was conducted to secure their southwestern borders. The scholar Dawa Norbu writes how from the late nineteenth century, Tibet was perceived by the imperial Chinese as a security threat. This perception continued during the nationalist period and was resolved by the Chinese Communists through their military takeover of Tibet. However, due to Tibet's unique status and the presence of a fully functional government, the Chinese signed the 'Seventeen Point Agreement for the Peaceful Liberation of Tibet' with the Tibetan government in 1951, which provided continued autonomy and the preservation of Tibetan religious and social traditions (McConnell 2016: 54). From 1951 to 1959, the Chinese Communists entered a 'united front' with the traditional Tibetan elites, which came to an end with the revolts in eastern and northeastern Tibet that culminated in the 1959 Lhasa uprising. The uprising was brutally crushed and led to the Dalai Lama and his coterie of religious and political officials coming into exile to South Asia. They were followed by tens of thousands of Tibetan refugees who were eventually settled in the numerous settlement camps in different parts of India, Nepal and Bhutan.

The presence of a sizeable refugee population, which increased over the years, led the Dalai Lama and his officials to create a CTA, which would provide relief and rehabilitation to the Tibetans. The establishment of the CTA would also challenge the Chinese takeover of Tibet and strive for the freedom of Tibetans. The CTA acted as an exile government that was a continuation of the Lhasa-based *Ganden Phodrang* government headed by the Dalai Lama. While this was intended to provide a continuity of government, alternatively, it was also a means to claim legitimacy in the eyes of the external world as well as of the Tibetans who remained inside Tibet. Significantly, the CTA provides governance to the Tibetans in exile and according to McConnell (2016), the CTA has in many ways emulated India's postcolonial mode of governance. These include combining capitalist principles with socialist-inspired centralised state-planned development, adopting managerial rationality through a formalised bureaucracy, and promoting the institutionalisation of democracy on a range of scales (McConnell 2016: 55).

The democratisation of the Tibetans in exile has been a major dream of the Dalai Lama, so much so that as mentioned earlier, in 2011, he relinquished the exercise of his political power for an elected leader. However, the seeds of democracy in exile were sown in 1961 when the Dalai Lama tasked his officials with devising a constitution that was based on democratic principles. Officially adopted on 10 March 1963, and closely following the Indian model, this was the first written constitution in Tibetan history. The new constitution combined Western concepts of parliamentary and popular democracy with principles of Tibetan Buddhism, laying the foundations for the formation of the CTA. It was only with the promulgation of the 'Charter of Tibetans in Exile' in 1991 that the three pillars of Tibetan democratic government (the executive, the legislature and the judiciary) were established. Accordingly, the Tibetan parliament in exile has directly elected members, with representation from the three historic provinces of Tibet (U-Tsang, Kham and Amdo), the religious schools of Tibetan Buddhism (including the pre-Buddhist Bon school) and Tibetans from North America, Europe and the region of Australasia. The parliament exercises broad legislative powers and responsibilities, which include overseeing the work of the CTA's departments, issuing policy decisions and managing the CTA's finances. During their sessions in March and September, the parliament hears public grievances and petitions of Tibetans in exile. The Tibetan judiciary was established in 1992 and is responsible for framing a judicial code and other civil procedures. The CTA has three independent statutory commissions to reaffirm the democratic status of the exiled establishment. These are the Election Commission, which conducts and oversees elections to the CTA, the post of *sikyong* and local assemblies in the settlements, and the Audit Commission, which appraises the accounts of the CTA's departments and other Tibetan public institutions (McConnell 2016: 55–57).

The power of the executive in the CTA is vested in the position of the *sikyong* (president), a post created in 2011 and the *kashag* (cabinet). Before 2011, it was the *kalon tripa* (prime minister) along with a cabinet who exercised the executive powers in the CTA. However, it can be stated that till 2011, the executive powers of the CTA rested with the Dalai Lama, even though direct elections to the post of the *kalon tripa* started in 2001. The *kashag* (cabinet) has *kalon*s (ministers) who head departments, such as the departments of finance, home, religion and culture, security and information and international relations. The CTA delegates bureaucratic officials to serve as Settlement Welfare Officers, who act as the medium between Dharamshala and the various settlements strewn across South Asia. The government in exile provides welfare and other services to the exiled population, providing a semblance of governance to the

Tibetans. Through delivering governance to Tibetans, the CTA claims itself to be the legitimate government of Tibet, thus challenging the claims of China. The exiled establishment has evolved over the years, with notions of governance strengthening over time. For instance, an example of the evolution in the CTA's mode of governance can be seen with an embracing of the digital by the Tibetan government in exile.

Digital Governance: The CTA Path to Politicisation

The CTA's tilt towards digital governance can be understood through the exiled government bringing out a translation of the English word 'e-governance'. According to the website tibterminology.net run by the CTA, e-governance is translated into Tibetan as 'གློག་འཕྲུལ་འཛིན་སྐྱོང་རྒྱལ་ཁབ་ཅིག་གི་ས་ཁུལ་གང་ཞིག་ཏུ་ཡོད་པའི་མི་སེར་ཞིག་ལ་དྲ་རྒྱ་དང་ཀམ་པུ་ཊར་ལ་སོགས་པ་བརྡ་འཕྲིན་འཕྲུལ་རིག་གི་ཡོ་ཆས་བཀོལ་ནས་སྤྱི་དམངས་ཞབས་ཞུའི་མཐུན་རྐྱེན་སྦྱོར་སྤྲོད་བྱེད་ལུགས།' (tibterminology.net), which means 'electronic administration providing welfare to the community through the internet and the computer'. In 2021, the CTA approved the creation of a Tibetan Population Information System (TPIS), which is a formal database that maintains a digital record of Tibetans in exile who are dispersed globally so as to maintain authentic Tibetan demographics for improved governance and delivery of services. Under this, PVC Identity Cards (ID) will be provided to all Tibetans who are registered in the TPIS database (*Tibetan Review* 2021).

According to a report published on the CTA's website (tibet.net), the purpose of issuing the ID cards is a means towards e-governance and also a step towards digitalising the whole demographic information system for all official purposes (*Tibetan Review* 2021). Through this initiative, the CTA wants to streamline the services provided digitally to its population. While the digitisation of the data of the exiled population is an ongoing process, it heralds a new form of governance by the CTA for the Tibetans, thus providing avenues for, and at the same time, strengthening digital politics in the exiled community. Another point that highlights the CTA's tilt towards digital governance is cooperation with the United States Agency for International Development (USAID) whereby the proposal is to build the CTA's capacity to effectively deliver services to Tibetans in India and Nepal and to strengthen the idea of community self-reliance. As a cooperative agreement valued at 14.5 million dollars, the five-year USAID/India-funded 'CTA-Capacity Building and Sustainability Initiative' will develop strategic plans to address policy needs, strengthen governance systems and processes, generate economic opportunities and conduct citizen outreach activities, including specific youth and women's engagement components and diaspora outreach. The proposed programme will focus on implementing new digital management systems (ICMA 2021). The objective of this proposal therefore is to strengthen digital governance in the community in exile.

A significant step taken by the CTA to 'ride the wave' of digital politics was the inauguration of Tibet TV in 2006. It is designed as a WebTV product which is also broadcast by local cable operators in Dharamshala and a few settlement camps in India. Termed as the official broadcasting channel of the CTA, its objectives are disseminating information on the activities and teachings of His Holiness the Dalai Lama, CTA and the current situation of human rights in Tibet, and about activities in the diasporic community (Department of Information and International Relations). Tibet TV is seen to be aiding the growth of digital politics in exile as the platform provides live coverage of the parliamentary proceedings from Dharamshala. The parliamentary sessions have been broadcast since 2005 via television and WebTV since 2006 so that every Tibetan is able to follow the political process in Dharamshala (Roemer 2009: 101). Through this, the exiled community can virtually participate in the discussions and debates of the parliament and witness the numerous policies being implemented by the exiled state. Here, a digital platform is seen to usher the politicisation of the Tibetan community.

The Tibetans in exile are not mute spectators, as through the use of internet platforms and social networking sites, they indulge in discussions regarding the proceedings of the parliament. The parliamentary debates garner massive views and shares on sites like Facebook, which provides the space for the viewers to comment and debate on the issues. The 17th Tibetan Parliament in exile's fourth session is a good example to highlight the role of digital media in Tibetan politics. The session was adjourned as 28 of the 45 MPs staged a walkout protesting the status of certain judges in the Tibetan Supreme Court. The online live comments from viewers were critical of the boycotting parliamentarians, with many calling for an end to the boycott. Interestingly, the majority of the parliamentarians are from the clergy and belong to the Do-toe (Kham) constituency. Thus, several comments were critical and called for banning the involvement of monks in politics. A YouTube channel 'Jho Jho Dorjee' with more than 5,000 subscribers uploaded a video of the 17th Tibetan Parliament in exile's fourth session which was titled 'The Tibetan Parliament adjourned as MPs Walk Out', that garnered 14,652 views.[1]

Secularism and Democratisation: In Exile

What is interesting is the growth in secularism in the Tibetan community with a rise in digital politics among the Tibetans. Although the understandings of secularism are many, here, it is understood in terms of the waning of the influence of religion in the lives of the people. As mentioned earlier, till 2011, Tibetan Buddhism was the mainframe of politics in exile, with the Dalai Lama assuming spiritual and temporal powers and the *kalon tripa,* who was a high-ranking Tibetan monk. In 2011, the Dalai Lama relinquished political power in favour of an elected leader—Lobsang Sangay, a layperson, thus strengthening secular politics in exile. With the 'visible' withdrawal of the religious from the political, the earlier censorship and 'self-censorship' imposed by religion among the Tibetans reduced, leading to an increase in voices that was affected mainly through digital media.

Holly Gayley illustrates the manner in which Tibetan language blogging websites such as Sangdhor (www.sangdhor.com), Amdo Tibet Blog (amdotibet.cn) and the exile-based Khabdha (www.khabdha.org) have provided a novel and significant space for secular critiques of the role of religion in Tibetan society (Gayley and Willock 2016: 25). While she writes in terms of the situation inside Tibet, her observations are pertinent for the notion of secularism in exile. Through the digital, especially social media, exiled Tibetans have called for a lowering of religious influence on Tibetan politics. Using Facebook or Twitter, demands have also been made to reduce the parliamentary representations of the various schools of Tibetan Buddhism. The same medium has been used to criticise the clergy being given the right to vote twice. Through online platforms, some exiled Tibetans have even criticised the role of the Dalai Lama and other higher religious elites. Digital media has also been utilised, especially by exiled Tibetans outside India, to demand an increase in their representation in the Tibetan parliament in exile.

As mentioned earlier, the number of Tibetans outside South Asia has increased, and parity has been reached. With these Tibetans settled in various corners of the globe, the digital medium becomes important for them to participate in the politics of the exiled state. To this effect, the Tibetans outside India had started online polls to garner support for the change in the composition of the legislature in exile. Ideas regarding the need to change the Tibetan legislature were debated online, which was titled 'The Way Forward on Democratic Reform: Research Scholars' Perspective', with the participants stressing the need to change the seat composition of the legislature (Democracy and Debate 2022). The role of the digital in Tibetan politics, especially during elections of the exiled parliamentarians and the *sikyong*, is understood through a statement made by Tashi, a resident of Dharamshala, who in an interview with the IANS simply stated how 'Technology is the new means: now we connect with the candidates directly. We don't have to wait for newspaper advertisements to make our choice' (IANS 2015). The same respondent further added that many candidates are declaring their nominations through social networking sites (IANS 2015).

Tibetans based in Europe, the US or other countries have created numerous online discussion forums and pages such as 'Toronto Tibetan Activities' with 889 members,[2] 'Tibetan American Media' with 1,600 followers[3] and the 'Tibetan Community in Germany' with 1,300 followers[4] which provides an avenue for political discussions and debates. For instance, the Facebook page 'Toronto Tibetan Activities' was created on 16 January 2009, and since then, its members have shared or uploaded several posts related to politics in exile. On 2 September 2021, to celebrate Democracy Day, a member of the exiled Tibetans uploaded an online debate on democracy in Tibetan Society between Kyinzom Dhongdue (former member of the Tibetan parliament) and Kelsang Gyaltsen (Former Envoy of His Holiness Dalai Lama). On 3

September 2021, a user named Tenzin Freedom Lungtok uploaded his video on the same page, which criticised the current president (*sikyong*) of the CTA, Penpa Tsering. In his critique of the current establishment, he mentions how democracy has provided him with the freedom to criticise the *sikyong*. The digital has been directly used in the context of 'Smart Vote Tibet', which is a user-friendly online application to aid Tibetans in making an informed decision regarding electing their parliamentarians. It is an initiative of the Tibetan association 'Project Democracy', which has mostly West-based Tibetan professionals and scholars.

Sonam Palmo Brunner, a member of 'Project Democracy', writes in a report that the online application helps Tibetan voters make an informed choice. She mentions how cyberspace is the only space available for Tibetans scattered around the globe to make an informed choice regarding their right to vote (Brunner 2021). According to the late scholar-bureaucrat Thubten Samphel, who was the first director of the Tibet Policy Institute (TPI) and the first research think tank of the CTA, the interlocking network of websites, newspapers, magazines and radio services has led to the emergence of a Fourth Estate with the clout to influence Tibetan thinking on issues such as candidates for the post of the *kalon tripa*, to advocating partisan politics in an increasingly pluralistic system (Samphel 2004: 184). The growth of the Tibetan exile media has a significant impact on the development of a democratic community. As a pillar of the exile body politic, the Tibetan media have access to the proceedings of the exile parliament.

Digital media has spawned a growing number of NGOs, mostly based in Dharamshala, which have their own websites and online platforms adding their distinct voices and concerns to the deliberations within the exile community and shaping their opinions. Thus, digital platforms have contributed to the growth of civil society in the exile community, which is needed for the emergence of a mature democracy. Thubten Samphel further states how the taking of firm roots of a free, boisterous press in the Tibetan refugee community has facilitated the Dalai Lama's own efforts at the democratisation of the exiled Tibetan polity. It has introduced a great deal of transparency in the workings of the exile administration. Thus, digital politics and governance have added a strong and decisive voice in the political participation of Tibetans, strengthening the cohesiveness and vibrancy of the community (Samphel 2004: 184).

Conclusion

The above observations by Thubten Samphel in *Virtual Tibet: The Media* (2004) present a positive image of media (including digital media) in exile, as it helps to boost democracy and its associated practices in the exile community. Along with democratisation, exiled Tibetan politics mediated through the digital has also sharpened secularisation in the community. However, an alternative argument can be framed with the 'digital' maintaining the influence of Tibetan Buddhism in the exile society. As mentioned earlier, religion provides legitimacy to the CTA, which has not decreased even though the Dalai Lama has relinquished his political powers. One sees this with TibetTV broadcasting the religious teachings of the Dalai Lama, including the recent teachings by the Tibetan reincarnate in Bodhgaya, India.[5] In a way, the CTA and politics of the exiled state cannot be distanced from culture, that is Tibetan Buddhism. Culture in the form of religion is seen to be influencing the digital politics of the exiled state. On the other hand, digital governance and a shift to digital politics by the CTA and Tibetans in exile is seen as a mode of embracing modernisation in governance practices, which helps in garnering legitimacy mainly from the West, which forms the bulk of their support. In a way, it can be stated that the project of adopting digital governance by Tibetans is a way to be embraced by Western powers. It can be seen as a way of expanding the 'politics at large' strategy of the CTA towards Tibetans, foreign governments and the PRC. As a political entity, the CTA employs the digital to accelerate governance, diplomacy and democratic processes. While stress on the digital has increased democratic voices and decreased religious hegemony in the exiled community, 'digital' hegemony has its own lacunas. Primary among them is the issue of 'digital illiteracy', which is the case with elderly

Tibetans and others who do not use smartphones and are therefore digitally impaired. Many of the settlement camps in India are located in remote regions of the subcontinent, where digital infrastructure is in a rudimentary stage. Thus, these Tibetans will be devoid of these new modes of governance and other services provided by the CTA. As noted earlier, the entry of digital platforms in Tibetan politics has certainly led to the flourishing of multiple voices, opinions and ideas, which are hallmarks of a democracy. However, it has also led to the emergence of opinions that are problematic and insensitive. For instance, several Tibetan YouTubers, who have other social networking pages, have simply crafted insensitive, one-sided narratives regarding politics and political leaders in the Tibetan community. Digital politics has also created trolls who whip up certain divisive sentiments in exile. While several are paid to serve the interest of the Chinese, many are intoxicated by the power provided by digital politics.

A major criticism of digital politics in exile is that it has widened the earlier historical divisions between Tibetans. While it cannot be directly held responsible for the cracks that have developed, still the platforms provided by the digital modes are seen to accentuate these problems. There is also a danger that the e-governance initiative by the CTA can be hijacked by superior cyber-attacks from opponents, especially through the machinations of the PRC. Furthermore, the maintaining of a digital record of Tibetans in exile is wrought with security issues that can be criticised along the lines of future surveillance by the state.

Finally, riding the wave of digital politics and governance by the CTA and Tibetans in exile is advantageous insofar as the exile population is settled in numerous countries and settlements within South Asia. Digital platforms also provide an easy mode for the government in exile to govern its diverse population. However, as seen in other states and societies, digital politics and other associated factors have crafted favourable conditions for the growth of 'post-truth', and a similar situation is present in the context of the Tibetans in exile. Hence, digital governance and politics for the exiled state can be seen as a double-edged sword, which needs to be utilised with much prudence and wisdom.

Notes

1 See Jho Jho Dorjee, 'The Tibetan Parliament Adjourned as MPs Walk Out', 2022, YouTube, https://www.youtube.com/watch?v=MI7Q90QpNOE (accessed 4 February 2023).
2 See Toronto Tibetans Activities. | Facebook (accessed 4 February 2023).
3 See Tibetan American Media | Facebook (accessed 4 February 2023).
4 See Tibetan Community in Germany | Facebook (accessed 4 February 2023).
5 See TibetTV, 'His Holiness the Dalai Lama's Teachings on the Praise of the Dharma', 2023, YouTube, https://www.youtube.com/watch?v=kbLesdV7YSM (accessed 30 December 2023).

References

J. Bray. 2012. 'Ladakhi and Bhutanese Enclaves in Tibet'. *Journal of Bhutan Studies*, 26: 1–20.

S. Brunner. 2021. 'For Stateless and Scattered Tibetans, a New Online Tool Helps Voters Make an Informed Choice'. *Rising Voices,* 21 April. Available at: https://rising.globalvoices.org/blog/2021/04/22/for-stateless-and-scattered-tibetans-a-new-online-tool-helps-voters-make-an-informed-choice/ (accessed 8 January 2023).

Department of Information and International Relations. 'TibetTV', *Tibet.net*. Available at: https://tibet.net/department/information/ (accessed 7 January 2023).

Democracy and Debate. 2022. 'The Way Forward on Democratic Reform: Research Scholars' Perspective', 13 December. Available at: https://www.youtube.com/watch?app=desktop&fbclid=PAAaZrUBXNEXjsJ-DEOAZJAnvXRfJoEFUZY2t6KsUQkSxlid99FaRfSTCFtvY&v=dVSbG628ej4&feature=youtu.be (accessed 1 February 2023).

G. Dreyfus. 1995. 'Law, State, and Political Ideology in Tibet'. *Journal of the International Association of Buddhist Studies*, 18 (1): 117–139.

Tibterminology.net. 'e-governance', *tibetterminology,* Available at: https://tibterminology.net/?s=e+governance (accessed 9 January 2023).

Holly Gayley and Nicole Willock. 2016. 'Introduction—Theorising the Secular in Tibetan Cultural Worlds'. *Himalaya—The Journal of the Association for Nepal and Himalayan Studies*, 36 (1), 12–21.

M.C. Goldstein. 2007. 'A History of Modern Tibet, 1913–1951—The Demise of the Lamaist State'. Delhi: Munshi Manoharlal Publishers.

ICMA. 2021. 'USAID/India Central Tibetan Administration Capacity Building and Sustainability Initiative (CTA-CBSI)', *icma.org*, 16 December.

Available at: https://icma.org/programs-and-projects/usaid-india-central-tibetan-administration-capacity-building-and-sustainability-initiative-cta-cbsi (accessed 8 January 2023).

IANS. 2015. 'Cyberspace Abuzz Ahead of Polls to the Tibetan parliament-in-exile', *Business Standard*, 12 August. Available at: https://www.business-standard.com/article/news-ians/cyberspace-abuzz-ahead-of-polls-to-the-tibetan-parliament-in-exile-115081200302_1.html (accessed 9 January 2023).

Lopes, A.C. (2015), *Tibetan Buddhism in Diaspora—Cultural Re-signification in practice and institutions*, New York: Routledge.

F. McConnel. 2016. *Rehearsing the State—Political Practices of the Government in Exile*. UK: Wiley Blackwell.

D. Norbu. 2004. 'The Settlements: Participation and Integration', in *Exile as Challenge—The Tibetan Diaspora*, edited by Dagmar Bernstoff and Hubertes von Welck, 186–213. New Delhi: Orient Longman.

J. Norbu. 2009. 'Wildlife and Nature Conservancy in old Tibet', *Phayul.com*, 8 December. Available at: https://www.phayul.com/2009/12/08/26164/ (accessed 10 January 2023).

T. Phuntsho. 2004. 'Government in Exile', in *Exile as Challenge*, 125–150.

S. Roemer. 2009. *The Tibetan Government in Exile—Politics at Large*. New Delhi: Routledge.

Tibetan Review. 2021. 'Exile Tibetan Administration to issue ID cards to all Tibetans for e-governance', *Tibetan Review*, 23 April. Available at: https://www.tibetanreview.net/exile-tibetan-administration-to-issue-id-cards-to-all-tibetans-for-e-governance/ (accessed 7 January 2023).

Staff Reporter. 2011. 'Tibetans Elect Dr Lobsang Sangay as *kalon tripa*', *Tibet.net*, 27 April. Available at: https://tibet.net/tibetans-elect-dr-lobsang-sangay-as-kalon-tripa/ (accessed 4 January 2023).

T. Samphel. 2004. 'Virtual Tibet: The Media', in *Exile as Challenge*, 167–186.

Samdhongrinpoche.com. 2014. 'A Brief Biography of Prof. Samdhong Rinpoche', 13 October, Available at: https://samdhongrinpoche.com/en/an-brief-biography-of-prof-samdhong-rinpoche/ (accessed 4 January 2023).

5

'King of the Jungle'

Digital Protest as Normative Disruptions in India's Northeast

Kaustubh Deka

Introduction: *We Were the Chosen Ones*

Although it contains a mere 3.6 per cent of India's total population and covers only 7.6 per cent of the land, the eight states situated in the northeastern part of India, collectively known as Northeast India (NEI) in academic as well as popular parlance, carries a significant status when it comes to cultural richness and geopolitical significance. It is home to tremendous ethnic, religious, and linguistic diversity, mirroring the region's highly diverse geographical terrain. Furthermore, the region's extreme geopolitical sensitivity (sharing turbulent international borders) puts it in paradoxical proximity to the centres of power: geographically and emotionally 'peripheral' in many senses and yet close to the national security apparatus. For some time, a rising phenomenon of digital activism through a plethora of means has been sweeping the region. From innovative YouTube channels to radical Instagram pages, India's Northeast is undergoing a liminal phase of social restructuring, largely routed through the digital space, where a section of the youth has begun to critically interrogate the normative boundaries that have come to construe the region.

These digital interventions have created interesting 'frictions' in the social discourse of the region and provoked varied responses from the power structures. In 2021, a hip-hop singer from the eastern parts of Nagaland, Nentong Konyak, released a title, 'KOJ (King of Jungle)'.[1]

He chose to sing it in Hindi, thereby making it evident that it was very much addressed to the 'nation' at large. 'You talk about crying, but you don't know. You talk about sufferings, but you don't know. You talk about dying, but you don't know. You don't know at all. Little too much on my shoulders. You don't know.' He goes on. It's a saga of the blood and tears of a conflict-torn people in a coal-mining area told in a powerful lyrical manner. Nentong speaks with confidence, assertion and grit, and the youth of the region grooves to him. He is one amongst a bunch of artists to have come out of the region in recent times who are good at utilising the digital space to put across their views, often stirring the prevailing normative notions on the region. The number of their kind seems to be growing with their content garnering substantial support in the digital space. In the language of the internet, their art and activism are going 'viral'.

Whose Digital? The Premiums and Paradoxes of Being Young in Northeast India

Being young in India's Northeast often translates into social interventions of different kinds. The youth, by design or by default, becomes vital social actors, performers of narratives and participants of paradigms. However, the story of the youth is also one of multitudes. Thus, youth activism in India's Northeast continues to be defined in various ways other than through the rubrics of conflicts and protests. A significant number of youth have been migrating out of the region in recent decades and an increasing number of them have been returning, too, with new found zeal. A certain sense of 'aspiration' is what explains such behaviour and one needs to bring in a discourse of social mobility to understand this new kind of activism. One argues that youth activism in NEI needs to be construed around the three broad and intertwined spectrums namely, assertion, aspiration and assemblages (Deka 2021). The three are intertwined, even if in an asymmetrical manner.

In the South Asian context, this has been explained as youth constituting the 'idiosyncratic generations… characterized not only by their aspirations for a better future, but also by their ability to experience collectively, yet in their own way, major political and social events' (Martelli and Garalytė 2019: 1). In the course of social changes sweeping through NEI, the youths are often found centrally involved. They are not only the early recipients of change; most often, they are the purveyors of it too. In essence, youth activism has an important role in the vernacularisation (Michelutti 2008) of politics in the region. This context of a 'relentless struggle' is vital to understanding the effects of the efficacy of an unfolding digital turn in the region at the moment.

Student-youth Politics as the Site of 'Relentless Struggle': the Historical Make-up in Northeast India

In recent times, the world has been witnessing a resurgence of student and youth movements. These movements have often shown tremendous resilience and significant political character. This resurgence has been also taken as a sign of students having gradually lost their special 'elite' status and identifying more with the rest of society (Zugman 2017). However, historically, student politics in India's Northeast has always been a site to articulate socio-cultural assertions, agendas and political ambitions of the different ethnic groups in the region, prompting the argument that students and the youths have become the agents of identity formation and student–youth movements have turned into de-facto identity movements or at least a strong articulation of identity politics (Deka 1996; Baruah 2002).

Student and youth organisations have provided crucial platforms for the articulation and performance of different identities in the societies of Northeast India at various levels. These have ranged from the 'inception' of identities within movements to the 'deliverance' of it in the form of accords as well as their further 'circulation' through continuing activism; processes that have been central to the discourse of political change in the region. Critical here is to understand how, through a process of political arrangement and negotiation, a category that identifies as a social group such as 'students' acquires a true political value only when it exceeds its own generational and sociological boundaries (Lanza 2012: 31–51).

In other words, the very production of the socio-political category of students in this context needs to be understood as part of a socio-political project. At this point, we also want to relate to Jenkins and Klanderman's observations elsewhere about social protest and the complex dynamics between state and social movements which can be applied in the case of Northeast India as well (Jenkins and Klandermans 1995: 1–13).

Activism as Aspiration and Access: the Internet as Empowerment

Look at me
I look little bit like a Chinese
Not so tall
But look little bit short
Being an Indian from inside
I live for money
During the election time
I sell my vote for a couple of thousand rupees.
I'm an Indian.
I'm a true Indian!

—K4 Keho from Arunachal Pradesh—'I am an Indian'[2]

Gilbertson, through her ethnographic studies on South India, tries to posit the concept of 'aspiration as one involving not just relative levels of capacity, but also relative levels of compulsion and consequence' (Gilbertson 2019: 21), where the Indian youth are 'compelled to aspire by the myth of upward mobility achieved through education in a rising India, and compelled to do so in particular ways by the fact that they are relatively unsheltered from the consequences of misjudgment' (ibid.: 31), For the youth in NEI too, social mobility has been a powerful driver of activism.

Traditionally, student–youth politics in the region, despite the dominant image of a critical force, have been in essence a platform for ambitions and a means to access the state. An empirical look at student activism in the region will affirm its character as a springboard for future leadership. Aspiration is also the bridge that seals the gap between the institutional with the non-institutional, as one observes that most critical social actors of the institutional frame are co-opted into those very institutions at some later point. Youth leaders of today become the policymakers of tomorrow, only to be affronted by the next batch of youth leaders. Thus the ecology of activism perpetuates. However, the cohorts of youth gathered under the banner of activism can also get into a limbo, a sense of waiting or procrastination. This can broadly turn into three directions, engagement in reactionary politics, channelling of energies into more progressive forms of democratic action or the emergence set of 'fixers' engaged in narrowly class-based, self-interested practices (Jeffrey 2010: 103).

The Digital Constituency Is Here and Now!

As per one report, the Northeast region has its share of 4 per cent of the youth population of the country in the age group of 15–35 years and also a relatively higher proportion of youth unemployment in the same age group compared to the all-India level (Amitav 2017). Guy Standing talks about the rise of the precariat, a 'dangerous class—characterized by deep anger, anomie, anxiety, and alienation' (Standing 2011: 113) and reminds us that since the youth 'make up the core of the Precariat', they are the ones who 'will have to take the lead in forging a viable future for it' (ibid.). The continuing angst, which certain youth activism can be seen as an expression of, needs to be explained by the perspective that 'the framework of infrastructure development (in NEI) has been conceived from the statist perspective, thus widening the gap between state and society' (Zilpao 2018: 486). As the situation of unemployment continues to deteriorate in NEI and the outmigration of the youth is on a constant rise, the conditions of the youth of the region turning into or having already turned into a constituency of the precariat is real.

There is this notion of the transformation of NEI from a 'a frontier into a corridor' through 'massive investment in connectivity' resulting in rapid urbanisation in the region.

At the same time, youth migration out of the region has intensified over the years. Karlsson and Kikon call it 'wayfinding' by the indigenous migrants, 'a journey without a map or pathway to follow, with no clear destination or end point' (Karlsson and Kikon 2017: 4), Duncan McDuie-Ra points out the emergence of 'adjacent identities' due to the increasing migration from the region, intensifying encounters between communities from the region and so-called 'mainstream' India (McDuie-Ra 2016). The often discussed structural factors behind this migration are high levels of insecurity and violence, lack of educational facilities, a stagnant economy, dependence on subsistence farming and unsustainable extraction of natural resources (Karlsson and Kikon ibid). Sanjoy Hazarika sees this transformation of the Northeast from a 'migrant-receiving region' to a 'migrant-producing area' as a sign of the Northeast people coming of age (Hazarika 2018). How does this unfolding experience reflect the trends of youth activism in the region? These are young people clued into and engaged with social media due to their circumstances. The internet for most of them is a means of escape as well as survival. For both categories—the 'migrants' from the region trying to make a mark outside as well as 'indigenes' in the region trying to assert their space within the region—the digital space becomes a prime area of operations.

Digitisation and Creativities: Activism of a Changing Time?

Let me go,
Let me be,
Wipe out all your sorrow
Don't hold me back this time
Let your eyes be dry
If I don't come back this time
Don't look out for me

> Here and there
> Am off to battle
> Am off to battle…

'Ronoloe Jau'[3] ('Am off to Battle', translation mine), a popular song by popular Assamese singer Shankuraj Konwar, known for his electronic rock music, garnered more than a million hits on YouTube in 2019. The year became a watershed moment for generations of youth in NEI, where they took to the streets in unprecedented numbers across the states. This was the activism of the millennials. Through creative music, poetry and other art forms, the youth in the region has been making a distinctive mark of late. This is activism of a new kind. The activism subculture has taken a new turn. There has been a marked digitisation of civic action globally and the youth of NEI have not been immune to it.[4]

Pandemic as Disruption: a Boost to the Digital Turn?

The pandemic presented a key moment for the discourse of social activism to turn towards the digital sphere in a significant way. During this course, the nature of the movement itself went through a sort of transformation: new spaces of solidarity and activism began to emerge, especially in the form of internet-based social activism. As is well documented elsewhere, the uses of social media in social campaigns usually have the potential to add some bit of radicalism and innovation to movements. At the same time, a 'digital turn' can also isolate a movement, constraining it to a clique well-versed in the language of social media. However, the fact that two important and largely effective online campaigns were run by the youth in Assam during the pandemic shows that with sufficient penetration of the internet and digital technologies, 'digital revolutions' seem to be a prospective reality even for spaces that remain peripheral on many counts. The campaigns revolved around two significant incidents of ecological importance that happened in Assam during the pandemic-induced lockdown.

One was the issue of a government-proposed land clearing for coal excavation within an elephant reserve and rain forest, a campaign against the Dehing Patkai coal mining proposal and the other was the campaign for adequate compensation and ecological protection in the wake of a massive gas leak, the Baghjan gas blowout incident. In addition to these campaigns, several social media vloggers emerged from all around Northeast India during this period. Their popularity reached an unprecedented level, measured by an ever-increasing number of 'views' and 'shares' of their content across social media platforms and the rising number of subscriptions to their channels. Showcasing aspects of local food, lifestyle and places, this phenomenon of young 'ethnic vloggers' is something interesting that has emerged strongly during the pandemic and continues to grow.

Scholars working on the discourse of social media and communicative rationality talk about the creation of a particular 'sociality' through (a) cognition (b) communication and (c) cooperation (Christian Fuchs 2014). One needs to place such theses in the context of the NEI, a situation of 'resource frontier' or 'militarised carbon landscape, with lives built around tea, oil, coal and coated with vernacular ideas of power, status, obligation' (Kikon 2019).

The Limits of Digital Infrastructure: the Digital Divide

> *I think you need to have a valid bank account first in order to open an account on Facebook.*
>
> —Student leader from an ethnic student organisation in Assam, when asked by reporters about his knowledge of Facebook, 2012.

The phenomena of protests or assertions using the digital medium have been rather recent in India's Northeast. In other words, traditional social movement organisations in the regions, such as the proactive student organisations were found less receptive in engaging with these emerging forums. One can recall here incidents as late as 2012 when reacting to allegations of derogatory remarks against their community on certain Facebook posts and thereby calling for a ban of Facebook in Assam, the ethnic student organisation leaders came across as clueless about the very concept of the social media platform. In contrast to this, gradually, the tech-savvy urban youth began to push the traditional student/youth groups to the margins by organising themselves through digital mediums around issues where the established organisations were found slow to respond. An example can be given of the 2013–2014 youth protests in Guwahati, Assam over the issue of women's safety. The substantial mass gathering and street action were largely mobilised through digital mediums like Facebook, and the protesting youth kept themselves outside the formal banner of any established organisation. Although internet penetration has moved significantly faster since then, the pandemic revealed a lot of distance was yet to be covered. The disquiet has been about whether the existing digital infrastructure is sufficient to meet the sudden requirements that the pandemic situation demands. This has made students worried and tense, almost slipping into depression, regarding their educational future.

As the lockdown placed a lot of emphasis on the prospects of switching to methods of digital education or a Technology Enhanced Learning (TEL) system, I ran a quick survey involving the students of my department in the initial days of the lockdown. The findings indicate that the internet can indeed be used widely for passing on essential information; however, when it comes to more in-depth interaction (classes, tutorials and so on), access seems limited and inequitable. Only 35 per cent of students claimed to have fast internet services needed for online classes, 30 per cent had personal laptops (important for doing assignments or reading big files) and less than 40 per cent had options to regularly 'recharge', that is, purchase the required volume of internet data for their devices. The scenario at the national level, as it existed prior to the pandemic, seemed to be rather grim, too. According to the 2017–2018 National Sample Survey report on education, only 24 per cent of Indian households had internet facilities through a computer laptop or tablet. While 66 per cent of India's population lived in villages, only a little over 15 per cent of rural households had access to internet services. For urban households, the proportion was 42 per cent. Smartphones were not considered in this survey (Deka 2023).

Conclusion: Surveillance, Curbs and a 'New Public Sphere'

In conclusion, fledgling and uncertain as it may be, a new public sphere with its dynamics of resilience wrought into it seems to have emerged in Northeast India through various digital forums. It's a space that essentially reflects the complex political subjectivities that inhabit this region in the throes of precarity. In a more direct sense, digital spaces seemed to have played a crucial role in the discourse of social protest in keeping the movements 'moving' by maintaining debates, supporting events, nurturing leaders during ebbs in movement activities, and more generally, helping produce submerged networks or latent social movements (Townsend 2004). In a more complex and wider sense, from engagements with ecological themes and sharp expositions on issues such as racial discrimination to various topics of existential strife, the digital lifeworld in the region has assumed an increasing vibrancy. The overarching sense of activism in the region around the themes of 'survival', 'acceptance' and 'dignity' (Fredy 2019: 65) has become irrevocably and intricately linked to the activities in the digital sphere. In various ways, these acts of protest, participation and assertion through the multitude of digital spheres have been disrupting the silos within which Northeast India and its people have been often put. In this sense, one can call the digital churning an act of re-imagination currently unfolding in the region.

Notes

1 See Nentong Konyak, 'King of Jungle', Alive Jam Studio, 2021, YouTube, https://www.youtube.com/watch?v=IOEpz-J8kOM, (accessed on 12 May 2023).

2 See K4 Kekho, 'I Am An Indian', AGT Production House, 31 August 2015, YouTube, https://www.youtube.com/watch?v=VMDhNLzKSFk, (accessed on 10 May 2023).

3 See Shankuraj Konwar, 'Ronole Jau', Baartalaap Records, 25 March 2019, YouTube, https://www.youtube.com/watch?v=CgiGZyRwaTY, (accessed on 1 May 2023).

4 See, for instance, the notions of 'animal rights' on the Instagram page 'noahs.ark.nagaland'(https://www.instagram.com/noahsark) (accessed on 12 May 2023)

or the page titled 'thewitchesofarunachal' that embodies ideas of intersectional feminism and radical sisterhood which questions embedded patriarchy (https://www.instagram.com/witchesofarunachal) (accessed 12 May 2023).

References

Khuntia Priyadarsan Amitav. 2017. 'Skill Development of Youth in North East India: Way Forward', V.V. Giri National Labour Institute. Available at: https://vvgnli.gov.in/sites/default/files/124-2017-P%20Amitav%20Khuntia.pdf (accessed on 10 September 2023).

Sanjib Baruah. 2005. *Durable Disorder: Understanding the Politics of Northeast India*. New Delhi: Oxford University Press.

Kaustubh Deka. 2015.'Youth Activism and Democratic Politics in India's Northeast: 2014 Election in Perspective'. Policy Report. No. 14, The Hindu Centre for Politics and Public Policy, Chennai. Available at: https://www.thehinducentre.com/scholars/kaustubh-deka-report-published/article64936035.ece (accessed 5 May 2023).

———. 2019. 'Youth and Infrastructure Development in Northeast India'. New Delhi: Heinrich Boll Stiftung. Available at: https://in.boell.org/en/2019/03/19/youth-and-infrastructure-development-northeast-india (accessed on 10 May 2023).

———. 2021. 'Vulnerable but Brave: The Case of Youth in Assam', in *Perspectives Asia: Fabrics of Society*. Singapore: Heinrich Boll Stiftung. Available at: https://th.boell.org/sites/default/files/2021-08/PerspectivesAsia10.pdf (accessed on 25 May 2023).

———. 2022. 'Youth Activism', in *Routledge Companion to Northeast India,* edited by T.B. Subba and Jelle P. Wouters, 280–285. London: Routledge.

Zugman Kara Dellacioppa. 2017. 'The Promise and Pitfalls of Horizontalism in the Occupy Movement', in *The New Global Politics: Global Social Movements in the Twenty-First Century*, edited by Harry E. Vanden, Peter N. Funke and Gary, 60–80. New York: Routledge.

Hans J. Freddy. 2017. *Conflict and Youth Rights in India: Engagement and Identity in the North East*. Palgrave Macmillan: Singapore.

Christian Fuchs. 2014. 'Social Media and the Public Sphere'. *tripleC Communication Capitalism & Critique Open Access Journal for a Global Sustainable Information Society*, 12: 57–101.

Amanda Gilbertson. 2019. 'Aspiration as Capacity and Compulsion: "The Futures of Urban Middle-Class Youth in India"', in *Anthropological*

Perspectives on Student Futures Youth and the Politics of Possibility, edited by Amy Stambach and Kathleen D. Hall, 19–33. New York: Palgrave MacMillan.

B.G. Karlsson and Dolly Kikon. 2017. 'Way finding: Indigenous Migrants in the Service Sector of Metropolitan India'. *South Asia: Journal of South Asian Studies*, 40 (3): 447–462.

Dolly Kikon. 2019. *Living with Coal and Oil: Resource Politics and Militarization in Northeast India*. Seattle: University of Washington Press.

Fabio Lanza. 2012. 'Springtime and Morning Suns: "Youth" as a Political Category in Twentieth-Century China'. *The Journal of the History of Childhood and Youth*, 5 (1): 31–51.

Jean-Thomas Martelli and Kristina Garalytė. 2019. 'Generational Communities: Student Activism and the Politics of Becoming in South Asia'. *South Asia Multidisciplinary Academic Journal*, 22. Available at: https://journals.openedition.org/samaj/6486 (accessed on 10 May 2023).

Duncan McDuie-Ra. 2016. 'Adjacent identities in Northeast India'. *Asian Ethnicity,* 17 (3): 400–413.

Willem van Schendel. 2002. 'Geographies of Knowing, Geographies of Ignorance: Jumping Scale in Southeast Asia'. *Environment and Planning D: Society and Space Volume*, 20 (6): 647–668.

Guy Standing. 2011. *The Precariat: The New Dangerous Class.* London: Bloomsbury.

Raile Rocky Ziipao. 2018. 'Look/Act East Policy, Roads and Market Infrastructure in North-East India'. *Strategic Analysis,* 42 (5): 476–489.

Section II

Nepal

6

Evolution of Nepal's ICT Policies

Through the Lens of Document Analysis

Nischal Regmi and Shailesh B. Pandey

Introduction

Nepal now has a sufficiently long experience with Information and Communication Technologies (ICTs).[1] Accordingly, plans, policies and by-laws that are specific to the ICTs have been developed by it. The earliest explicit mention of ICTs is found in the sixth Five-Year Plan of the Nepal Planning Commission (1980) which addresses issues of expanding telecommunication infrastructure. The seventh plan (1985) forwarded its computer policy, while the ninth plan (1997) dealt with the internet for the first time. Specific policies dealing with the internet and information technology (IT) began to appear only after 2000. In between, different acts and by-laws related to ICTs have also been published. In this regard, the ICT policy regime in Nepal could be described as a vertically and horizontally linked set of documents with the constitution at the top, guidelines and directives at the bottom and plans, policies, acts and regulations located in the intermediate layers (Martin Chautari 2014: 2).

A peculiarity in the major plans and policies, from the eighth plan of 1992 onwards, is that the plan documents are firmly convinced of the favourable developmental impacts of contemporary ICTs ranging from economic growth, justice, poverty reduction and good governance to vague terminologies like 'healthy, civilized and cultured society' (Pandey and Regmi 2020: 21). Researchers have criticised the overtly optimistic claims of Nepali ICT policies along several lines. Pandey and Raj (2016: 10) argue that policies should be based on household-level statistics that describe the end users and focus should be equally given to why people do not use ICTs. Regmi and Pandey (2015) highlight how insufficient energy infrastructure could dwarf the vision of digitising the nation. Regmi (2017) argues that the prerequisites for observing ICTs' developmental benefits might not hold in Nepal and criticises the policies for overlooking the quality dimension. Pandey and Regmi (2018) criticise the policies from the perspective of distributional inequity of ICT access and use. Subsequently, Pandey and Regmi (2020) link the time-trend of ICT imports in Nepal with the rise and fall of global optimism on ICTs' potential. The crux of these criticisms is that the Nepali context is missing in Nepal's ICT policies.

Here, we seek to examine the plans, policies, by-laws and acts[2] related to ICTs, from 1965 to 2019, so as to trace the main themes that these documents have addressed. While earlier studies have critically reflected on Nepal's ICT policy, they have not explored how the central themes of the policies evolved, and how it is linked with changes in the global technological discourses. To eliminate our biases that could result in a faulty enumeration of the policy themes, we use the computational method of topic modelling. We re-validate the arguments engendered from the topic modelling by using the technique of n-gram analysis. This thematic examination of Nepal's ICT policies is the unique contribution of the current study. In doing so, the study is organised as follows: the next section describes the methodology, the data and its organisation, including the details of topic modelling and n-gram analysis and the following section describes the findings which then link with extant literature, thereby developing the argument of this study.

Methodology

Data Collection

The data for this study is a collection of plans, policies, and by-laws related to ICTs in Nepal. Our collection contains documents from 1965 to 2019, and we have considered the English version of the documents, mainly due to the difficulty in processing Devanagari fonts. As many of the Nepali versions are scanned copies, document processing becomes difficult. Our choice of documents is mainly based on the policy landscape presented in a research brief by Martin Chautari (2014: 2). Later documents have been added to it, and the English versions of some of the documents listed in Martin Chautari (2014: 2) are unavailable. A complete list of the documents used in this research is provided in the endnotes.

Document Analysis

Document analysis in this study is based on two popular methods—topic modelling and n-gram analysis. Topic modelling is a computational technique that takes the document corpus and number of topics as input and outputs a set of keywords that is equal to the number of topics (Ramage et al. 2009: 1). Depending on keywords, the human analyst assigns meaningful titles to each of the sets, that is, topics. In the context of social sciences, the choice of the number of topics is up to the researcher, who usually selects the number in such a way that the resulting topics are meaningful. Topic modelling is preceded by the removal of 'stop words', which are the words such as pronouns and conjunctions that have no conceptual relevance to the problem being considered.

The term 'n-gram' refers to consecutive words appearing in a document.While n-grams are used internally in many language processing algorithms, simple counts of n-grams in a document collection can provide invaluable insights. In this study, we analyse bigrams and trigrams, that is, terms comprised of two and three consecutive words, respectively. As with topic modelling, n-gram analysis is preceded by the removal of stop words.

For topic modelling, we have used the Latent Dirichlet Allocation algorithm available in the Java software, Mallet (Graham, Weingart and Milligan 2012). The n-gram analysis was done mainly using the R package 'ngram' (Schmidt and Heckendorf 2014).

Findings

Inferences from Topic Modelling

We applied the topic modelling algorithm by setting the number of topics to 5, 10, 15, 20, 25 and 30. After manual inspection, we decided to select the number of topics to be identified as 15 which could be interpreted as groups of certain keywords. The 15 sets of keywords that were received as generated by the algorithm have been labelled by the authors and that is shown in Table 6.1. The 15 sets of keywords output by the algorithm were labelled by the authors, as shown in Table 6.1. We can note that the topics mostly centre around infrastructure and its regulation, two exceptions being the topics 'ICT in Education' and 'Sectors'.

Table 6.1: The 15 Topics Identified Using Topic-modelling

S.N.	Topic	Description
1	Cybercrime and security	Crime and security issues related to ICTs.
2	ICT infrastructure operation	The operation and management of the telecommunications infrastructure
3	e-services	Development and deployment of e-government, and e-services for health, tourism and citizen databases.
4	Electronic Transactions	Issues related to authorisation and certification of digital transactions.
5	Spectrum	Issues related to radio spectrum distribution and management
6	Regulation	Licensing and regulation of telecommunications
7	Access to ICTs	Access to broadband and telecommunications services
8	Older ICTs	Issues related to older ICTs, mainly postal service, radio-television transmission and press.
9	Copyright and Patent	Copyright and patent issues in a broader sense, also encompassing audio-visuals, broadcasting and computer programmes
10	Sectors	Application of ICTs to other sections such as agriculture, health and tourism
11	Access to IT	Access to the internet and related services
12	Licensing	Licensing new operators and service providers
13	Themes for ICT	Presumed overall benefits of ICT
14	ICT in Education	Implementation of ICT in the education sector
15	Landline infrastructure upgrade	Upgrading the backbone of telecommunications infrastructure

Source: Compiled by the authors using Topic-modelling

Table 6.1 clearly reflects that the problem of technology-induced inequality and other societal side-effects have been overlooked by policy documents, as not a single topic emerged that could be related to inequality and other undesired consequences of the ICTs. Now, one would naturally ask what these documents talk about most often. Of course, each document in our collection could be related to more than one topic. Table 6.2 shows the most relevant topics for documents published year-wise.[3] We can observe that the issue of infrastructure and regulation has been the most relevant topic for almost all documents. Only a single document published in 2019 has 'Sectors' as its most relevant topic.

For each document published in a particular year, we identified the most important topic and displayed it in the table. In some of the years, more than one document has the same most relevant topic.

Table 6.2: Timeline of Most Relevant Topics

Year	Most Relevant Topics	Year	Most Relevant Topics
1965	Copyright and Patent	2004	Access to IT, Copyright and Patent
1980	Landline infrastructure upgrade	2007	Electronic Transactions, e.g. digital signature, access to IT, ICT in education
1985	Access to IT, Landline infrastructure upgrade	2008	Regulation, Electronic Transactions
1992	Older ICTs	2012	Regulation, Spectrum
1993	Copyright and Patent	2015	e-services, Access to ICTs
1997	Older ICTs, Licensing	2016	Cybercrime and security
2000	Access to IT	2019	Sectors, Access to IT
2002	Access to IT, Copyright and Patent		
2003	Older ICTs		

Source: Compiled by the authors based on their topic model on the plan documents (1965–2019)

To make the findings more lucid, we now explore how the policy focus has shifted in each decade. Table 6.3 shows the most relevant topics for the decades of the 2000s and 2010s. This is not to suggest that they were not relevant in the earlier decades. For example, Table 6.3 shows

'Spectrum' as a topic for the 2010s. This means that 'Spectrum' is the most relevant topic for one of the documents in the 2010s, but is not the most relevant topic for any of the documents in the earlier decades. The same table also shows the topic that has been the most relevant one for the largest number of documents in each decade in the third column (i.e. most reiterated topic). In other words, the most reiterated topic for the decade reflects the highest priority given by the policy documents in the corresponding decade. The decade-wise inclusion of new topics describes how the policies have been incorporating newer themes. We argue in a later section that the inclusion of new topics has been influenced by the dominant narrative of the decade. Table 6.3 also reflects that infrastructure expansion has always been the central focus of the policies.

Table 6.3: Inclusion of New Topics in the Policies and the Most Reiterated Topic for Each Decade

Decade	Most relevant topics for the documents of the decade, but not for the earlier decades	Most reiterated topic in the decade
Pre-1990s	(Not applicable)	Landline Infrastructure Upgrade
1990s	Older ICTs, Licensing new operators/providers	Older ICTs, Licensing new operators/ providers
2000s	Electronic Transactions, ICT in Education, Regulation	Access to IT
2010s	Spectrum, e-services, Access to ICTs, Cybercrime and security, Sectors	Access to ICT

Source: Compiled by the authors based on their topic model on the plan documents

Inferences from N-gram Analysis

While the output of topic modelling presented above traced the evolution of different themes in the document collection, an n-gram analysis would be important to observe if certain terminologies are more frequent than others in the collection. We now present word clouds for different decades. In word clouds, texts with higher font sizes are the terms that have a larger effective frequency[4] in the document collection for the decade. Terms with similar importance are displayed using the same colour.

Figures 6.1 to 6.4 show the decade-wise word cloud for the bigrams. The word clouds reconfirm many of the observations we made from topic modelling. First, one can note that the frequent bigrams for all the decades are infrastructure or regulation-related terms. In the pre-1990 period (Figure 6.1), we find bigrams like 'telephone exchange' and 'local telephone' have been highlighted, reflecting the fact that expanding the landline telephone system was the main concern of the policies in this period. The word cloud for the decade of the 1990s (Figure 6.2) is somewhat diverse compared to the earlier decade, owing to the fact that we have a larger document collection. Nonetheless, we can observe that the telecommunications infrastructure is still the main focus. The word cloud for the 2000s (Figure 6.3) shows that the interest has shifted towards information technology, that is, the internet. Note that the bigrams 'digital signature' and 'electronic record' have appeared in the word cloud, indicating that these terms have been sufficiently reiterated in the decades of the 2000s. The word cloud for the 2010s (Figure 6.4) still highlights many infrastructure and regulation-related bigrams. Here, we should observe that apart from 'information technology', the bigram 'ICT education'[5] has been highlighted, again reflecting the technological view that the ICTs would be able to transform the education system. In addition, the word cloud also indicates that the policies have become more capacity-centric, which can be inferred from the bigram 'high speed' that has been highlighted.

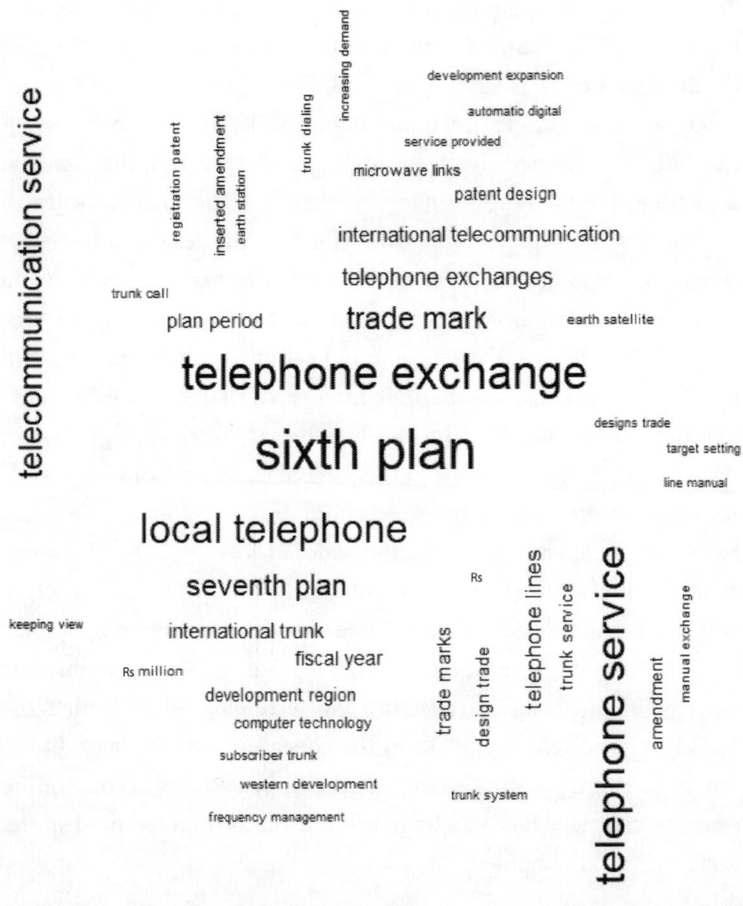

Figure 6.1: Bigrams for the pre-1990 period. The larger and darker terms are more important compared to the smaller and blurred terms in this and the following word clouds.

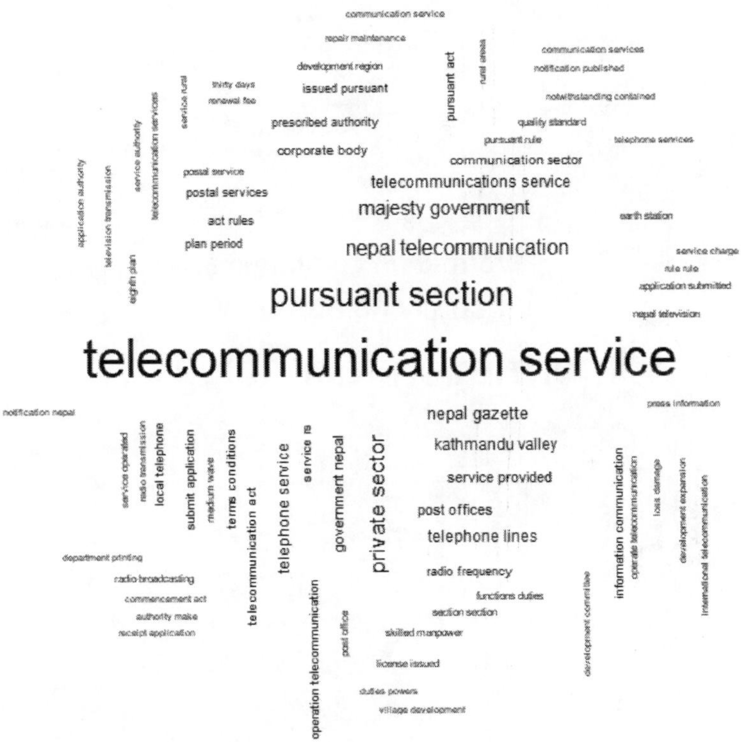

Figure 6.2: Bigrams for the 1990s decade

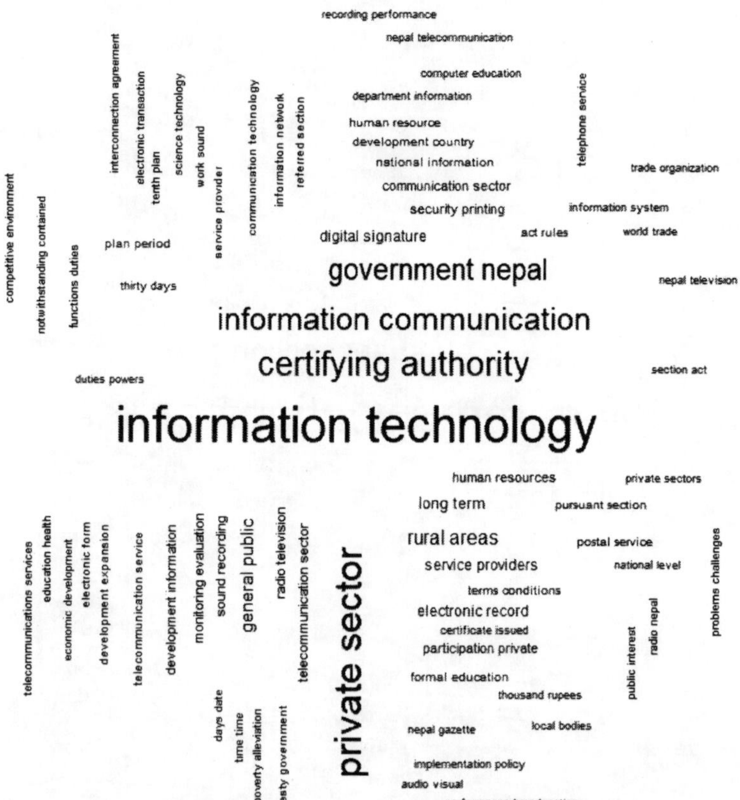

Figure 6.3: Bigrams for the 2000s decade

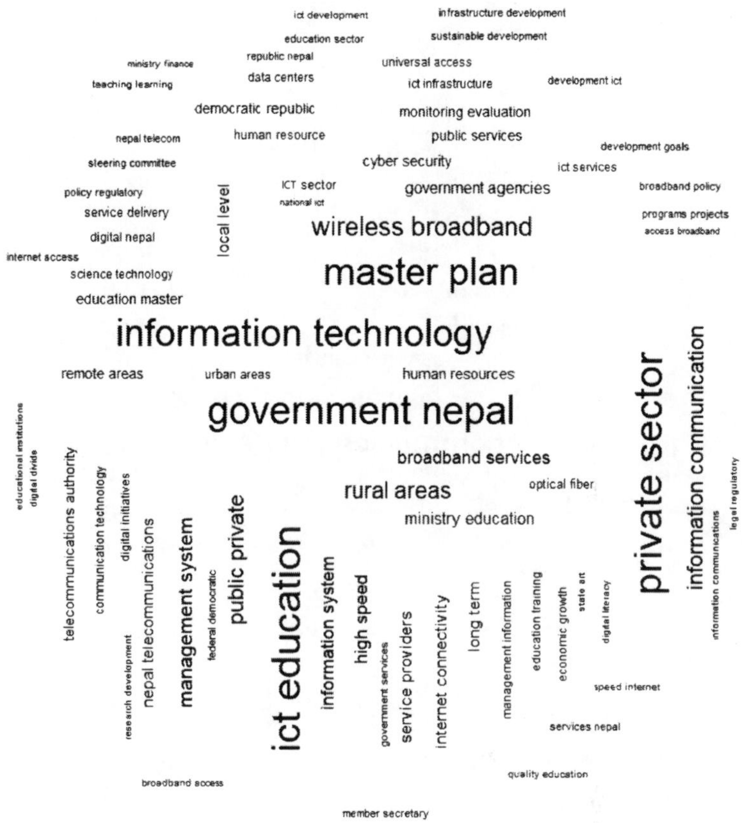

Figure 6.4: Bigrams for the 2010s decade

Figures 6.5 to 6.7 show the word clouds for newly added bigrams in each decade's documents. The word cloud for new bigrams in the 1990s (in Figure 6.5) agrees with our earlier observation in Table 6.3 that the documents in this decade have mostly focused on the issues related to older ICTs like post and telephone communication. Similarly, the word cloud in Figure 6.5 shows that internet-related terms such as 'digital signature' and 'electronic record', along with corresponding regulation terms such as 'certifying authority' and 'monitoring evaluation', have been included in the 2000s decade. In the 2010s (Figure 6.7), the noticeable new terms relate to the broader concept of ICT, its capacity and the application of ICT in the education sector.

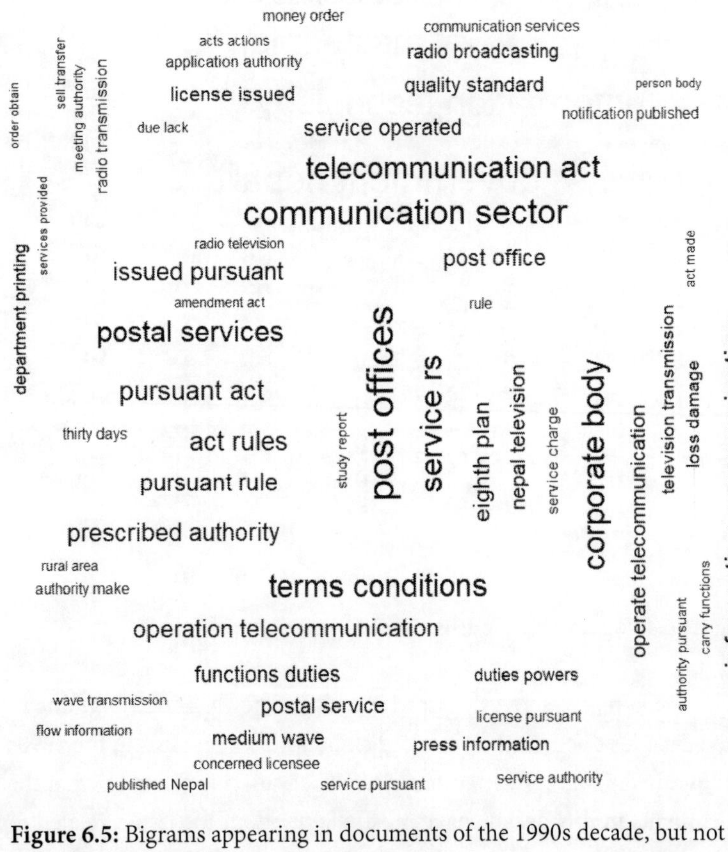

Figure 6.5: Bigrams appearing in documents of the 1990s decade, but not in the earlier documents

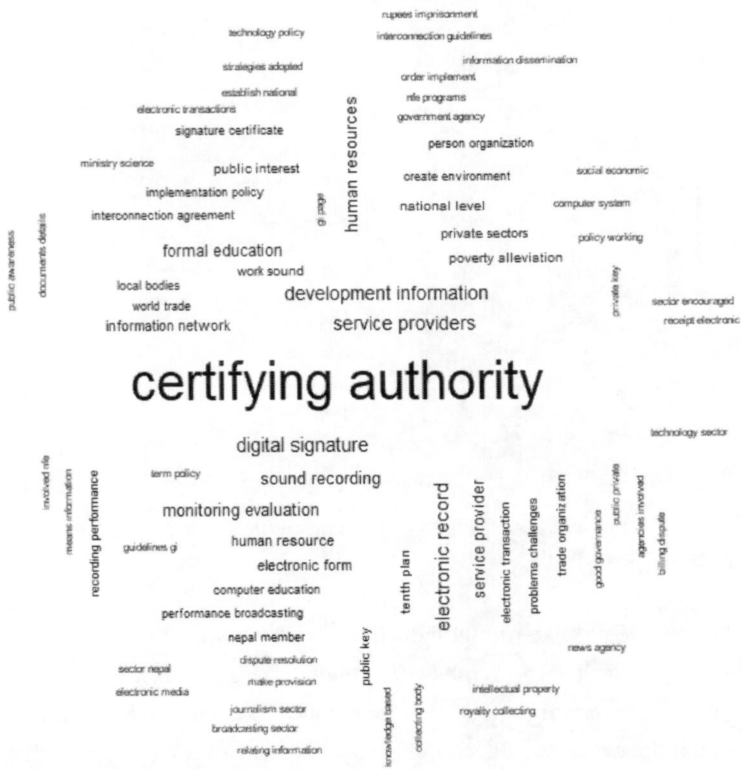

Figure 6.6: Bigrams appearing in documents of the 2000s decade, but not in the earlier documents

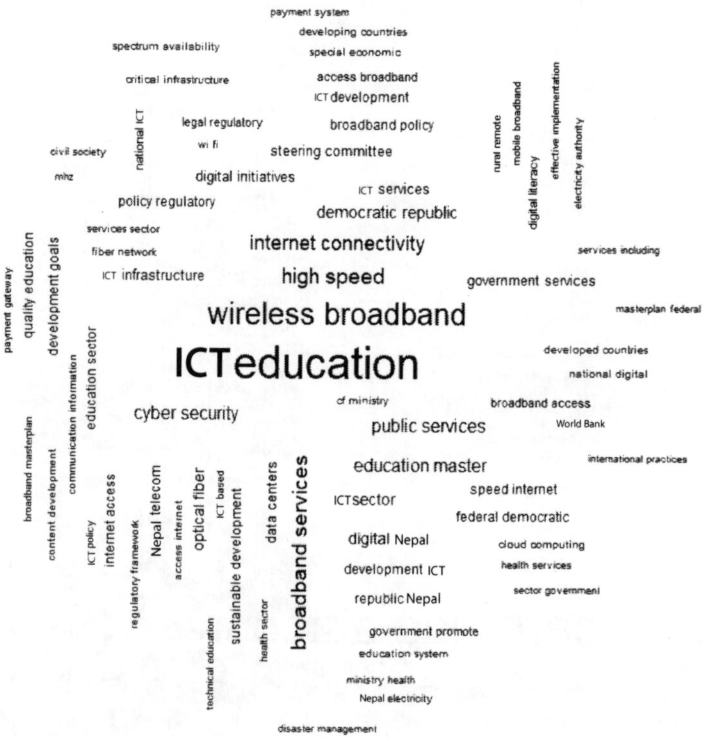

Figure 6.7: Bigrams appearing in documents of the 2010s decade but not in the earlier documents

Here, we would like to highlight that the chronology of newly added bigrams revealed from the wordclouds of Figures 6.5 to 6.7 also aligns with our argument that the policy documents have always been influenced by the technological constructs of the corresponding decade. We also examined trigrams, and decade-wise inclusion of bigrams- and trigrams in the document collection. The results do not reveal any further insights, thus we have not included them.

Some Specific Terms

In the preceding analysis, we considered the bigrams and trigrams having a high effective frequency as the important ones. But we think there could be some terms in the document collection, that despite having a low effective frequency, are significant. Such terms could provide different insights about the narratives in the documents being considered. In this section, we examine the occurrences of a few such terms that would be relevant to build our argument further.

The bigram 'digital divide' has appeared in a single document that was published in 2007 and seven other documents in the 2010s. The frequency of this bigram is too low to be highlighted in the word clouds. In addition, the 'digital divide' has been taken as the binary gap in access to the ICTs. There are a few other terms that refer to digital divide and inequality. The terms 'digital skill development' and 'skill development initiative' appear 35 and 34 times respectively, but only in a single document, which is the latest document in our collection, that is, The Digital Nepal Framework of 2019. The bigrams 'digital literacy' and 'ICT skills' are found in five and three documents, respectively, of the 2010s. Here, we highlight that the occurrences of the terms that could refer to the digital divide and inequality are too low. This is the reason why the topic-modelling algorithm did not produce any results that could refer to the concept of inequality.

The bigram, 'internet things' (internet of things), appears in two documents, that is, the e-Governance Master Plan of 2015 and the Digital Nepal Framework of 2019. The later document is also the single document that includes the term 'digital transformation'. The term 'economic growth' appears in 10 documents from 1997 to 2019 and the term 'knowledge-based society' appears in 8 documents from 2000 to 2019.

Analysis

Following the global trends

ICT policies in developing countries have been following the global narratives about the potential of technology, what Friederici and others call the 'mirage of inclusive digital development' (Friederici, Ojanperä and Graham 2017: 1). Friederici Ojanperä and Graham argue that the African ICT policies are influenced by grand ideas such as the internet forging economic, social and political inclusions that are supposed to be self-evident. Similar criticisms have been raised against the ICT policies of Nepal. In particular, Pandey and Regmi (2020) examine the ICT import data and describe how global discourses have shaped its policies. They show how ICT imports increased rapidly during the dot-com bubble and declined sharply after it burst. After the second half of the 2000s, they observed that the increase in ICT imports correlated with the transformative narratives about mobile broadband. In this section, we shed further light on how the global narratives and technological advancements have been influencing Nepali policies more minutely, referring to documents published over a much longer period of time.

A crucial narrative that has been reiterated time and again is that ICTs lead to development, where 'development' is mostly taken in an economic sense. This is seen as the occurrence of the term 'economic growth' appearing in a majority of documents since the 1990s.[6] The terminologies in the narratives, nonetheless, have changed over time, echoing popular contemporary buzzwords. Documents of the 1990s used the terms 'internet', 'information technology' and 'information and communication'. For instance, the ninth Five-Year Plan (1997) strongly contends that the internet leads to economic growth, and as an auxiliary benefit, serves the 'overall socio-economic development'. In the later decades, the terminology shifts from the 'internet' to the 'ICT'. Anyway, it is observed that the influence of the global narratives is intact throughout the decades that are considered.

Figure 6.8 shows the time-trend of the popularity of some relevant terms using the Google Books Ngram Viewer. The idea that the internet leads to development is captured by the terms 'internet for development' and 'IT for development'. A conceptualisation of the developmental benefits of the internet beyond economic growth is the 'knowledge-based society' that has appeared in our document collection since the 2000s. It can be observed in the figure that the usage of the terms 'IT for development', 'internet for development', and 'knowledge-based society' began to increase in the 1990s and peaked during the early 2000s. On the other hand, the usage of the term ICTD (ICT and development) began to increase sharply in the early 2000s and peaked after 2010. The global popularity of terminologies and ideologies has a clear influence on the policies.

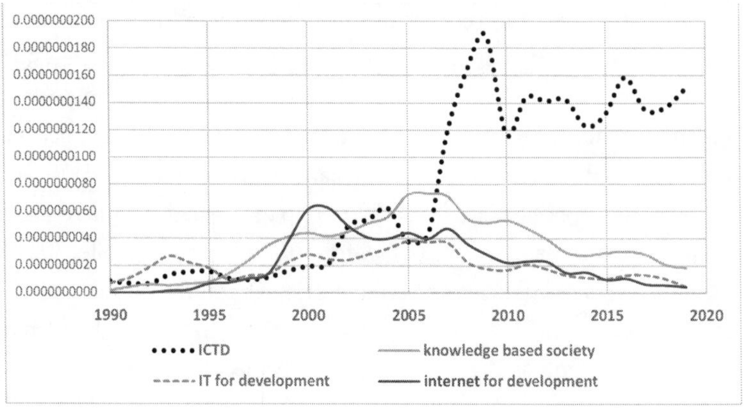

Figure 6.8: Time trends of the popularity of different terms generated using Google Books Ngram Viewer.[7]

To illustrate how the policies have followed contentious global narratives, if not unfounded, we digress here on the question of the developmental effects of ICT, more specifically, on the contribution of ICT to economic growth. An interesting case here pertains to the World Bank. In one of its publications (Qiang, Rossotto and Kimura 2009: 45), it claimed that a 10 per cent increase in broadband penetration leads to a ratio of 1.38 per cent increase in the GDP growth for developed economies. This claim has fuelled the ambitions of ICT policies in developing countries, including Nepal (Pandey and Regmi 2020). However, in 2016, the World Bank retracted its claim by asserting that the developmental benefits of ICTs are not observable in the nations that lack the 'analogue complements of the digital economy', which are favourable business environment, strong human capital and strong governance (The World Bank 2016). The questions regarding the ICT and development nexus are still an active area of research. A recent review (Vu, Hanafizadeh and Bohlin 2020) concludes that despite the higher number of academic publications mentioning favourable impacts of ICT on economic growth, reliable empirical studies are required to confirm the hypothesis.

Impacts of the global trends on the policies appear, in addition to the belief in ICTs' development potentials, also on the choice of the technology itself. Figure 6.9 shows the time trend of some technical terms that were observed in the decade-wise unique bigrams of Figures 6.6 to 6.7. We can observe that the usage of the term 'television transmission' was high in the 1990s and thus emerged as an important bigram for the 1990s. Similarly, the usage of 'digital signature' peaked during the early 2000s and is an important bigram of the decade. Usage of the terms 'data centre' and 'cloud computing' are high after 2010, and consequently, they are important bigrams for the document collection of the 2010s. This re-confirms an earlier argument that the Nepali policies are 'capacity centric' (Pandey and Regmi 2020), that is, the focus has always been on importing and using the latest technologies.

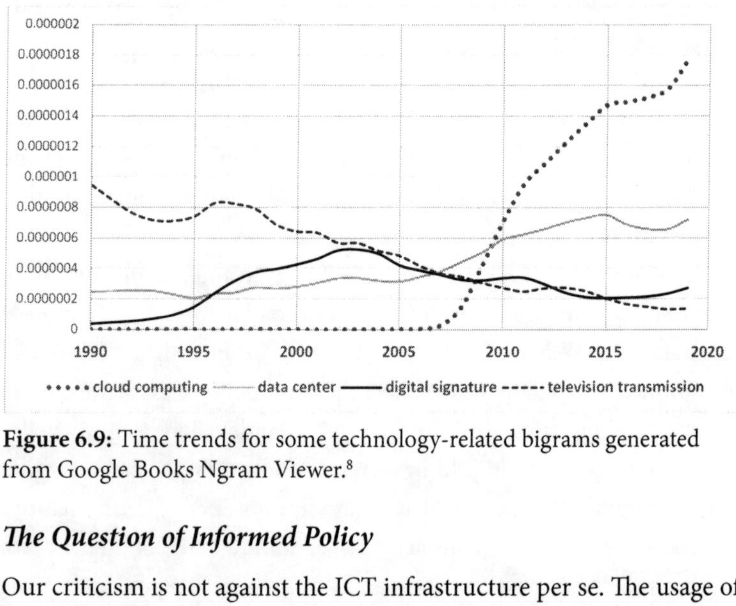

Figure 6.9: Time trends for some technology-related bigrams generated from Google Books Ngram Viewer.[8]

The Question of Informed Policy

Our criticism is not against the ICT infrastructure per se. The usage of the latest technologies could be probably justified from the perspective of engineering so as to make the infrastructure responsive to the needs of the future. Points that are usually missed are the distributional benefits of the ICT infrastructure and the prerequisite infrastructures that facilitate its sound functioning so that all the potential benefits can be reaped. Development projects without a proper requirement analysis and an assessment of the ground realities are prone to fail. In the case of information system projects, Heeks (2002) has reminded us of the importance of requirement analysis as early as 2002.

Heeks contends that information system projects fail due to what he calls 'design-actuality' gaps. This argument applies to infrastructure projects in general.

Prior research in Nepal's context has pointed mainly to two issues that need to be addressed before formulating realistic ICT policies. First is the lack of understanding about ICT users, their requirements and their demographic backgrounds (Pandey and Raj 2016). Second is the question of the availability of the prerequisite infrastructure, mainly energy; it is observed that energy requirements of the ICT infrastructure in Nepal have already been gigantic and comparable to the transportation sector (Regmi and Pandey 2015). Our topic modelling did not yield a single topic that is closer to either of the two themes, that is, the necessity of ICT users' profiling and the massive energy demand of ICT. The n-gram analysis also did not highlight a single term which could indicate that policies were aware of ICT users' profiling and energy and related infrastructural prerequisites.

This missing Nepali context implies that the policies are generic but not tailored to the nation's requirements and realities. In this regard, a later document, the Digital Nepal Framework of 2019, tends to acknowledge some of the challenges for a properly functioning ICT infrastructure. However, the acknowledgements are apparently only cosmetic as the document does not delve deeper into the challenges to the conception of a 'Digital Nepal'. The Digital Nepal Framework, 2019, is more comfortable in painting the benefits of ICTs as the earlier plans and policies have done. For example, the Digital Nepal Framework, 2019, still does not differentiate the digital divide, which is differential in access to ICTs, from digital inequality, which is inequality in skills, use and the benefits of the ICTs (DiMaggio and Hargittai 2001). The question of tackling the multifaceted digital inequality therefore remains as it is.

The Curious Case of Missing 'Digital Inequality'

The missing of digital inequality, or even its earlier avatar, the digital divide, as a topic of discussion in the policies is annoying. The digital divide was already a pressing issue at the end of the twentieth century (Jurich 2000). In the early years of the 2000s decade, researchers had also already introduced the complexity of digital inequality (DiMaggio and Hargittai 2001), and the volume of inequality research proliferated rapidly in the later years.

As mentioned earlier, the term 'digital divide' appeared in Nepal's policies after 2007, though its effective frequency is not high enough to be highlighted in the word clouds. The policies have rather taken the simplistic aim of reducing the gap in access to the ICTs. On the contrary, the target of reducing digital inequality is 'persistent and dynamic' (Martin Chautari 2018: 2). This means that inequality is ever persistent, but it reappears in newer forms. Even if we close the access gap, inequality would emerge in other dimensions like skills, use and benefits.

Official statistics in Nepal show that household broadband penetration is around 32 per cent, and mobile broadband access is almost universal (NTA 2022). These statistics, however, do not reflect the distributional aspects of ICT access, use and skills. In an earlier analysis based on the data from the national census of 2011 and Twitter usage, Pandey and Regmi (2018) revealed a huge geographic gap in household internet access as well as mobile broadband use. The unfair distribution of ICT access has not changed much thereafter. A later report based on a survey of 12,800 households (CBS 2020: 96) reveals significant gaps in household internet penetration when compared across the provinces of Nepal. Bagmati province, the province with the capital city, has household access of 68.7 per cent, whereas the far-western province of Sudoor Paschim has 24.3 per cent. Within the Bagmati province, the urban–rural gap is surprisingly high, with household access of 81.8 and 35.2 per cent, respectively. The gaps in ICT skills and use are even more pronounced and manifested across gender and other dimensions; readers are referred to the CBS report (2020) for the details. The method used for assessing ICT skills and use in CBS (2020) is simplistic when contrasted with the detailed methodology prescribed in Van Deurson et al. (2014). A thorough assessment could have painted a starker picture of digital inequality.

In recent years, digital inequality has become even more intricate, as concerns have been raised about the broader class of inequalities termed 'emergent inequalities', that are 'spawned by the platform economy, automation, big data, algorithms, cybercrime, cybersafety, gaming, emotional well-being, assistive technologies, civic engagement, and mobility' (Robinson et al. 2020) Since these newer kinds of inequalities are also being observed in industrialised countries, without precautionary measures, these are bound to appear in the developing nations that follow the technologies of advanced economies. Our analysis in this study indicates that Nepal's policies are miles away from this realisation.

Guessing the Narratives of Future Policies

With the rapid evolution in computing sciences and technologies, technical jargon like 'big data', 'internet of things' and 'digital transformation' have emerged in academic and popular debate after the later years of the 2000s decade. Figure 6.10 illustrates how the uses of these three terms have exponentially increased after 2010. In principle, big data analytics, in the context of development, refers to the gathering of usage data from the ICT end-users and processing them to infer policy decisions (Hilbert 2016). The internet of things (IoT) connects every possible digital divide to the internet, thus acting as a medium for collecting big data. 'Digital Transformation' has been defined in several ways. Vial (2021: 1) gives a general definition of digital transformation as 'a process that aims to improve an entity by triggering significant changes to its properties through combinations of information, computing, communication, and connectivity technologies'; clearly, this definition is imprecise and could have several interpretations.

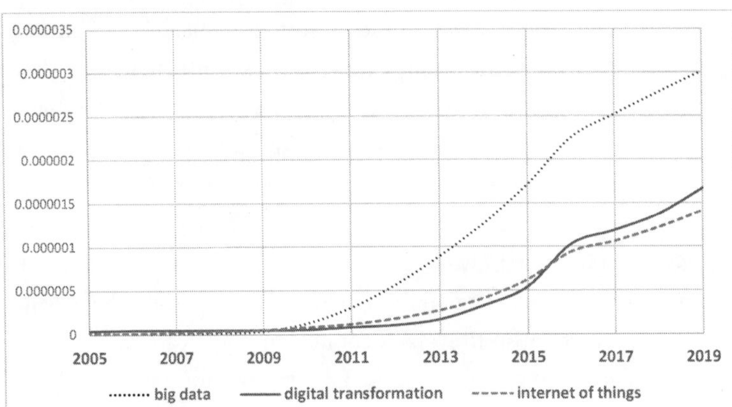

Figure 6.10: The usage of the terms 'big data', 'digital transformation' and 'internet of things' has surged after 2010.[9]

Assuming the business-as-usual scenario, it is straightforward to speculate what narratives the future ICT policies would put forward. Unsurprisingly, the terms big data, IoT and digital transformation have begun to reverberate in the policy discussions, as can be seen in the later documents in our collection. In this regard, the Digital Nepal Framework 2019 expresses its belief in the potential of artificial intelligence and internet of things as 'emerging business models and disruptive technologies such as artificial intelligence (AI), robotics, and the internet of things (IoT) are transforming the way work is done. These digital technologies are allowing governments and enterprises globally to unlock the potential to achieve exponential growth' (17).

The same document continues to justify the role of big data in policy making stating, 'equally important is the need to factor in the role that big data analytics can play in fundamentally reshaping policy-making processes' (154).

An earlier document, the e-Government Masterplan of 2015, also expresses its capacity-centric view by noting that 'taking the lead of 5G will put Nepal at the forefront of the ongoing digital transformation' (49). These statements are clear indications that following the style of their predecessors, future policies will embrace vague terminologies and continue to believe contentious hypotheses as self-evident.

Consider the example of big data. In the context of socio-economic development, big data analytics would gather massive data from end-users' ICT devices and process the data to get inferences for the policy makers (Hilbert 2016). However, the presumed applicability of big data is not straightforward in a society that is inflicted with inequality. There is a two-way relationship between big data analytics and the digital divide. First, the inferences from big data analytics could be biased in the presence of the digital divide as the data gathered from ICT usage does not represent the whole population. Second, big data itself is creating a newer form of digital divide; the 'divide in data-based knowledge to inform intelligent decision making' (Hilbert 2016: 1). Thus, the benefits of big data are doubtful in Nepal's context, and one can make similar arguments against the vague notion of digital transformation.

The argument presented in the preceding paragraph highlights the necessity of understanding digital inequality before promoting newer technologies like big data and IoT. Without a complete profiling of the general end-users of the ICTs, any technologically ambitious project is bound to benefit only the small portion of the population who are already advantaged. The irony is that the later documents have signalled that technological determinism has been and will be the central philosophy of the ICT policies. It would not be wrong to argue that forthcoming ICT legislations and policy will be fuelled by the optimism of big data, IoT, artificial intelligence and digital transformation.

Conclusion

Infrastructure expansion has always been the central objective of Nepal's ICT policies. Rather than building the development objectives on the grounds of empirical data on the end-users' requirements and preferences from the very beginning, the ICT policies have relied on contemporary narratives on the potentials of digital technologies and the related buzzwords. Policy documents published in the latter half of 2010s decade reveal their fascination with technologies like big data and the internet of things and notions like digital transformation. We can conclude that in the business-as-usual scenario, forthcoming policies will uncritically cling to the presumed capabilities of big data, the internet of things and digital transformation.

In this study, we focused mainly on understanding the evolution of different themes and linking them with the contemporary global narratives on ICTs and society. Critical discussions of policy implications were not the objectives of this paper. We nonetheless stressed that the better path is to first identify the drivers and consequences of digital inequality, and the adequacy of energy along with other prerequisite infrastructure, before setting any unrealistic goals. Such an assessment will help to gauge the benefits, and more importantly the adverse effects, of any new technological infrastructure.

Annexure I: List of Documents Used in the Study

The following documents have been used in the study.

Year	Document
1965	The Patent Design and Trademark Act, 2022
1980	Sixth Plan (Telecommunications section)
1985	Seventh Plan (Computer Policy chapter)
1985	Seventh Plan (Telecommunications chapter)
1992	Eighth Plan (Communication chapter)
1993	The National Broadcasting Act
1997	1997 Ninth Plan (Information and Communication chapter)
1997	Telecommunication Rules, 2054
1997	Telecommunications Act, 2053
2000	Nepal Information Technology Policy, 2057
2002	Tenth Plan (Information and Communication chapter)
2002	Tenth Plan (Information Technology section)
2002	The Copyright Act, 2059
2003	Long Term Policy of Information and Communication Sector, 2059
2004	Copyright Rules, 2061
2004	Telecommunication Policy, 2060
2007	Electronic Transactions Rules, 2064
2007	Eleventh Plan (Information and Communication chapter)
2007	Eleventh Plan (Information Technology section)
2007	Nepal Non-formal Policy
2008	Interconnection Guideline, 2065
2008	The Electronic Transactions Act, 2063
2012	Directives for Laying and Maintaining Optical Fiber Network
2012	Wireless Broadband Master Plan
2013	ICT in Education Masterplan, 2013–2017
2015	e-Governance Masterplan
2015	ICT Policy
2015	Nepal Broadband Policy, 2071 (Draft)
2016	National Cybersecurity Policy (Draft)
2019	Digital Nepal Framework
2019	Fifteenth Plan

Notes

1 In this paper, ICT is taken in its broadest sense to include all computing and communication technologies.

2 We use the word 'policy' to collectively represent plans, policies, acts and by-laws, unless stated otherwise.

3 For each document, the algorithm generates a list of numeric weights for the topics. The most relevant topic for the document is the topic having the highest weight. We note here that in some of the years, more than one document had the same topic as the most relevant topic. Thus the number of documents published each year could be larger than the number of the most relevant topics for the year. Two out of the 15 topics listed in Table 6.1 do not appear as the major topic for any of the documents. These topics are 'ICT infrastructure operation' and 'Themes for ICT'.

4 We have defined the 'effective frequency' of n-gram as its number of occurrences in the whole collections multiplied by the number of documents where the n-gram appears. Use of simple frequency, that is, the number of occurrences of n-gram, could be misleading because it may have very high occurrence in a single document, but nil in the rest of the documents. We thus contend, in the context of this study, that the effective frequency correctly quantifies the importance of the term.

5 This bigram actually represents 'ICT in education'. The preposition 'in' has been removed as it is a stop word. Similar bigrams/trigrams appear in the forthcoming discussion, and need to be understood accordingly.

6 Effective frequency is low and thus not noticeable in the word clouds.

7 The vertical axis corresponds to the frequencies of n-grams in Google's book corpus. The scores for 'IT for development' and 'internet for development' have been multiplied 5 and 10 times, respectively, for clarity.

8 The scores for 'television transmission' has been multiplied 10 times for clarity.

9 The scores for 'digital transformation' and 'internet of things' have been multiplied 5 times for readability.

References

CBS. 2020. *Nepal Multiple Indicator Cluster Survey 2019*. Kathmandu, Nepal: Central Bureau of Statistics (CBS) and UNICEF Nepal.

Martin Chautari. 2014. 'Universal Connectivity in Nepal: A Policy Review'. *Kathmandu: Martin Chautari.*

———.2018. *Moving Beyond Access—The Landscape of Internet Use and Digital Inequality in Nepal*. 23. Kathmandu: Martin Chautari.

Paul DiMaggio and Eszter Hargittai. 2001. 'From the "Digital Divide" to "Digital Inequality": Studying Internet Use as Penetration Increases'.

Princeton: Center for Arts and Cultural Policy Studies, Woodrow Wilson School, Princeton University 4 (1): 4–2.

Nicolas Friederic, Sanna Ojanperä and Mark Graham. 2017. 'The Impact of Connectivity in Africa: Grand Visions and the Mirage of Inclusive Digital Development'. *The Electronic Journal of Information Systems in Developing Countries* 79 (1): 1–20.

Shawn Graham, Scott Weingart and Ian Milligan. 2012. *Getting Started with Topic Modeling and MALLET*. The Editorial Board of the Programming Historian.

Richard Heeks. 2002. 'Information Systems and Developing Countries: Failure, Success, and Local Improvisations'. *The Information Society* 18 (2): 101–112.

Martin Hilbert. 2016. 'Big Data for Development: A Review of Promises and Challenges'. *Development Policy Review* 34 (1):135–174.

Sonia Jurich. 2000. 'The Information Revolution and the Digital Divide: A Review of Literature'. *TechKnowLogia* 2 (1): 42–44.

NTA. 2022. *Nepal Telecommunications Authority MIS Report (15 May 2022–14 June 2022)*. Nepal Telecommunications Authority (NTA).

Shailesh Pandey and Nischal Regmi. 2018. 'Changing Connectivities and Renewed Priorities: Status and Challenges Facing Nepali Internet'. *First Monday* 23 (1).

———. 2020. 'If You Build It, Will They Come? Exploring Narratives That Shape the Internet in Nepal'. *Science, Technology and Society* 25 (3): 444–464.

Shailesh Pandey and Yogesh Raj. 2016. 'Free Float Internet Policies of Nepal'. *Studies in Nepali History and Society* 21 (1): 1–60.

Christine Zhen-Wei Qiang, Carlo M. Rossotto and Kaoru Kimura. 2009.' Economic Impacts of Broadband'. *Information and Communications for Development 2009: Extending Reach and Increasing Impact* 3: 35–50.

Daniel Ramage, Evan Rosen, Jason Chuang, Christopher D. Manning and Daniel A. McFarland. 2009. 'Topic Modeling for the Social Sciences', in NIPS 2009 workshop on applications for topic models: text and beyond, vol. 5, 1–4.

Nischal Regmi. 2017. 'Expectation vs Reality—a Case of Internet in Nepal'. *The Electronic Journal of Information System in Developing Countries* 82 (7): 1–20.

Nischal Regmi and Shailesh B. Pandey. 2015. 'A Regression Analysis into Nepali ICT's Energy Consumption and Its Implications', in *2015 9th International Conference on Software, Knowledge, Information Management and Applications (SKIMA)*, 1–8.

Laura Robinson, Jeremy Schulz, Hopeton S. Dunn, Antonio A. Casilli, Paola Tubaro, Rod Carvath, Wenhong Chen, Julie B. Wiest, Matías Dodel,

Michael J. Stern, Christopher Ball, Kuo-Ting Huang, Grant Blank, Massimo Ragnedda, Hiroshi Ono, Bernie Hogan, Gustavo S. Mesch, Shelia R. Cotten, Susan B. Kretchmer, Timothy M. Hale, Tomasz Drabowicz, Pu Yan, Barry Wellman, Molly-Gloria Harper, Anabel Quan-Haase and Aneka Khilnani. 2020. 'Digital Inequalities 3.0: Emergent Inequalities in the Information Age'. *First Monday*. doi: 10.5210/fm.v25i7.10844.

Drew Schmidt and Christian Heckendorf. 2014. 'Guide to the Ngram Package'.

The World Bank. 2016. *World Development Report: Digital Dividends 2016*. The World Bank.

Van Deursen, AJAM, Ellen J. Helsper and Rebecca Eynon. 2014. 'Measuring Digital Skills', From Digital Skills to Tangible Outcomes Project Report.

Gregory Vial. 2021. 'Understanding Digital Transformation: A Review and a Research Agenda', in *Managing Digital Transformation*, 13–66.

Khuong Vu, Payam Hanafizadeh and Erik Bohlin. 2020. 'ICT as a Driver of Economic Growth: A Survey of the Literature and Directions for Future Research'. *Telecommunications Policy* 44 (2): 1019–1022.

7

Digital Re-fashioning of Identity

Insights from the Nepal Picture Library

Rahul Ganguly

Introduction

It has almost become a commonsensical assertion that we now live in a digital world. However, when a phenomenon becomes a part of the everyday lexicon, there is a tendency to stop thinking critically about it, and its meaning is often taken for granted. What does it mean to live in a digital world? What are its implications and possibilities? How does the digital allow us to re-think our pasts, presents and futures? These are some of the broad questions this chapter will engage in through a study of the Nepal Picture Library (hereafter, NPL). The NPL is a digital archive that attempts to critically engage with the histories of the Nepali nation–state. De Kosnik (2016: 53) shows in her work the ways in which digital archives and digital archivists are renewing the traditional category of 'archives', and hence generating new forms of cultural engagement and conflict. Digital archives are important for this paper because they are largely opposed to the canonisation of certain kinds of cultural texts and also challenge the workings of print-based cultural memory (De Kosnik 2016).

The reason for choosing this particular archive as the entry point here is because it provides scope to examine how digital spaces can emerge as sites of democratic deliberations which potentially challenge the boundaries of accepted histories and social orders. This kind of interrogation also opens up new pathways for hitherto marginalised groups and individuals to make their presence felt and documented. In doing so, this study will also explore the manner in which digital spaces such as the one provided by the NPL can enable creative ways of (re) imagining national identities and belongings beyond state-mandated ways of 'seeing'. Drawing on Benedict Anderson's (1991) idea that the nation is an 'imagined community', this chapter argues that the Nepali nation–state was a particular kind of imagined community, based primarily on the caste Hindu ideas of kingship. This exclusionary imagination has fostered marginalisations along multiple axes—all of which have nevertheless been challenged and critiqued in multiple ways.

The NPL can be seen as a sort of community archive that challenges such exclusionary imaginations of what it means to be 'Nepali'. This process, of course, has a larger history including the Maoist movement, the Janajati movement, and the most recent People's Movement of 2006. However, this chapter argues that the digital nature of the challenge is the point of departure since it opens up the possibilities of recovering newer forms of history and politics. In other words, the digital emerges as a new site of organisation, deliberation and contestation with its own dynamics and possibilities that can add significant meanings to the 'physical' realm of politics.[1] Based on this understanding, the chapter is organised into three sections.

In the first section, the essay discusses how the digital can be seen as a site for democratic interventions and re-thinking. The second section deals with the broad social history of the Nepali nation–state in order to understand the ways in which it has emerged, consolidated and engendered the practices of structural exclusions. In the third section, there is a discussion of select material from the NPL in order to show how it critiques and challenges the hegemonic understanding of what it means to be Nepali. The discussion also points to the manner in which such a critique posits the possibilities of re-inscribing identities that have been systematically rendered invisible in the Nepali public sphere.[2] Finally, I will argue about the ways in which such digital archives can contribute to the democratisation of history writing and the possibilities that digital futures may hold.

Democratic Possibilities of the Digital

In contemporary times, there can be no illusion that the digital space or ecosystem is democratic in an unqualified way. Numerous examples of data hacking, government interventions and the impacts of big corporations and far-right groups in the digital space have shown how these spaces can be resolutely undemocratic. However, that does not mean that we throw the proverbial baby out with the bath water. It is, in fact, the openness of the digital space that permits such an extreme spectrum of possibilities, ranging from openly undemocratic to deliberatively democratic. The aim here is to uncover the democratic possibilities within the digital and explore the ways in which it can remain an important space for the practise of progressive politics and social commentary.

To state in a binary way that the digital is either democratic or undemocratic is profoundly un-sociological and un-historical. Rather, what is required is an analysis of those agents and networks who make use of the potential of the digital and give it their specific meanings. Witschge (quoted in Baldwin 2015: 33) argues that the internet holds huge potential to challenge hegemonic power structures and bring to life agonism, given the sheer number of contradictory and digressive viewpoints. Baldwin (2015) further states that the specific and novel features associated with online deliberative spaces have the ability to challenge and redefine the ways in which citizens make use of their tools in order to improve their efforts and spread their messages. In this regard, Spinner (2012) argues that information and communication technologies possess the capacity to reduce the costs of traditional forms of political and social participation. As the internet increasingly becomes less costly and easier to use, a greater number of civic groups begin to make use of it. Shirky (2009) (quoted in Spinner 2012: 83) shows that the increasing complexity of the online communication space renders it more participatory, allowing the networked population to get better access to information. Such a phenomenon plays an important role in increasing public participation as well. This perspective holds for the NPL.

Being an online platform with an extremely popular Instagram page, apart from their website, allows the NPL to spread across networks that are transnational and perhaps engage with groups across the world who are working for indigenous populations and marginalised groups. This has a positive impact on the democratisation of knowledge and posits the possibilities for building transnational alliances. Apart from the digital benefits, social media also contributes to creating an empathetic experience, which is important in forming a community, whether it is physical or virtual (Spinner 2012: 84). A critique of the public sphere, as theorised by Habermas (quoted in Spinner 2012: 86), has been that it has often privileged the rational over the affective, resulting in the narrowing of the kinds of participation that are possible. However, as Spinner (2012) and Gimmler (2001) show, digital spaces have the capacity to go beyond such binaries, forming communities of effect and deliberative rationality. Kreide (2016: 6) argues that new media are created through the participation of the many and continue to retain many of the characteristics of an enlightened public including free access, plurality of themes, equality among participants and no restrictions on the number of those who can participate. Kreide (2016) further notes that social media sites like Twitter (in our case, Instagram as well) make use of the power of existing distant connections between activists, in fact strengthening them. New social media platforms are often able to make existing social orders stronger and more efficient as they can go beyond the restrictions imposed by the need for face-to-face interactions and physical presence.

This does not mean that the digital can become a substitute for the physical. Rather the two should be seen as mutually co-constitutive in forging new modes of social and political participation. I argue that digital spaces help in the re-shaping of subjectivities. But what is the nature of this subject? Gimmler (2001) points out that the political subject is one who simultaneously attains a personal and collective identity as a part of complex relationships with other individuals. It is this fundamental social identity that becomes the terrain on which the struggle for recognition in the public sphere is enacted. The NPL can be seen as a similar space, working to establish the recognition of those who have been systematically denied this right of recognition, in the Nepali public sphere. Deliberative democracy understands the public sphere as a public space where citizens can debate over issues that are relevant to them. Gimmler (2001: 24) notes that the deliberative democracy model of the public sphere performs a critical function in opposition to the traditional public sphere dominated by the state or mass media. In this context, the internet can help strengthen deliberative democracy.

This is because it structurally supports the equality of access to information and promises an unrestricted means of access. I further argue that the internet provides a space for knowledge production that may not be realised in traditional sites. It is not just the access to information, but the nature of information as well that is democratised.

The NPL is also an important site of visual history. According to Bleichman and Schwartz (2019), visual histories are extremely important in expanding source bases[3] and images must be seen as makers of history in their own right. This implies that images should not simply be seen as recording history but as actively making or constructing it as well. Such an understanding corresponds to the NPL's attempts to visually re-construct and challenge the traditional history of Nepal. Further drawing on Taylor (2015), we can argue that the camera allows for a greater range of social classes, places and moods to be recorded. This is something that the NPL tries to do as well—humanising marginalised groups by rendering them historically visible.

The above discussion shows us how and why the digital can be seen as a space for the consolidation of democratic practices through a challenge to hegemonic ways of 'seeing' and 'being'. Methodologically, this study will be using critical discourse analysis in order to examine how the NPL works as a space filled with the democratic potential of the digital which has been discussed above. This is because such a method helps us to find the ways in which words and images have specific meanings in specific historical, social and political contexts (Mogashoa 2014: 106). Locke (quoted in Mogashoa 2014: 105) mentions that critical discourse analysis makes it possible to explore relationships of causality and determination between discursive practices and texts, and their broader socio-historical structures. The next section will discuss the historical emergence and consolidation of the Nepali nation–state and the ways in which it has systematically and legally rendered minorities invisible from the national imagination.

History of Exclusions: The Nepali Nation–State

The history of modern Nepal, right from its founding under Prithvi Narayan Shah to the present day, can be read as the historical trajectory of an upper-caste Hindu state. While there have been formal changes, with the abolition of kingship and the transition to democracy, the substantive impacts of these changes remain questionable at best. Whelpton (2005: 56) shows that in the *Dibya Upadesh*, Shah saw his kingdom as the unpolluted land of the Hindus, markedly different from 'India' which had been polluted first by Mughal rule and then by the British.

The Rana regime which followed the Shah's for an interim period of almost 100 years institutionalised the Hindu nature of the Nepali nation–state through the Mulki Ain of 1854. The primary aim of the Mulki Ain (territorial law) was to commit the state to ensure the enforcement of a uniform caste-based moral and legal code throughout the country. It entailed the assimilation of lower-caste and non-caste ethnic groups to the values and morals of upper-caste Hindus (Whelpton 2005). This led to the criminalisation of many practices of these groups such as beef-eating and fostered an erasure of their cultures, languages and histories. In the twentieth century, the official ideology of 'Panchayat democracy' was based on the two axes of Hinduism and the Nepali language. The unity envisioned by this ideology was driven by the customs and values of the high-caste Parbatiyas who had dominated the Nepali state throughout its history.

The 1962 Constitution explicitly defined Nepal as a Hindu state, reaffirming its continuity with the vision of Prithvi Narayan Shah and the Ranas (Whelpton 2005: 84). Hangen (2010) further argues that the process of state-building in Nepal resulted in a hierarchical stratification of different ethnic and caste groups based on a model of superiority of upper-caste Hindus. Hangen (2010) shows that many members of the Hindu upper castes benefited materially and socially from their interactions with the emergent state occupying the upper echelons of business and administration. At the same time, the lower castes and ethnic groups such as the Gurungs, Magars and Tamangs were enlisted to meet the labour and fiscal demands of the expanding state. The women's movement in Nepal has been largely organised around a homogenised idea of the 'Nepali woman' and dominated by upper-caste Hindu and Newar women as well (Tamang 2009). Gellner (2007) shows that the national identity propagated in schools and through various government media was experienced as highly exclusionary and oppressive by lower castes and ethnic groups. Gellner (2007) further argues that the hills–plains divide became an important basis of discrimination towards those residing in the plains of southern Nepal (the Terai region), who were often accused of harbouring pro-India sentiments based on their ethnic similarities with those living in India.

Frydenlund (2019) explains that social mobility and access to resources are shaped by ethnic positioning within a racialised order. She further notes that lower-caste Hindus and non-Hindus have been devalued in historical, political, social and cultural contexts through legal as well as extra-legal forms of discrimination. Comaroff (1996) contends that ethnicity usually has its origins in relations of inequality and operates in a field of contestation over power that is simultaneously political, material and symbolic. Such an approach helps us understand the ways in which the Nepali state has systematically and normatively ensured ethnic discrimination and marginalisation. Frydenlund (2019) also shows how the Nepali state's racialised ethnic projects used land reforms as a way to transfer non-Hindu lands to upper-caste Hindus, thereby transforming the Nepali uplands and in part causing widespread migration to India.

The religious origin of the Nepali nation–state entrenched the status of Dalits as Untouchables, both in laws and policies until the middle of the twentieth century (Bahadur 2013: 10). To note, the Mulki Ain (1854) legally sanctioned untouchability and caste discrimination. Bahadur (2013) further shows in his ethnographic work that Dalits continue to have bitter experiences of caste discrimination when they openly use their caste identities, compelling them to hide their surnames. Such an act is both a phenomenological experience of humiliation as well as an enforced erasure of personal history. This brief overview helps us understand that the imagined Nepali nation was based on the exclusion of lower castes and non-caste ethnic identities. This has entailed serious material, social and psychological consequences for groups not belonging to the upper castes. It has also meant that their histories, cultures and experiences had little to no place in the publicly and privately imagined idea of being Nepali. However, this does not mean that there has been no opposition to such a system or that changes have not taken place. For instance, the new constitution of Nepal (2015) has outlawed untouchability in Article 24 (5). Nepal has also become a signatory to the International Labour Organisation (ILO) Convention 169, which enables the transfer of ownership and management of natural resources to indigenous people and allows them to direct the development of educational and health facilities among others (Jones and Langford 2011). However, Jones and Langford (2011) argue that there remains a discrepancy between high-level political commitments to the ILO Convention and the UN Declaration on the Rights of Indigenous Peoples on the one hand and the political will to honour and implement these commitments on the other.

However, despite the lack of substantive changes, there have been significant efforts made by different marginalised groups in Nepal to claim their place in history. It can be argued that the NPL draws on such an existing legacy, both directly and indirectly. The works of Des Chene (1996) and Onta and Humagain (2017) help us see how the rise of Janajati magazines in the 1990s contributed to the creation of a subaltern Janajati counter-public. Such magazines attempted to both critique the existing historical and cultural narratives in Nepal and carve out counter-discourses. In the context of the booming heritage industry in Nepal, Kunreuther (2017) shows how individual attempts at archiving family histories in the Kathmandu Valley reveal complex relations between the personal, the home and the state. The rise of ethnic movements and the restoration of formal democracy in Nepal provided an opportunity to rigorously question and challenge the foundational cultural, social and historical bases of the Nepali nation (Lawoti and Hangen 2013). The NPL must therefore be seen as a part of a broader tradition that has tried to establish counter-publics and construct narratives and cultural forms (such as the Tamus that Des Chene (1996) talks about) that question the marginalisation of non-upper-caste groups in Nepal. In doing so, it is the digital nature of the NPL that is its point of departure.

The Nepal Picture Library (NPL): Digital Histories for the Future

The NPL is a digital photo archive that seeks to create a broad and visual archive of Nepali social and cultural history. This section will include some of their projects which show the ways in which the NPL attempts to create an inclusive and corrective archive of the Nepali nation. As mentioned earlier, there exists geographical differentiations and discriminations in Nepal which favour the hills over the plains. In their exhibition titled 'Skin of Chitwan', the NPL attempts to foreground the experiences of the plains through a conversation around indigeneity, change in climate, traditional knowledge, ideas of development and progress and indigenous notions of futurity. A series titled 'Furnishing Papers' (Nepal Picture Library 2022), curated by Diwas Raja, reads as follows:

> Identification documents, like most state artefacts, are notably commonplace. But they are, in fact, wonders of alchemy. They belie the spectral way in which personhoods transform and states become real. The people of Nyeshang, a place nested in the mountains between Tibet and Nepal, have for long lived lives that were not territorially bound… Displaying the original IDs and photographic archives of Nyeshang travels, collected by Karma Tara Gurung, this exhibition seeks to highlight how Nyeshange negotiations with Nepali citizenship created new effects on identity, mobility, and territoriality. The materiality of the paper is an important enabler of this process. Not only the attributes of graphical iterability and portability, but it is also the medium of the single sheet that visually merges the indexicalities of the individual with the inscriptions of the state and creates a spatially unified experience of documentary life.

Another one titled 'The Feminist Memory Project' of the NPL displays photographs of Tharu women from Karjahi, Dang:

> who led a peasants' revolt against the abuses of local landlords in 1980. The landlords had started intimidating peasants and vandalized their property with police help following the land tenure reform of 1979, compelling these women to take action.

One of the images from their collection titled 'Dalit: A Quest for Dignity', shows scenes of Dalit protests in Kathmandu from 2000–2015 with the following caption:

> Nepalis increasingly contend that caste is a thing of the past or at least on its path to dissolution. Why raise old demons when they are already

> dying? This is what many think when Dalits organize, protest, and insist on the salience of caste in the present moment. No one cares more for the disappearance of oppression and humiliation than those who are oppressed and humiliated. But how naïve it would be to think that people with power and privilege are not actively responding to the threat of their own obliteration. History makes no guarantee of equality and justice. The Dalit movement is, thus, an urgent need of not only Nepal's present but also its future. (*Dalit: A Quest for Dignity*, Nepal Picture Library 2019)

Similarly, another photo showing how documents become a site of struggle for both material and personal dignity is captioned 'Documents play a complex role in the oppression of Dalit communities'. Documents, their documentation, and therefore, by extension, archives, are the means that are regularly activated at the point of contact with the state or other figures of authority.

Dalit: A Quest for Dignity tried to highlight how documents have been both a tool of caste oppression as well as an important strategy for evidencing caste atrocities and injustice. The photograph taken by journalists Ekal Silwal and Kalasiya Devi Khatwe from Mahottari shows the documents for a loan a husband had taken to migrate abroad for work. The moneylenders were attempting to seize the tiny piece of land that the family owned. Here, the notion of debt is an essential basis on which the caste system is able to continue reproducing its coercive structures. A photograph from the Mohammadi Siddiqui collection of the NPL highlights her work as one of the most prominent women working on Muslim women's rights in Nepal. She was one of the first Muslim women to get into Nepali politics and founded the Fatima Foundation, an NGO based in Banke, working to empower Nepali women. Another photo from the Feminist Memory Project focuses on Leela Kattel, who was a prominent leader of the communist uprising in the Terai in the 1970s, better known as the Jhapa Revolt. It is captioned as follows:

> Women have contributed significantly to the movement, but their presence remains almost invisible or in the periphery. Leela Kattel was one of the women at the forefront of the Jhapa Revolt. We found very few traces of her materially during our research, but she existed

> so strongly in people's memories of the movement. Her political involvement started when she joined the Mechi Campus as a student. The campus was considered as a hub for student activism dominated by Communist ideologies. She was arrested after the Panchayat regime started the crackdown on the movement. After her release, she distanced herself from politics and started teaching again. She and her husband Shriram Giri, who was her fellow comrade during the movement, died in a fatal road accident in 1991. Leela Kattel's underground name was Tara. (Feminist Memory Project, 2018)

Nepal Picture Library as the New Lens

The preceding section shows us the ways in which the NPL is actively working to introduce and inscribe identities that have remained marginalised in Nepal to the Nepali public imagination. Students of history are often taught that one must read archives against the grain, for the silences in the archive speak louder than what is present in the archive. While this is indeed an extremely helpful way of deconstructing hegemonic texts which speak from the position of power, digital archives such as the NPL provide us with an additional model of working against power. Rather than requiring the reader to unearth the silences, such archives materialise and humanise these very silences. By documenting the histories of women, Dalits, ethnic minorities and revolutionary movements among others, they provide us with a new lens to view the substantial history of the Nepali nation. The NPL deconstructs the idea that Nepal is a naturally Hindu nation by showing the violence and exclusions that go into maintaining such a myth. Such an archive also helps us see the various other histories that contest the meanings of the Nepali nation and by extension to understand what it means to be 'Nepali'. Rather than privileging the state as the producer of history, it shows the ways in which those who constitute the nation challenge the state's definitions of history and its writing.

Then again, it is not just the contents of the archive but its form as well that allows it to be such a potent medium for the democratisation of Nepali history. Based as a website, along with an Instagram account, the archives are largely free (some series are behind a paywall) to access images that are available from anywhere in the world. This facility, combined with the pictorial nature of the archive, makes for its easy viewing and helps in spreading its message. Further, the visual texture of the archive adds a degree of humanisation and liveliness to the message that may not always be found in written texts.

As discussed, the internet is an important site of deliberative democracy because of the easy ways of access and participation and because it provides the scope and space to voice antagonisms. All of this holds in the case of the NPL, which challenges the notion that to be Nepali is to be either an upper-caste Hindu or to assimilate with that identity both culturally and religiously. This is not to say that such digital archives are solutions to all of the problems faced by various groups across Nepal. In fact, it may be only a very small step towards addressing these problems.

Conclusion

As mentioned at the beginning, the emergence of the digital sphere as an important cultural and political medium cannot be ignored in the contemporary period. Drawing on the work of De Kosnik (2016), we can see how the digital emerges as an antagonistic space challenging the conventional notions of the canonical and archival. Through this chapter, I have tried to show how the digital and visual mediums employed by the NPL provide a way of challenging the hegemonic historical discourses in Nepal. The history of Nepal has been based on a number of foundational exclusions which continue to inform social, cultural, and political life in Nepal. The NPL can be placed in a longer tradition of attempts to construct counter-publics and identity claims that challenge such exclusions. This chapter shows that the digital nature of the NPL provides it with a dynamism and reach that was not available to previous efforts that were largely print-based. This chapter is therefore an attempt to contribute to the discourse(s) around the digital as a site of democratisation along with its tremendous possibilities and limitations.

Notes

1 The distinction between physical and virtual is a theoretical one in order to make sense of certain categorical differentiations. It does not mean that they always hold in practice.
2 Due to the possibility of copyright issues, images from the library will not be used. Based on consent from those running the NPL, I will be using the captions of the images which describe in detail what the images are.
3 Source base here refers to the traditional primary sources used in historical work such as texts and artefacts.

References

B. Anderson. 1991. *Imagined Communities: Reflections on the Origin and Spread of Nationalism*. London & New York: Verso.

A. Bahadur. 2013. 'The Stigma of the Name: Making and Remaking of Dalit Identity in Nepal'. *Baha Occasional Papers*, 6: 1–60.

B. Baldwin. 2015. 'Democratic Potential for a Multiplicity of Public Spaces: A Content Analysis of Media-Hosted Discussion Boards', PhD Thesis, University of Massachusetts, Amherst: Department of Communication.

D. Bleichman and V. Schwartz. 2019. 'Visual History: The Past in Pictures'. *Representations*, 145(1): 1–31.

J. Comaroff. 1996. 'Ethnicity, Nationalism and Politics in an Age of Revolution', in *The Politics of Difference: Ethnic Premises in a World of Power*, edited by E. Wilmsen and P. McAllister. Chicago & London: University of Chicago Press, 162–184.

A. De Kosnik. 2016. *Rogue Archives: Digital, Cultural Memory and Media Fandom*. Cambridge, Massachusetts and London, England: The MIT Press.

M. Des Chene. 1996. 'Ethnography in the Janajati-yug: Reading Rodhi and other Tamu Writings'. *Studies in Nepali History and Society*, 1(1): 97–161.

S. Frydenlund. 2019. 'Situationally Sherpa: Race, Ethnicity and the Labour Geography of the Everest Industry'. *Journal of Cultural Geography*, 36(1): 1–22.

D. Gellner. 2007. 'Caste, Ethnicity and Inequality in Nepal'. *Economic and Political Weekly*, 42(20): 1823–1828.

A. Gimmler. 2001. 'Deliberative democracy, the public sphere and the internet'. *Philosophy & Social Criticism*, 27(4): 21–39.

S. Hangen. 2010. *The Rise of Ethnic Politics in Nepal: Democracy in the Margins*. Abingdon: Routledge.

P. Jones and M. Langford. 2011. 'Between Demos and Ethnos: The Nepal Constitution and Indigenous Rights'. *International Journal on Minority and Group Rights*, 18: 369–386.

R. Kreide. 2016. 'Digital Spaces, Public Places and Communicative Power: In Defense of Deliberative Democracy'. *Philosophy & Social Criticism*, 42(4–5): 1–11.

L. Kunreuther. 2017. 'Politics of Heritage and Domestic Archives among Urban Nepalis of the Valley', in *Political Change and Public Culture in Post-1990 Nepal*, edited by M. Hutt and P. Onta. Cambridge: Cambridge University Press, 253–272.

M. Lawoti and S. Hangen, ed. 2013. *Nationalism and Ethnic Conflict in Nepal*. London and New York: Routledge.

P. Onta and D. Humagain. 2017. 'Janajati Magazines and the Contents of the Subaltern Public Sphere during the 1990s,' in *Political Change and Public Culture in Post-1990 Nepal*, edited by M. Hutt and P. Onta, 99–123. Cambridge: Cambridge University Press.

T. Mogashoa. 2014. 'Understanding Critical Discourse Analysis in Qualitative Research'. *International Journal of Humanities Social Science and Education*, 1(7): 104–113.

M. Spinner. 2012. 'The Effects of Social Media on Democratization', M.A. thesis, City College of New York.

J. Taylor. 2015. 'Visual History: A Neglected Resource for the Longue Duree,' in *Environment, Trade and Society in Southeast Asia: A Longue Duree Perspective*, edited by D. Henley and H. Nordholt, 181–202. Leiden and Boston: Brill Publications.

S. Tamang. 2009. 'The Politics of Conflict and Difference or the Difference of Conflict in Politics: the Women's Movement in Nepal'. *Feminist Review*, 91: 61–80.

J. Whelpton. 2005. *A History of Nepal*. Cambridge: Cambridge University Press.

Section III

Bangladesh

Chapter 8

Digital Politics in Bangladesh

Interactive Dynamics between Practices, Public and Policy of the Internet

Ratan Kumar Roy and Preeksha Malhotra

Introduction

The 2008 general elections in Bangladesh saw one of the oldest political parties of the country, the Awami League, promise a thrust towards digitalisation. The party's election manifesto introduced the idea of seeing their nation step towards the digital revolution that seemed to engulf the world—the idea of a 'Digital Bangladesh'. This manifesto painted a new picture for the nation, a shift from its current analogue present towards a vibrant Digital Bangladesh with new opportunities and possibilities. It took the ideals of a hunger- and poverty-free prosperous Bangladesh painted by the country's founder and married it with the ideals with digitisation, with the thrust from the springboard of a new Digital Bangladesh (Chowdhary 2021).

Global initiatives like the World Summit on Information Society (WSIS)[1] have led to the idea of building an information society reaching countries, including Bangladesh. However, the impetus of the initiative has been limited. The 2008 election manifesto promise of a Digital Bangladesh is seen as a more concrete step towards the actualisation of achieving greater levels of digitisation. The idea behind the programme is to leverage Information and Communication Technology (ICT) to harness socio-economic development. As per the Bangladesh Awami League, this is a step towards furthering the country's development in the face of globalisation and making it a developed nation. The programme is also seen as a 'reincarnation of the vision of "Sonar Bangla"' (Golden Bengal) (League 2021). It aims to use ICT as the medium to achieve this vision, especially for the poorer section of society. The programme wishes to integrate this digital revolution into all aspects of the day-to-day lives of people. They have identified four pillars to leverage the tenets of the programme on an immediate basis.

This chapter critically scrutinises the ambitions and achievements of the project of Digital Bangladesh, keeping an eye on politics, policy, and the public around internet culture. Needless to say, the understanding of internet culture is not limited to the media's effects on society and culture but fathoms cyberculture as a new cultural domain. In this domain of cultural (re)production and consumption, the internet cannot be seen only as a tool for creative prosumers[2] or a technology of information and communication but also as a new social field with mediated practices and politics. Couldry (2004) outlined the practice theory to understand media as 'embedded in interlocking fabric of social and cultural life' and engage with the questions of power and complex mediated practices. Therefore, we find the practice framework befitting to explore the digital media politics that is shaped by multiple actors and actions of the policy realm, public participation and practices in relation to the internet.

According to Ardévol and Gómez-Cruz (2014: 8),

> New media landscape forms new means of production, circulation, and consumption of media products that intertwine with significant practices of representation and reproduction of social identities. In this sense, the use of digital technologies is part of a process of appropriation, which develops as people incorporate these technologies in everyday life.

The framework of interactive practices of policy, public and practices helps us pay close attention to everyday life where politics is played out at various layers. Digital politics in Bangladesh is, therefore, not only a meta-narrative of the vision 2021 packaged as 'Digital Bangladesh' to achieve an ICT-based society that ensures electronic delivery of social services. Along with the master narrative of statecraft, policy implications and public reactions, we also find it important to outline the micro-practices that are stimulating and vibrant to the social system.

Digital Bangladesh: Promise Delivered?

As per the electoral manifesto, the ruling government promised to transform Bangladesh into a 'Digital Bangladesh', and they officially claim that the promise has been delivered. However, there are various undercurrents to such a claim, as one looks into the ground reality of the grand vision of 'Digital Bangladesh'. The four pillars of the programme have been identified as—Human Resource Development, Connecting Citizens, Digital Government and IT Promotion (Bangaldesh ICT Division, 2019). These pillars also hint at the integration of technology in every aspect of the day-to-day transactions of a citizen. Right from online education, remote working opportunities and e-governance to telemedicine, e-commerce and e-agro, every service is delivered through the medium of the internet (BTRI Portal 2009). The shift here is not merely to a society where digital means of interaction, governance or education have been adopted, but it is an attempt to shift towards a knowledge-based economy. A robust ICT system and massive internet penetration are two bedrocks of this kind of economic order (The World Bank 2013). Data by the Bangladesh Bureau of Statistics estimates that 27.3 per cent of the population in 2022 owned a smartphone (BBS 2022: 15). The government has set up a 'National Web Portal', which is a website that redirects to 25,000 government websites to access information or basic services such as paying utility bills, taxes, health etc. (CRI 2018: 19). E-service centres across 64 districts were established in 2011 to start the work on online data-sharing and decision-making.

Global consultancy McKinsey has noted that the 'Bangladeshi freelancer community has further supplemented the IT exports by close to US$7 million in 2010—with Bangladesh appearing consistently in top freelance work locations on sites like oDesk, eLance and the likes.' As per a report by the firm, the Digital Bangladesh initiative has helped enhance infrastructure in the country to support the setting up of operations by international players. Efforts to indigenise and localise the internet ecosystem by paying attention to expansion in the use of Bangla through the development of a spell-checker, a text-to-speech (and vice-versa) software and the development of a standardised Bangla keypad have been undertaken. A national content repository called e-Tathyakosh to enable public and non-state actors to share information has also been created. An effort to establish stronger infrastructure to support modernisation efforts can also be seen through the coming up of multiple hi-tech smart parks across the country. The government wishes to establish Bangladesh as a major outsourcing destination for IT companies. This requires a steady supply of graduates trained in the domain of Information and Communication Technologies. Efforts to expand courses in the domain would thus help make this a viable reality.

Looking at sector-specific penetration of digitisation, Bangladesh Bank has given approvals to mobile finance service providers in the country. A total of 15 providers like ROCKET by Dutch Bangla Bank Ltd, bKash by bKash Ltd., MYCash by Mercantile Bank Ltd, etc. (Bangladesh Bank) have come up in the space. The launch of Nagad, a state-run carrier and digital transaction service maintained by the Postal Department of Bangladesh, has been actively competing with other ventures since 2019. Sprouting e-commerce ventures like Daaraz, Amar Desh e-shop (Amar Desh shop), Ajkerdeal and Chaldal that provide doorstep delivery of goods show that e-services are coming up in the country. These could help facilitate online spending by customers and thus boost online transactions in day-to-day product delivery. It is important, however, to note that a number of such popular platforms were found involved in fraud and mishandling of funds in the name of digital commerce.[3] There was a lack of legal and regulatory mechanisms for operating e-commerce in the beginning. Stakeholders urged for it since there were cases of fraudulence and misconduct. In order to systematise the operation of digital commerce and provide users with trust and solutions, the Ministry of Commerce introduced the Digital Commerce Operation Guidelines, 2021, as a successor of the National Digital Commerce Policy, 2018. While it is still too early to assess if the implication of such a policy wins back the trust of the consumers or the confidence of the e-commerce players, various kinds of micro- and mini-commercial ventures are going on using social media platforms beyond the purview of any regulatory framework.

The government has outlined a draft of the Bangladesh Telecommunication Regulatory Commission Regulation for Digital, Social Media and OTT Platforms, 2021, which acts for the overall regulation of the digital sphere. The Digital Security Act (DSA), 2018,[4] is actively in place to control the speech and fake news online but is criticised heavily within and beyond the nation as a tool for repressing dissent and free speech. We will return to this point shortly, however, it is imperative to zoom in our lenses on multiple actions and activities in relation to the rise of digital in Bangladesh including the backlash to 'Digital Bangladesh'.

'We Don't Want Digital Bangladesh': The Love and Hate of Digital Politics

The digital domain was filled with expressions such as 'We don't want Digital Bangladesh, we want safe Bangladesh'. Both on the streets and online, students carried the slogan indicating their priority of safety over digitisation during a protest that erupted towards road safety in the wake of two students being killed by a speeding bus in Dhaka in 2018. Road safety has been a concern voiced by many citizens in the past as well, but in vain. Thus, when a group of children decided to take to the streets to protest, they were supported by their guardians who themselves came out to show solidarity and support. Over the course of time, university students and various other activist organisations participated and came to support the mobilisation. Social media was widely used for information dissemination to mobilise such movements. But the platforms also saw a surge in fabricated and impulsive messages about the protests. These led to extreme conflict and violence on the ground.

Virality, an inherent component of social media, played a role in fuelling mobilisation on the streets. Protestors and activists, while expressing their aversion to 'Digital Bangladesh', were essentially using digital platforms to circulate protest information to gain wider support. The law-enforcing bodies identified students with charges of dissemination of provocative information on social media. The injury of hundreds of protestors, agitation and confrontations made an unruly situation, making the regulatory authority shut down mobile internet. An actress was arrested for a 'rumourous' Facebook post amidst the protest, and renowned photojournalist Shahidul Alam was detained for his statement to the international media deemed by the regulatory forces as 'provocative'. Government agencies and leaders of the party in power expressed their deep concern for the 'spread of rumours and fake news' via social media platforms. Keeping the national election of December 2018 in consideration, the government activated various wings and bodies to monitor the circulation of misinformation and harmful content to maintain law and order. Content filtering, blocking of social media sites, intensified surveillance and arresting individuals for allegedly provocative social media activities became normalised. Introducing DSA as an effective tool to spread fear among the users of social media and control of the digital domain made the political climate around the digital sphere more complex.

From 2008 to 2018, a decade full of dramatic expressions of love and hate for the digital can be traced while exploring digital politics in Bangladesh. In parliament and public processions, leaders of the ruling party often claimed credit for providing people with mobile phones and the internet. Taking such speeches out of context, ordinary Tik-Tokers made humorous video clips. While ordinary users made hundreds of popular memes to make fun of 'Digital Bangladesh', opposition party leaders often claimed that the ruling party has been successful in 'digital theft' and 'digital corruption' to appropriate the often-cited digitalisation. When the 'digital' continued to feed into the discourses of Bangladesh, be it good or evil, fun or serious, polemic or affirmative, a significant shift in mainstream politics took place with the enhanced online participation by political actors. Every political party in the country boosted their resources to make digital politics vibrant. Political leaders and activists paid special attention to building and maintaining their social media persona for larger public support.

Social media-led socio-political mobilisations can be considered significant events through which the love and hate of digital politics have been expressed in contemporary Bangladesh. Right from the Shahbag protest in 2013, which was organised around the war crimes tribunal, to the no VAT movement or the 2018 road safety protest—these were all socially motivated movements.[5] However, they desired to influence the political landscape by gaining social currency and acceptance from the masses. internet-based activism played a key role in all these episodes of mobilisation. These are movements whose initiation, ideation and implementation have come to resemble each other, where the use of social networking sites to mobilise people to join protests was common. All such movements are initiated from the realm of the digital. Thus, what started with the Shahbag movement has now snowballed into influencing other protests to create a post-Shahbag milieu where such socio-political movements are part of the same rosary tied together by the thread of the digital. Thus to understand how these protests are structured, understanding the Shahbag movement is a good point of origin. The movement started with the agitation by online activists and bloggers in 2013 expressing their dissatisfaction with a verdict against a 'war criminal'. The youth activists demanded a supreme penalty for the accused for being involved in 'genocide' or 'crimes against humanity' during the 1971 War of Liberation of Bangladesh. The movement is the namesake of the Shahbag intersection in Dhaka city, which was occupied by the protesters for weeks and used as a stage to communicate the incidents around the issue. The youth mobilisers maximised the usage of social networking sites to facilitate the conversation from their own perspective. The blogs successfully transcended the digital space to make an impact in the physical world by inspiring people to join the physical protests. This synergy between a socio-political retaliation and the digital ecosystem implies a need to delve deeper into the role of the media in social mobilisations in society (Roy 2021).

The intended usage of a social media platform and its actual usage by users on the ground always evolves and changes. In the case of this incident, we see the usage of Facebook evolves with the requirements of the protestors. Originally intended as a platform to share photographs and short texts of personal updates with family and friends, the platform was used for something beyond this scope by the protestors in Shahbag. And we have also seen other movements like the 'No VAT[6] in Education' in 2015 use social media to spread the word about their cause. The movement started in 2015 to protest for no-value-added taxes in education in private universities. In fact, digital media became the space of congregation for the protestors to discuss their ideas. As avid social media users, these youngsters recognised the importance of the digital domain in helping them garner support. The role of media, however, goes beyond just mediating between the potential audience of a protest and the organisers. It becomes a co-creator of the protest and, in turn, also plays a role in the influence the movement has on society. This, thus, makes it a part of the politics of representation of this protest culture. Owing to its power and ability to reach a mass audience, media, and especially, social media holds the power to sensitise people towards politics, and the role of power relationships in society. In the process of thus mediating the movements, it also reproduces certain sociocultural relations, and also shapes social forms (Roy 2019).

However, with positives, there are also some negatives associated with such use of social media. The downsides of the uses of the internet to mobilise such movements have come up in the form of fake news, rumours and vitriol. Thus, in response to the use of the media for spreading the aim of such movements, we also saw the spread of fake news and rumours surrounding them. In addition, the digital democratisation process has also come under question. And to understand this we now zoom out and shift our lenses to the realm of digital policy.

Policy Pitfalls

The vision of Digital Bangladesh was to accelerate service delivery, governance and everything that is needed to achieve the status of a developed nation for Bangladesh. But apart from the positives, there are also concerns that surround digitisation. With the growing use of the digital, the policies around it have also started to evolve. Initially, the country regulated the internet through the Penal Code of 1860 (Remura 2019) This changed post the enactment of the Information & Communication Technology Act, 2006. This was introduced with the aim of regulating cyber-crimes and e-commerce disputes. It deals with aspects such as fake electronic publishing, hacking of electronic devices and computer-related offences (Parliament 2006). Despite the intended uses, it has been widely used to suppress freedom of speech and expression. Critics have widely noted the misuse of its provisions under Section 57 (Liton 2018). It was originally enacted by the Government of Khaleda Zia in November 2006 and was amended in 2013 by the government of Sheikh Hasina. The 2013 amendment is said to have made the law stricter and more stringent.

This expansion in the scope of the powers of the state was under the contentious Section 57 of the Act. The section was criticised in its previous 2006 version as well, and it was found to be detrimental to freedom of speech and expression in the country. As per the amended law, the police gained the authority to arrest without warrants; there were a number of cases against journalists under the provisions of the act in 2017 alone (Adhikary 2018). In a report brought out by Human Rights Watch in 2018, titled 'No Place for Criticism: Bangladesh Crackdown on Social Media Commentary', many such cases of detention are outlined. It has reported the arrest of Monirul Islam, a rubber plantation worker in Srimongol, southern Bangladesh, on 13 April 2017, for allegedly liking and sharing a Facebook post by someone else relating to the then Bangladeshi prime minister's visit to India. According to the ICT amended law of 2013, such acts of commenting and liking posts on Facebook were considered offences. The accused were booked under the non-bailable section of the act, and the prison sentence was extended from 10 to 14 years under the amended version of the act, making it all the more concerning.

This situation was further aggravated with the introduction of the Digital Security Act, 2018 (DSA). Rights activists and critics found DSA more troubling and threatening to freedom of expression. According to Riaz and Rahman (2021), 'The DSA, enacted by the government of Hasina in October 2018, incorporates the Official Secrets Act of the colonial period with stringent new provisions. Fourteen of its twenty provisions are non-bailable and police can arrest on suspicion and without a warrant'. As per the Center for Governance Studies' tracker for DSA, over 1,500 cases have been filed under the law in three years, 2018–2021 (Riaz 2021).

The unintended uses of the provisions of policies and laws, like the Digital Security Act have 'inhibited debate and dissent' in Bangladesh and led to many questioning the fairness of the policies made under the pretext of digitisation in society, and how these measures are rather a biased political intervention (Aziz 2021). Section 21 of the DSA gives the law enforcement bodies absolute power to initiate investigations into anyone whose activities are considered a threat. If we connect this section with the Shahbag protests (2013) discussed earlier, we can only imagine that the protest would probably not have survived the government's crackdown under the DSA. Since mere 'suspicion' over any social media activity is deemed reason enough to make arrests without warrants, the protest could have been effectively deemed illegal.

These vulnerabilities in the legislative and regulatory structure have been termed 'digital pitfalls' to highlight the 'engendering of new vulnerabilities and power hierarchies within Bangladeshi society' (Aziz 2021). Creating such 'digital pitfalls can take support from two kinds of measures: online censorship and digital surveillance' (Stoycheff 2018). Surveillance measures create an information imbalance between the rulers and the ruled, which promotes a top-down governance structure.

Bangladesh is a signatory to the International Covenant on Civil and Political Rights (ICCPR), putting it under the obligation to uphold international standards of civil and political rights in all its domestic regulations. However, acts such as the DSA, 2018, have made people question this commitment to international standards, in light of the stifling of freedom of speech and expression under such laws. While Article 39 of the Constitution of the country guarantees the freedom of speech and expression to its citizens, it also puts reasonable restrictions on this freedom (Azad 2021). Such reasonable restrictions can be put in place under Article 19 (3) of the ICCPR as well; however, they must adhere to three aspects. First, restrictions must be 'provided by law', secondly 'restrictions must only be imposed to protect legitimate aims' which are further specified under the article, and lastly, 'necessary to protect one or more of the legitimate aims'.

Surveillance and online censorship are deeply intertwined with the democratic political practice and the regulatory structure of the country and thus are not mere technological concerns (Aziz 2021). We can see that while Digital Bangladesh is heralding the internet as a medium of the future, it is only investing in expanding its usage in economic aspects and not in other areas like communication (Aziz 2021). In February 2021, a writer, Mushtaq Ahmed—arrested in a Digital Security Act case for spreading 'rumours' on social media, allegedly tarnishing the image of the founding father of the nation and hurting the spirit of the Liberation War of 1971—died in prison. He was arrested along with another cartoonist Kabir Kishore; both of them were admins of a satirical Facebook page called 'I am Bangladeshi'. As per the regulatory forces, they have circulated various politically provocative posts relating to the nation-state that threaten the law and order and communal harmony of the country. As DSA took Mushtaq Ahmed away for writing on Facebook, there were other instances where citizens were killed by mobsters for their social media posts. There were a series of killing and hacked-to-death cases of bloggers and online activists from 2013 to 2018 in Bangladesh (Roy 2021).

In 2019, an engineering student of the Bangladesh University of Engineering and Technology (BUET), Abrar Fahad, was brutally killed by members of the ruling party's—Awami League—student organisation Bangladesh Chhatra League (BCL) in the university hostel for his Facebook post. In this post, Abrar was critical of the bilateral agreement signed between Bangladesh and India during the visit of then Prime Minister Sheikh Hasina to India. With reference to some historical facts and instances, he questioned the decision to allow India to withdraw water from the Feni River of Bangladesh. In this case, not under the DSA or by the law enforcers, the BCL men allegedly interrogated him for hours before killing him for a post deemed critical of the then prime minister. Needless to say, the DSA has failed to safeguard the citizens, including the minority communities, who have been victims of communal violence fuelled by social media posts. There have been a series of attacks on minority groups by unruly Islamist mobs in reference to 'blasphemous' social media posts or images in contemporary Bangladesh. In many such cases, it was found that the posts were fabricated and intentionally made in the name of a Hindu Facebook user to blame for the blasphemy. Curiously enough, DSA is applicable to the person who is accused of posting such content but has hardly been used to prevent the wider circulation and spread of the same content for instigating the masses into mob violence. It is, therefore, important to examine the scope and limitations of DSA beyond the scheme of 'freedom of speech' and further elaborate on the other social media phenomena that define digital politics.

More recently, the government has proposed Telecommunication Regulatory Commission regulation for digital, social media and OTT platforms to draft rules to regulate Over-the-Top (OTT) content services in the country. The rules are suspected (Foundation 2022) to be inspired by the Indian version of the 'Information Technology (Intermediary Guidelines and Digital Media Ethics Code) Rules, 2021' (MeitY 2021), which have themselves garnered criticism for their overarching regulatory measures. As far as policies regarding the internet and the digital domain are concerned, the government's vision of safety is being equated with control by observers. It is yet to be seen what route policies take in the long run and how it would be possible to bridge this perception gap between the citizens' requirements and the government's anticipated needs for them. To ensure that the government can step outside of its image as an Orwellian State—a metaphor rampantly used for states seen to be ebbing towards becoming a surveillance state in the purview of digitisation efforts—a more collaborative approach to the future needs to be deployed.

John Trenchard argued at the end of the seventeenth century that the 'government is a mere piece of clockwork' and the aim is to make the 'springs and wheels' work in a manner that is to the public's advantage. Thus, if we look at the government itself as a piece of technology, here 'one technology is affected by another technology (digital forms of producing and circulating information and communication)' (Coleman and Freelon 2015: 2). This perspective to understanding the interaction of technology with the government lends us the advantage of seeing the government itself as a mechanical entity which is technologically and socially constructed (Orlikowski 1992: 406 as cited in Coleman and Freelon 2015: 3).

Scope of Digital Politics: Policy, Public and Practice

The above discussion made it quite evident that the government is confident with its hegemonic claim of succeeding in creating a Digital

Bangladesh that amounts to infrastructure and economic growth, with some service sector improvements. The other axis of the digital is all about control, regulation and curbing freedom of speech centred around the DSA. Digital politics, however, is a much more contested field spread across, within and beyond, the binary of good and bad of Digital Bangladesh. As Coleman and Freelon (2015: 1) put it, 'It is one thing to say that politics is affected by digital communication. It is quite another thing to say that digital communication fundamentally reshapes politics. The truth lies somewhere in between those two statements.' To explore this truth further in the context of Bangladesh, first, we identify three broader scopes of online politics in Bangladesh, namely, party politics, ordinary politics and politics of confrontation. Then, we shed light on the interactive dynamic between policy, public and practices of the internet.

Party Politics

With the advent of the internet, slowly and steadily, the medium made its place in the political ecosystem. It gave people the medium to communicate their grievances, their concerns and at the same time voice their opinion on current measures by the government. And with this increased avenue for participation, the dynamics in the political space evolved in the digital age. Almost all the mainstream political parties have extended their Information Technology (IT) and digital media cells to garner support and spread their ideologies. The official social media handles of the mainstream political parties are far more active than before, even though none of the top political figures, such as the president of the Awami League and the former Prime Minister Sheikh Hasina and former chairperson of Bangladesh Nationalist Party and former Prime Minister Khaleda Zia are on Facebook.

Everyday politics prior to the internet has seen a top-down approach to message delivery. Politicians deliver their message to the people through the medium of speeches and make promises for delivery. However, with the advent of the digital, an efficacious channel of communication has opened up between the people and the politicians (Al-Zaman 2020). Thus, politicians can no longer afford to merely deliver sermons and expect reception amongst the masses. They have had to increase their online presence and build a relationship with their voter.

Ordinary Politics

Digitisation, despite its obvious stone blocks like literacy and infrastructural access, has been accepted in some way or the other by so many after overcoming these hurdles. With the advent of the digital and its acceptance by the masses, we have seen the ushering in of a new era of the politics of people, thus creating a new political public sphere in Bangladesh. This is a space where the people are not mere receivers of top-to-down welfare schemes but are a part of the decision-making process. Thus, the 'independence and interdependence' of institutions like political and media organisations is changing. The dominance in agenda setting, a kind of 'establishment collusion' that the political institutions and the media maintained has been 'interrupted by grassroots articulations of public interests and values' (Coleman and Freelon 2015: 3).

Political interaction has taken a multidimensional colour through the digital because various entities can participate actively in the discourse which was earlier limited to only the powerful. The social divide that further fuels the digital divide, however, plays a significant role in the expansion of this sphere of politics. If the control of the new digital mediums also remains confined in the hands of a few elite or urban people as opposed to equity with the poor and the rural, we will see the digital further instate the hierarchies of the traditional media,which are an extension of the society.

Politics of Confrontation

Online spaces are a new battlefield for confronting groups and communities. Often virtual spaces in Bangladesh are filled with texts and images of atrocities against minorities. There is also a rise of activism culture with vibrant visibility of individuals and various religious groups. The convenience offered by the combined efforts of the internet and smartphones helped individuals and groups to be active online and partake in public discourse with regard to religious identity and ideology. Facebook and YouTube have become natural platforms for religious propaganda and publicity in Bangladesh, be it preachings by the Islamic orators or concerns of Hindu minority groups.

On 30 October 2016, a rumour spread that a juvenile named Rasraj had posted a photo on Facebook where the Hindu god Shiva had been attached to the Kaaba—a sacred place for Muslims. This fuelled absolute mayhem—at least five Hindu temples and countless houses were destroyed. Eventually, Rasraj got arrested. However, after his release, he claimed that he did not even know how to use Facebook and was not familiar with the concept of a password. There has been a routine mobilisation by various Islamic groups in different parts of the country that began with spreading rumours about allegedly blasphemous posts or images on Facebook pages run by Hindu minorities. All these can be traced back to 2012, when allegations of posts defaming the Quran on Facebook led to a series of attacks on Buddhist monasteries and inhabitants in Ramu, Cox Bazar, Bangladesh. A mob composed of Muslim males and youths destroyed age-old Buddhist temples and houses in reaction to a Facebook post from a fake account under a Buddhist's name.

Another nationwide atrocity against the Hindu minorities was conducted on the news that the Holy Quran was found at a temporary Durga Puja celebration premises at Cumilla. It was interpreted as a sign of disrespecting the sacred text of Islam, and very soon chaos erupted. The temple was attacked, and the idols of goddesses were destroyed. But most importantly, the image of the Quran placed near the idols of goddesses was widely circulated to provoke the Muslim masses, and that worked magically. Later, it was found that the person who was responsible for placing a Quran at the temple was not a Hindu; he was a Muslim whose name was Iqbal Hossain. Social media posts and visuals have fuelled a number of communal conflicts in contemporary Bangladesh. Keeping an eye on online activism and religious politicking, it can be argued that there is vibrant digital politics in the line of communal conflict and friction between the majority Islamist group and minority Hindus.

Digital politics cannot be fully understood by these three scopes, it must take into consideration various political discourses around policies and practices. The political is 'deeply embedded in constitutional and institutional protocols'. But it also 'simmers under the surface', where it is shaped by the cultural dynamics around it and at the same time influences them as well (Coleman and Freelon 2015: 1). It is also about policymaking, the processes through which a policy is made, implemented, sustained, denied and debated.

It must include the participation of political parties, from those who are in power and those in opposition, their narratives and reflections. In the age of media abundance, we see that 'professionalization of political advocacy' has increased significantly, thus making media not an 'add-on' but an 'integral part of the processes of political outreach' (Blumler and Kavanagh 1999: 214). Here, the objective thus becomes to get the most coverage for 'your agenda on your terms' and 'to put critics and opposition party on the back foot' (ibid). Muzzling the opposition's voice in a democracy is detrimental to its growth. And it has to be ensured that the traditional power hierarchies do not penetrate the digital media as well. The opposition as well as the party in power need to have equal opportunity to voice themselves.

How the public and their everyday relation with digital technologies are maintained in the context of the digital economy, digital labour and digital laws are much debated. An interactive dynamic between the policy, public and practices, therefore, enables us to broaden the scheme of digital politics that is continuously in the making. Digital politics in Bangladesh does shape the political culture of contemporary times and vice-versa while it co-creates the dominant political discourses since the internet facilitates everyday politics, and *digital* is key to its development.

Conclusion

In this evolution of the digital, we see the lived culture and actions of its users play a significant role in harnessing its future. The extensive use of the internet for communication—amongst citizens, between citizens and the state, as well as between citizens and media—demonstrates its power being utilised across the spectrum of stakeholders in a democracy. But the credit for the democratisation of the internet lies with its users from the grassroots. They have truly transcended the traditional hierarchies of power to voice their concerns and reclaim their power as citizens in a democratic structure.

However, these successes in communication and mobilisation have been met by strong regulatory interventions like the Information Communication Technology Act, 2013, and the DSA,

2018. While the intended use of both legislations has been to regulate the internet to make it a safer space, practical experience shows that they have been misused by the state to silence criticism. Such regulatory practices highlight that these measures are reactive rather than proactive, hinting at the government's reluctance to let the digital spread further than some mere infrastructural and commercial purposes. The avenue to strengthen democracy through the robust use of ICTs for feedback and expressing criticism is not looked upon favourably as the various examples of misuse of regulation in the area prove.

But despite these measures, what cannot be ignored is that with the expansion of the digital, its interaction and influence on everyday lives and politics (and vice-versa) is inevitable. As we highlight in the three spheres, we see this influence particularly play a role, namely party politics, ordinary politics and politics of confrontation.

These three broad scopes are not exhaustive in mapping the complex interplay of players in the digital sphere, but they lend a critical lens to nudge us to take into consideration lived experiences encompassing culture, politics and policies to understand this new digital milieu in Bangladesh. The internet is a user-driven space that is shaped through interaction between its various users. Thus, not factoring them in as the premise of this idea of governance is not the right fit for the medium.

Now that we have rolled out this technology, we need to work on the impact it has on people. The age of surveillance has become very real, and the need for privacy is pertinent. It becomes the responsibility of the stakeholders who took on the onus of introducing people to the internet, to now responsibly govern it. For them to back out at this stage is certainly a very capitalistic and non-democratic way of functioning, something that the internet by its very nature vouches to stand against.

Notes

1 Through resolution 56/183, the United Nations General Assembly adopted a resolution on the World Summit on Information Societies. The idea was to

globally discuss the opportunities around Information and Communication Technologies. The WSIS has been implemented in two stages in 2003 and 2005, and will meet again in 2025 to review the process. The first edition focused on chalking out a clear workable plan for the WSIS, while the latter was focused on looking at viable ways to implement this plan. See https://en.unesco.org/themes/building-knowledge-societies/wsis#:~:text=The%20UN%20General%20Assembly%20Resolution,16%20to%2018%20November%202005 (accessed 21 February 2023).

2 A term referring to an individual who both consumes and produces information.

3 See for details: https://www.newagebd.net/article/158509/e-commerce-in-bangladesh-faces-rough-ride-in-2021-as-scams-shatter-growth (accessed 5 March 2023).

4 This act has been replaced by the Cyber Security Act, 2023 (CSA). The CSA, 2023 has also been criticised to not be very different from its 2018 counterpart.

5 The most recent addition to this list being the July 2024 protests by students against the reservations in government jobs in Bangladesh. Organised by students across the capital city, these protests gained steam and were mobilised through the extensive use of social media applications, notably closed messaging platforms. The significant role that the internet played in bringing these protesters together can be understood from the government's decision to country-wide shut down the internet during the protests. Such was the impact of this anti-reservation student movement turning to anti-government that the then Prime Minister Sheikh Hasina had to resign and flee from the country.

6 Value Added Tax.

References

Amar Desh Shop. (n.d.). Available at https://twitter.com/amardesheshop?lang=en (accessed 17 November 2023).

T.S. Adhikary. 2018. 7 July, *The Daily Star*. Available at: https://www.thedailystar.net/frontpage/bangladesh-ict-act-the-trap-section-of-57-1429336 (accessed 17 November 2023).

R. Ali and R. Sajjadur. 2021. *Center for Governance Studies*, January. Available at: https://bdmediaowners.com/reports-2/ (accessed 22 November 2023).

S. Al-Zaman. 2020. 'Digital Media and Political Communication in Bangladesh: A New Wave of Democratic and Pluralistic Politics?' *Arth-Journal of Social Sciences*, 1–19. Available at: https://doi.org/10.12724/ajss.53.1.

A. Azad. 2021. 27 May. Available at: https://www.etd.ceu.edu/2021/azad_ananya.pdf (accessed on 16 November 2023).

A. Aziz. 2021. 'Digital Pitfalls: The Politics of Digitalization in Bangladesh'. *Communication, Culture & Critique*. doi:10.1093/ccc/tcab037 .

Bangladesh Bank. n.d. Available at: http://rtn.bcc.net.bd/index.php/information-on-mobile-banking (accessed on 29 December 2023).

Bangaldesh ICT Division. 2019. Available at: https://investindigitalbd.gov.bd/page/digital-bangladesh-vision-2021 (accessed on 29 December 2023).

G.O. Bangladesh. 2019. CITR, September. Available at: https://www.cirt.gov.bd/wp-content/uploads/2020/02/Digital-Security-Act-2020.pdf (accessed on 29 December 2023).

B.B. BBS. 2022. Survey on ICT Use and Access by Individuals and Households 2022. Available at: http://bbs.portal.gov.bd/sites/default/files/files/bbs.portal.gov.bd/page/b343a8b4_956b_45ca_872f_4cf9b2f1a6e0/2023-01-08-07-00-667cde6536494c707e86d483c0b618a5.pdf (accessed on 29 December 2023).

J. Blumler and D. Kavanagh. 1999. 'The Third Age of Political Communication: Influences and Features'. *Political Communication*. Available at: http://www.communicationcache.com/uploads/1/0/8/8/10887248/the_third_age_of_political_communication-_influences_and_features.pdf, 209–230 (accessed 17 November 2023).

BTRI Portal. 2009, 5. Available at: http://btri.portal.gov.bd/sites/default/files/files/btri.portal.gov.bd/page/a556434c_e9c9_4269_9f4e_df75d712604d/Digital%20Bangladesh%20Concept%20Note_Final.pdf (accessed 17 November 2023).

A. Chowdhary. 2021. 25 December, UNDP. Available at UNDP: https://www.undp.org/bangladesh/blog/digital-bangladesh-innovative-bangladesh-road-2041 (accessed 20 November 2023).

S. Coleman and D. Freelon. 2015. *Handbook of Digital Politics*.

CRI. 2018. 'Bangladesh's Digital Revolution'. Available at: https://cri.org.bd/publication/digital-revolution/Bangladesh's%20Digital%20Revolution.pdf (accessed 20 November 2023).

Elisenda Ardévol and Edgar Gómez-Cruz. 2014. 'Digital Ethnography and Media Practices'. Elisenda Ardévol and Edgar Gómez-Cruz. 2014. 'Digital Ethnography and Media Practices'. The *International Encyclopedia of Media Studies* Edited by Fabienne DarlingWolf. Volume VII: Research Methods in Media Studies. Wiley.

I.F. Foundation. 2022. Available at: https://internetfreedom.in/report-on-bangladeshs-regulation-of-digital-social-media-and-ott-platforms-and-it-rules-2021/ (accessed 21 November 2023).

I. Khan. 2021. February, available at: https://spcommreports.ohchr.org/TMResultsBase/DownLoadPublicCommunicationFile?gId=27845 (accessed 21 November 2023).

Awami League. 2021. Available at: https://www.albd.org/articles/news/35867/Digital-Bangladesh---Vision-2021:%0D%0AThe-Secret-of-Bangladesh%E2%80%99s-Transformation (accessed 22 November 2023).

S. Liton. 2018. 25 July, International Press Institute. Available at: https://ipi.media/ipinetwork/bangladesh-abuse-of-cyber-law-finds-no-limit/ (accessed 21 November 2023).

MeitY. 2021. February, available at: https://www.meity.gov.in/writereaddata/files/Intermediary_Guidelines_and_Digital_Media_Ethics_Code_Rules-2021.pdf (accessed 22 November 2023).

Bangladesh National Parliament. 2006. October, available at: https://samsn.ifj.org/wp-content/uploads/2015/07/Bangladesh-ICT-Act-2006.pdf (accessed 23 November 2023).

T. Remura. 2019. 20 October, available at: https://tahmidurrahman.com/cyber-law-of-bangladesh-internet-law-web-ict-act-rules-regulations-punishment-and-rights-in-bangladesh/#:~:text=In%20Bangladesh%2C%20the%20ICT%20Act,computer%20technology%20or%20cyber%20crime (accessed 21 November 2023).

A. Riaz. 2021. December, Carnegie Endowment. Available at: https://carnegieendowment.org/2021/12/09/how-bangladesh-s-digital-security-act-is-creating-culture-of-fear-pub-85951 (accessed 21 November 2023).

E.B. Stoycheff. 2018. 'Online Censorship and Digital Surveillance: the Relationship between Suppression Technologies and Democratization across Countries'. *Information, Communication &Amp; Society*, 23(4): 474–490. Available at: https://doi.org/10.1080/1369118x.2018.1518472.

The World Bank. 2013. Available at: https://web.worldbank.org/archive/website01503/WEB/0__CO-10.HTM (accessed 21 November 2023).

9

Hashtagification of Political Slogans

Catalysing Propagation of Political Narratives

Rizvan Saeed

Introduction

Over the past few decades, the global shift towards digitisation has been rapid, and Pakistan has been no exception to this transformative trend. In the country, the rapid growth of the telecommunication sector in the early 2000s and the subsequent diffusion of social media in the early 2010s have played pivotal roles in improving connectivity and depleting communication barriers at the public level. The widespread penetration of communication technology has facilitated this shift, fundamentally altering social connectivity. Political parties and human rights activists leveraged these changes to engage with a broader audience and expand their social networks through social media platforms, especially Twitter (Saeed 2023).

Three factors catalysed the process of digital politics in Pakistan over the last decade: the emergence of a networked society (Saeed 2021) because of social media penetration; the presence of youth bulge that actively adopted the technology; and the instrumental use of social media by political parties, human rights activists and religious groups.

The core focus of this chapter is on the techniques and tools of digital politics in Pakistan. This aspect will be elaborated on based on the analysis of primary Twitter data. The data analysed and presented in this chapter was collected over four years (from 2019 to 2022) against the top trending hashtags on the country's Twitter Top Trends panel.

Twitter's Technological and Social Affordances

Twitter offers technological and social affordances, making this platform a convenient and effective medium for propagating political narratives. Twitter's technological and social affordances include ambient awareness facilitation, accessibility through the @ mention feature, connectivity through following and followed ties, reply and quote options, content categorisation through hashtags, reproducibility of the content through retweets and framing of political stances through hashtags.

Twitter is a microblogging website that allows exchanging messages of up to 280 characters for non-verified accounts. Although text-based messages have a restriction in characters; users can share videos, photos and links to content outside of the blogging site. Therefore, Twitter allows the expansion of the message by linking additional content. Moreover, the recent developments regarding the platform's content policy let verified accounts go beyond the limit of 280 characters and share videos lengthier than 2:22 seconds ('Counting Characters' n.d.).

Twitter's key characteristic is ambient awareness facilitation, making it a fast, real-time news-sharing platform. Ambient awareness has been mentioned as a critical characteristic of microblogging websites (Kaplan and Haenlein 2010). Ambient awareness is sharing details of one's actions or feelings at the moment so that one's near and dear ones can learn about them despite their physical distance (Kaplan and Haenlein 2010). This characteristic makes Twitter a valuable tool for sharing content and spreading information quickly. Along with information sharing, Twitter facilitates networking among users. Twitter users can connect with others by following them or sending direct messages.

Over the course of its evolution, Twitter has transformed from primarily being a news-spreading platform into a significant space for individuals to connect, share news and amplify their voices on social issues (Ahmed et al. 2020). Initially recognised for its role in disseminating news, Twitter has garnered increasing attention as a platform for social activism and mobilisation.

A pivotal moment highlighting Twitter's potential for mobilisation occurred during the Arab Spring uprising in Egypt, where the platform played a crucial role in organising and uniting protesters. This contrasted with the framing of the uprising by the country's mainstream media, emphasising the divergent narratives presented by traditional news outlets (Wasike n.d.).

The concept of Hashtag Activism, as explored by Jackson, Bailey and Welles (2020) provides an insightful compilation of hashtags and corresponding analyses that exemplify Twitter users' efforts to raise their voices against various forms of discrimination. Notably, hashtags like #BlackLivesMatter emerged as a powerful tool to shed light on the systemic discrimination faced by Black communities in America—similarly, Jackson, Bailey and Welles delved into hashtags used to address the pervasive issue of sexual harassment, with #MeToo serving as the movement's symbolic hashtag.

In this evolving landscape, Twitter has broadened its scope beyond news dissemination. It has become a dynamic platform where users can advocate for social causes, challenge societal norms and contribute to collective movements against discrimination. Twitter's technical features as a social media platform make its role crucial in digital politics in Pakistan. A platform's social usage and features depend on the technological affordances of the platform (Ellison and Boyd 2013). Therefore, the key features are discussed here.

Twitter Profile

A Twitter user profile has three main components: The user chooses a username followed by an @ sign. The username is unique to each user; two pictures are allowed to be used as part of the profile: one passport-size profile photo and a header photo. The use of the image(s) is optional to the profile completion, and biographical information is allowed within a given word limit of 280 characters ('Counting Characters' n.d.). The features of having a profile picture and biographical information can be used to propagate a political narrative. In Pakistan's case, PTI supporters put Imran Khan's photo as their profile picture to make a statement. So, if someone is merely scrolling down their Twitter feed, they can see the presence of PTI without even reading the tweets.

Users can add a location and link to their website or social media accounts in this section. The user can turn on the option to share a 'live location' while tweeting. This component is also optional. Tweets are instantly shared with the world. Twitter users also have the privilege of protecting their tweets. They can turn on security settings and restrict tweet access to approved individuals only. If no restriction is turned on, their tweets and retweets are instantly visible to all Twitter users and appear in their timelines.

Connecting Ties: Accessibility Affordance

Twitter offers easy accessibility to other Twitter users and reproducibility and amplification of any available tweet. On Twitter, users can establish ties or connections with other users by simply liking, replying and retweeting any tweet. On the senders' part, Twitter offers easy accessibility through the @mention function. If a sender wants to make their message visible to the followers of a particular individual, the sender can use @mention at the beginning of the tweet. This function not only notifies the receiver of the Twitter handle but also makes the tweet visible on the timelines of the followers of the targeted individual. When any tweet receives a 'like', 'reply' or 'retweet', the sender of the tweet gets a notification along with information about the user who 'liked' or 'retweeted' it (if the sender has turned on the notification).

Similarly, the reproducibility or amplification of available tweets can be done by pressing 'retweet'. This function resends the tweet with the new user's id. 'Quote' is a feature where any tweet can be retweeted with the addition of commentary. The 'quote' option makes it easier for the user to support or challenge any person's opinion.

Twitter Hashtag: Framing and Amplifying Device

Twitter categorises topics by using hashtags. A # sign symbolises a hashtag. Any word or phrase written without spaces and preceded by the symbol # makes a hashtag on Twitter. The hashtag is a symbol used by Twitter to categorise topics. By default, Twitter shows trending hashtags from ongoing global discussions (Kwak et al. 2010). These hashtags are recommended based on the user's location and the person the user follows. Twitter also allows suggestions to be tailored based on personal interests and relevance.

Twitter's categorisation of topics by hashtags makes content organisation easier. A hash symbol '# marks a hashtag' is a unique tool that allows quick connection with network users, developing connections and disseminating information to the general audience. In other words, hashtags are short phrases that help identify all related posts or messages (Brock 2012). Twitter's ability to highlight information through hashtags helps people quickly reach out to any networked user or community. For example, Qin (2015) employed hashtags #assange, #wikileaks and #p2 to find posts on Twitter tied to Edward Snowden's case. Another study by Hamdy and Gomaa (2012) looks at Egypt's January 2011 uprising taking Egypt's state-run, independent and social media. They use a unique dataset of Arabic language content from sources such as newspapers and social media posts which were collected during the protests. It was observed that semi-official (governmental) newspapers had examined the events using the hashtags such as #Egypt, #Thawra and #25jan hashtags which were aimed to connect all the messages.

Despite the increasing attention to hashtags as framing tools, further research is needed, particularly with a focused investigation into the dynamics of this framing device. While studies, such as those conducted by Qin (2015), have contributed to our understanding, more comprehensive examinations are required. For instance, Moscato delved into the realm of hashtag activism, recognising the significance of hashtags in facilitating and promoting online social movements (Moscato 2016). This study centred its investigation on the #IdleNoMore movement, employing it as a case study to elucidate how online activists, leveraging hashtag activism, have shaped public and social policy discussions within the media landscape. The analysis involved meticulously examining various emerging frames; each was subsequently scrutinised independently to discern disparities across different media outlets. The primary outcome of this analysis indicates that social media plays a pivotal role in providing substantial support and promotion for social movements, thereby functioning as a catalyst for positive social activism.

Central to this study's inquiry was exploring how online social activism, propelled by social media platforms, alters the dynamics of debates within traditional media. Moscato (2016) contends that hashtags, as framing devices, have evolved into revolutionary search tools, with #IdleNoMore as a paradigmatic example. This transformation has significantly elevated the prominence of social media platforms like Twitter compared to traditional media outlets, emphasising the transformative impact of hashtags on shaping contemporary discussions and influencing public discourse.

Twitter Following

Twitter's functionality enables users to subscribe to the tweets of specific individuals. If user A wishes to view tweets from person B, they can click the 'follow' button on B's profile. Reciprocally, anyone has the liberty to follow user A. However, Twitter offers a feature that allows users to control who can follow them. When this restriction is activated, users will receive a follow request, and only upon acceptance will the follower gain access to future tweets.

In contrast to platforms like Facebook, Twitter's following mechanism is not mutual. Granting permission for B to follow A does not automatically result in A following B. The decision to reciprocate the following is entirely at the discretion of user A. It is crucial to note that accepting a follow request on Twitter does not imply a friendship, as is the case on Facebook. Statistics underscore this distinction, revealing that merely 22.1 per cent of Twitter users follow each other (Kwak et al. 2010).

The concept of mutual following holds particular significance within the Pakistani Twitter landscape. This mutual agreement is the foundation for individuals to be considered 'friends' if they follow each other. This mutual connection is pivotal for Pakistani Twitter users as it amplifies their tweets' reach, with a broader follower base contributing to a wider outreach. Research (Saeed 2021) indicates that on Pakistani Twitter, the users engaged in inauthentic coordinated behaviour tend to exhibit a relatively higher percentage of *friends* compared to the globally established percentage of *friends*—22.1 per cent (Kwak et al. 2010).

Case Studies

In the following section, I will talk about two case studies based on Twitter primary data collected between 2019 and 2022. The first case study is about a hashtag (#ImportedGovernmentUnacceptable) aggressively propagated on Pakistani Twitter in April 2022 by supporters of PTI, and this hashtag became a symbol of political resistance in the country. The second hashtag was #AuratMarch (#Women'sMarch), whose active propagation started in 2019. Since then, this hashtag has become a symbolic cultural artefact of women's struggle for their rights.

Case Study 1 - #ImportedGovernmentUnacceptable

In Pakistan, the Pakistan Peoples Party (PPP), Pakistan Muslim League Nawaz (PMLN) and Pakistan Tehreek-e-Insaf (PTI) are the three biggest political parties. In 2014, the Pakistan Tehreek-e-Insaf (PTI) began using social media for political campaigns. Since then, it has steadily increased its presence in this space and developed a strong position. Using hashtags strategically, PTI has significantly created and spread political narratives in this digital era, primarily on Twitter.

PTI came into power after the 2018 general elections, and Imran Khan became the prime minister. During his tenure, he put a noticeable emphasis on using different social media platforms to propagate his narrative. For this purpose, he interacted with social media influencers during his premiership (Irfan n.d.). This coordinated effort demonstrates the party's understanding of social media's and influencers' critical role in influencing public opinion and promoting an engaging and vibrant political dialogue.

On 8 March 2022, a significant political event unfolded in Pakistan as a Vote of No Confidence (VoNC) motion was initiated against Prime Minister Imran Khan (Chaudhry 2022). Following constitutional procedures, the prime minister was mandated to seek a vote of confidence from the National Assembly, requiring a two-thirds majority to retain the position. However, Imran Khan fell short of the needed votes, leading to his removal from office (Chaudhry 2022). Subsequently, Shehbaz Sharif from PMLN assumed the role of the new prime minister.

The PTI blamed the incumbent government (a coalition of more than 10 parties) as stooges of foreign powers. Imran Khan said he was ousted due to a foreign conspiracy that local abetters supported. His political narrative took the form of the hashtag #ImportedHakoomatNaManzoor (#ImportedGovernmentUnacceptable). This hashtag became a symbol of political resistance. The Party asked every active PTI supporter and worker on social media to tweet with the hashtag. On 9 April, the hashtag appeared on Pakistani Twitter's Top Trending Panel and remained there for over a month. Since then, this hashtag has become a signature for PTI's political campaign.

There were a staggering number of tweets with the hashtag TweetBinder—a social media analytics platform that presented statistics about the most monumental hashtag in Twitter's history—#ڈٹروپما_ روظنماں_تموکح (translated as #ImportedGovernmentUnacceptable). According to TweetBinder, until 25 April 2022, 106,433,419 tweets were sent with the hashtag.

Despite the immense volume of tweets generated, it is noteworthy that the hashtag never attained inclusion in Twitter's global trending hashtag panel. Several factors could contribute to this absence, and among them, the discernible presence of an inorganic component in the propagation of the hashtag emerges as a plausible explanation.

The analysis of the hashtag presented in the following section is based on the primary data collected from 9 April to 24 April 2022. The data was collected by using Twitter APIs through two sources. One dataset of 5,36,000 tweets was collected through VOSONDash version 3.5. This dataset contained tweets sent between 8 and 14 April 2022. The second dataset, including 1.3 million tweets sent between 8 and 14 April, was collected using Netlytic. Both datasets were combined, and the duplicates were removed for analysis. The final dataset returned 1.5 million tweets with 108,355 unique posters (Twitter users). On average, one user sent 14 tweets. If I try to put these statistics in another way, if 108,355 users sent 1.5 million tweets, then how many users would be needed to send 106,433 419 tweets? Going by the most superficial estimation using the percentage of accounts to the total number of tweets, the users make up 7 per cent of the total. By this parameter, we would need 7.4 million users to send the number of tweets quoted by

TweetBinder (Tweet Binder [@TweetBinder] 2022). However, the daily analysis of the percentage of unique users (from 8 March to 24 April) followed an almost linear pattern where the number of unique users posting with the hashtag kept dropping each day after 12 April. On 12 April, the percentage of unique users was 22 per cent, which fell to 10 per cent in the dataset collected on 24 April. Posting 100 million tweets in two weeks requires an average of 6.6 million daily.

Discussing unique posters and the total number of tweets highlights two critical issues. First, there was inorganic activity in propagating the hashtag. Second, Twitter algorithms allowed the 'manipulation' of the platform on the one hand. On the other, the algorithms looking for the most popular hashtags globally did not recognise the hashtag as a globally trending phenomenon despite the highest number of tweets.

The pattern of account opening indicates that 15 per cent of accounts were opened in just one and half months (Table 9.1)—between 8 March and 24 April 2022. Till 2018, on average, 6,000 accounts were opened annually. However, the percentage of new accounts increased when PTI was in government. Of all accounts participating in the hashtag propagation, 53 per cent were opened when PTI ruled the country. The moment the vote of No Confidence was moved (8 March 2022), PTI opened Twitter accounts in bulk to spread its narrative. They resisted the regime change in online space by propagating a historic hashtag, #ImportedGovernmentUnacceptable.

Table 9.1: Number of Twitter Accounts Created Annually

Timeline	No. of Accounts Opened	% Of Accounts Opened
Mar 8– April 24, 2022	16122	15%
2022 (Till Mar 7)	4781	4%
2021	17624	16%
2020	10763	10%
2019	9024	8%
2018	6687	6%
2017	5972	6%
2016	4887	5%

Timeline	No. of Accounts Opened	% Of Accounts Opened
2015	4959	5%
2014	7002	6%
2013	5726	5%
2012	5333	5%
2006–2011	9475	9%
Total	108355	100%

Case 2—Women's Movement and Attempts to Police Their Resistance

In Pakistan, women's struggle for their rights is as old as the country's. However, the feminists divide the struggle into different phases or waves where the latest phase, the fourth wave, started a few years before the debut of the Aurat March (Women's March) in 2018 (Saigol and Chaudhary 2020). This new wave of women's rights in Pakistan revolves around the bodily rights and sexual autonomy of individuals (Shaheed 2019). In 2019, women used digital platforms to amplify their voices against patriarchy.

In 2019, feminists and LGBTQ community members introduced hashtagification to the women's rights movement. They initiated the digital wave of the women's movement that adopted social media as a powerful tool to push their rights agenda. Within social media, these feminists introduced the use of technological and social affordances of social media platforms for digital visibility and connectivity. Using hashtags as a device for framing and amplification worked well in creating a debate on women's rights in the country.

However, women's rights activists' digital presence and widespread messaging stirred the digital world. In this section, I will talk about hashtags as framing devices by women's rights activists and their opponents who attempted to police women's resistance and even presence in online spaces.

In the following section, I will analyse critical hashtags from 2019 to 2022 around International Women's Day about women's rights in Pakistan. The analysis is based on the data collected between 2019 and 2022 during February and March every year. The data was collected through the VOSON Dashboard. This dashboard is an interface based on the VOSON SML R package that collects data from Twitter, YouTube and Reddit using Twitter. APIs (VOSON Lab | Virtual Observatory for studying Online Networks, n.d.). VOSON Dashboard returned data in '.rds' and '.graphml' files. '.rds' is complete data from Twitter, stored as an R data frame object. 'graphml' is a file format for storing network data with edge attributes. In 2019, the data was collected for two months, from February to March 2019, using all the top trending hashtags on Pakistani Twitter. However, in the following years, the data collection was more specific to particular hashtags about women's march and their opposition. Throughout the years of data collection, #AuratMarch was included in every year's data collection, along with year-specific pro- and anti-women's march hashtags. For instance, in 2020 and 2021, #ExpiredKhusray (#ExpiredEunuchs), #ForeignFundedMarch and #HayaMarch were propagated, respectively. Likewise, in 2022, #StopFahashiMarch (translation: #StopSpreadingObscenity) and #روزنامہ_چرام_ترورع (translation: #AuratMarchUnacceptable) were propagated, and the data were collected against these hashtags along with the signature hashtag of #AuratMarch (and its variant hashtags in Urdu and English).

The social network analysis method was used to analyse the online structures of networks. In this method, various structural properties of a network are measured to understand the importance and influence of a node in the network and its role in facilitating the flow of information within the network and subnetworks.

#AuratMarch

Over the last five years, #AuratMarch has become a signature hashtag on Twitter that remains part of everyday discussions on women's rights, patriarchy, violence against women and gender discrimination. However, close to International Women's Day (8 March), the number of tweets with the hashtag increase manifold. Every year, the organisers of the Women's March use this hashtag along with year-specific hashtags to disseminate the agenda of the Women's March for that year and amplify the visibility. So is the case with the opponents who run a series of hashtags in response to the defaming, discrediting and policing of resistance.

It is hard to precisely identify when the hashtag #AuratMarch was used on Twitter. However, the hashtag gained prominence in February and March 2019. The word 'Aurat March' was used as a title in 2018 by a group of feminists in Karachi who organised a women's march on International Women's Day. In the following year, in 2019, women's marches named Aurat March were organised in different cities. To publicise the March date, venue, and agenda, the organisers propagated the hashtag #AuratMarch on Twitter.

The relationship between offline incidents and the emergence of online hashtags targeting the women's march is a nuanced exploration that unfolds across the years 2019, 2020 and 2021 on Pakistani Twitter. In 2019, the march garnered attention for specific placards that challenged existing gender norms, provoking male users to express their discontent through abusive language. Although no particular counter-hashtag emerged during this period, it set the stage for subsequent digital engagements.

2020 witnessed a televised debate between writer Khalil ur Rehman Qamar and Marvi Sirmad. Qamar passed a derogatory comment that MarviSirmad's physical appearance was not feminine enough ('Khalil Ur Rehman, Please Sit—Comment', n.d.). The misogynists picked this derogatory comment, and they created the hashtag #ExpiredKhusray while talking about Sirmad. In 2020, when the women's march organisers started tweeting with the signature hashtag #AuratMarch to disseminate information about the year's march, the opponents also started propagating the #ExpiredKhusray to silence the women's rights activists.

Similarly, in 2021, a few weeks before Women's March Day (8 March), a video surfaced on Pakistani Twitter accusing one of the key organisers of the women's march, Nighat Dad ('Interior Ministry Complaint Alleging Nighat Dad's Misuse of Digital Rights Foundation Funds Is Misleading' 2021). Dad is associated with an organisation that works on the promotion of women's digital rights. She was accused of tax evasion and receiving foreign funding. Coinciding with this, the hashtag #ForeignFundedAuratMarch emerged, linking the women's march to NGOs and prompting discussions around financial impropriety.

These instances illuminate the relationship between offline events and online discourse surrounding the Women's March. The association of the women's resistance and their yearly symbolic march on 8 March with foreign-funded vulgarity and against cultural norms is reflected online and offline. Hashtags serve as digital manifestations of societal attitudes and controversies, impacting the socio-political landscape surrounding women's activism in Pakistan.

Ease of Content Generation and Reproducibility

The organisers of the Women's March used Twitter's technological affordance of easy reproducibility of the content, automated temporal posting and low transaction cost as a tool to propagate the hashtag #AuratMarch. Twitter allows different apps to send tweets automatically at a specified time. The frequency of the tweet posting can also be adjusted through the apps. Tweet Deck, Hootsuite Inc, PeriScope, Social Champ and other apps were used to propagate the hashtag #AuratMarch (Saeed 2023). Some 600 tweets were sent using these apps. Although this number makes up merely 2 per cent of all the tweets sent or retweeted with the hashtag, it reflects the ease of reproducibility of the content. To send 600 tweets manually can take time and human resources, while with the affordances of content generation and reproducibility, the hashtag got propagated in less time with lower efforts.

Accessibility: An Affordance Facilitating Group Formations and Narrative Propagation Centres

The following sub-section focuses on the data analysis of hashtags propagated in favour of or in opposition to the women's rights movement. The analysis is built on Twitter's affordance of accessibility through mention, reply (and retweet/quote) ties. I have taken @AuratMarch as a sample node and analysed its Ego Networks across four years.

Women's marches are organised by activists in their capacities, although many of the organisers are affiliated with different organisations. There is no registered organisation named Aurat March. However, the organisers created Twitter handles to voice the annual women's march agenda. These handles included @AuratMarch, @AuratAzadiMarch, @AuratMarch2019, @AuratMarchKarachi and @AuratMarchLahore. Starting in 2019, these Twitter handles, especially the @AuratMarch, became a representative voice of women's rights activists in the following years. Therefore, I have taken @AuratMarch as the central representative node of the women's digital movement and compared its network's structural properties to understand the social support and opposition this node (Twitter handle) received over the years. However, for the first year—2019, I analysed the network properties of @AuratMarch, @AuratAzadiMarch and @ AuratMarch2019. These three nodes were collectively termed 'wg' (women groups). The network characteristics of these Twitter handles can be used to increase understanding of the online group formations and propagation of political narratives through hashtags as the connecting factor among these nodes was the use of #AuratMarch.

The following analysis of 2019 data is based on the dataset that collectively contained 4,628 nodes, with a distribution of 63 per cent men, 32 per cent women, 0.15 per cent identifying as gay/trans and 4 per cent representing accounts categorised as either company or blocked/suspended accounts (Saeed 2023).

Table 9.2 shows that wg received 16 per cent of all inbound ties received by all genders and wg collectively. Although the Twitter handles were newly generated in 2019, the volume (16 per cent) of inbound ties reflects the attention these handles received. Among wg Twitter handles, @AuratMarch was the biggest individual receiver of in-degree at 12 per cent of the total in-degree. Considering the total number of nodes, which was 4,628, just three nodes (wg) receiving 16 per cent of the whole inbound ties reflects how deeply the Twitter users felt about the messages generated by these Twitter handles. It is crucial to consider the backdrop of Pakistani Twitter between February and March 2019. Within this timeframe, three pivotal historical events unfolded in Pakistan. Firstly, Prince Muhammad Bin Suleman of Saudi Arabia visited the country, a visit of political significance for Pakistan. The government, which had assumed office in October 2018, eagerly anticipated the visit, seeking support from the Saudi Crown Prince. As highlighted in the previous sections, PTI's government actively propagated its political narrative on social media. So, like any politically important event, the Prince's visit was also propagated on Twitter. Secondly, the Pakistan Super League, a prominent cricket event featuring international players, captivated the attention of Pakistanis, garnering significant traction on Twitter. Thirdly, heightened tensions between India and Pakistan arose due to the Indian Air Force's intrusion into Pakistan's airspace, leading to retaliatory measures by Pakistan. This conflict sustained an elevated state throughout the entire data collection period. Despite all these events, the @AuratMarch received voluminous attention on Twitter.

Table 9.2: In-Degree Centrality (percentage) of wg (Women Group) Twitter Handles

Username	In-Degree (%) among Men, Women and Trans
AuratMarch	12.31
AuratAzadiMarch	2.27
AuratMarch2019	1.21
Total	15.79

The betweenness centrality for wg was 19 per cent of the total betweenness centrality. This is an indication of the bridging role the wg played on Twitter. The higher betweenness centrality indicates the greater bridging social capital (Saeed 2023) and shows more control over the flow of information within the network (Freeman 1977).

Table 9.3 shows the ego network size and density of the wg nodes. @AuratMarch, @AuratAzadiMarch and AuratMarch 2019 had 83, 23 and 36 nodes, respectively, with network densities equal to 0.06, 0.23 and 0.12. The wg nodes had the highest network sizes.

Table 9.3: Ego Network Size and Density of wg (Women's Groups) Twitter Handles

Username	Ego Network Size	Ego Network Density
@AuratMarch	83	0.07
@AuratAzadiMarch	23	0.24
@AuratMarch2019	36	0.12

Network Structures Explain Connectivity Patterns and Accessibility

Connectivity and accessibility are among the critical affordances of Twitter. A social network analysis of online networks reveals the connectivity patterns of the users who tweeted with the hashtag #AuratMarch or engaged with @AuratMarch to support or oppose them. The visual representation of the data helps to understand how Twitter users align themselves in online space. Figures 9.1 and 9.2 show 1.5 and 2.0 Ego Networks of @AuratMarch respectively. In both graphs, the clusters are around @AuratMarch because 2019 was the first year the hashtag #AuratMarch became prominent. The users who were against the women's march (most of them were men, as the qualitative analysis of the tweets showed) replied to or mentioned @ AuratMarch to register their opinions. However, in the following years, the opponents organised themselves. They started using their separate hashtags against the women's march organisers and clustered around the prominent anti-women's march Twitter handles.

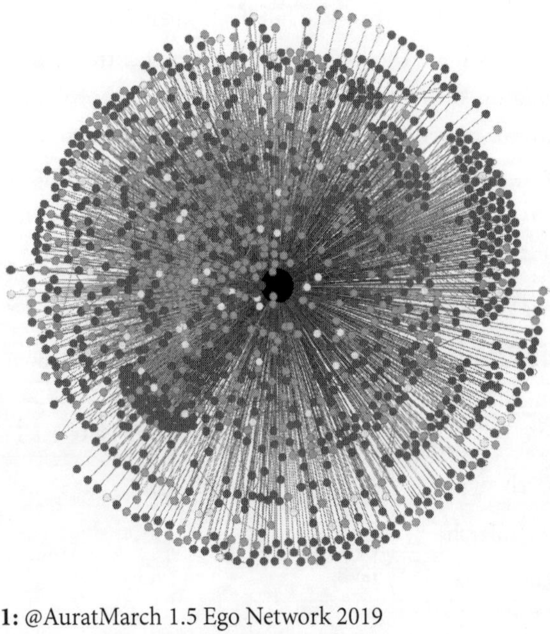

Figure 9.1: @AuratMarch 1.5 Ego Network 2019

Ego Networks of 2019 Women's March

Figure 9.1 is Ego Network 1.5 of @AuratMarch in 2019. This network contained 29 per cent (1,333 nodes) of total nodes and 35 per cent (8,588 ties) of all the ties established around Women's March 2019. The figure shows a big black circle that represents @AuratMarch. Around the black circle, there are multiple small dark and light grey circles. Dark grey circles are male users, and light grey circles are female. Most dark grey circles are connected to the big black circle or light grey circles. The light grey circles are clustered closer to the big black circle, while dark grey circles are more scattered. This visualisation (Figure 9.1) shows that women were connected closely as they were propagating the same hashtag or supporting each other by retweeting or quoting. However, men seem to engage with the big black circle (@AuratMarch) or cluster around light grey circles. The ties (connecting lines) between dark grey circles were rare as men engaged more with women than with other men. However, this connectivity pattern changed in the following years when men started propagating their hashtags against the Women's March.

In the same year—2019, @AuratMarch's Ego Network 2.0 exhibited 2,846 nodes and 16,567 ties (Figure 9.2). This volume accounted for 61 per cent of all nodes and 72 per cent of ties within the network, as Figures 9.1 and 9.2 depicted. These visual representations indicate a notable absence of a substantial number of sub-networks, revealing that most Twitter users were directly connected to the central node.

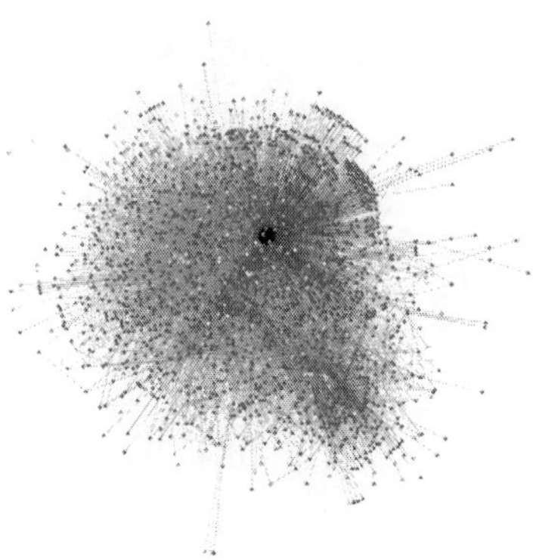

Figure 9.2: @AuratMarch 2.0 Ego Network 2019

In 2020, two significant shifts occurred regarding hashtagging about women's marches. The organisers of the women's march started using the yearly theme of the rally and their signature hashtag #AuratMarch. Second, the opponents of the women's march got more organised, and they started using their distinct hashtags against the women's rights activists.

The structures of online social networks of the Ego Networks (1.5 and 2.0) of @AuratMarch from 2020 data showed relatively smaller ego network sizes and lower number of inbound ties than the previous year—2019.

In 2020, the Ego Network 1.5 of @AuratMarch comprised 766 nodes and 4259 ties (Figure 9.3). In percentages, the nodes in Ego Network 1.5 had 7 per cent of all the nodes, and the percentage of ties was 20 per cent. Meanwhile, the Ego Network 2.0 of @AuratMarch comprised 5033 nodes and 13265 ties. In percentages, the nodes in Ego Network 2.0 had 46 per cent of all the nodes, and the percentage of ties was 63 per cent. Compared with 2019, the 1.5 Ego Network of AuratMarch shrank from 29 per cent of total nodes in 2019 to 7 per cent in 2020. Likewise, the ties' volume decreased from 35 per cent of all ties in 2019 to 7 per cent in 2020. Comparing Ego Network sizes from 2019 and 2020 showed the shrinking volume of the networks, where nodes' volume decreased from 61 per cent in 2019 to 46 per cent in 2020. This decrease explains why opponents started building their separate social networks on Twitter. The network structure of the hashtag #ExpiredEunuchs, which was propagated by the opponents of the women's march, showed the clustering of opponents in separate networks with fewer inter-network ties with @AuratMarch.

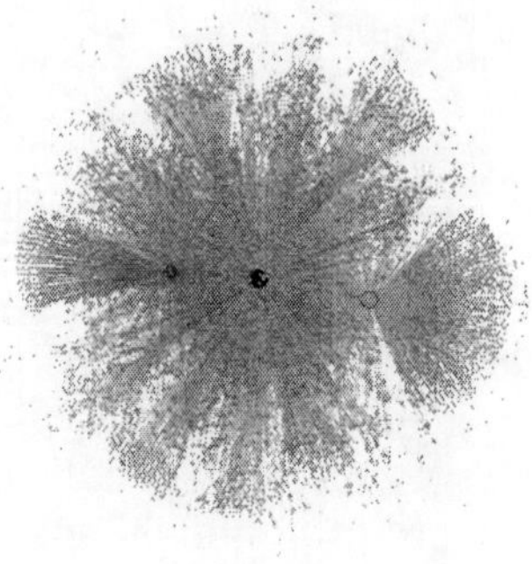

Figure 9.3: @AuratMarch 1.5 Ego Network 2020

Figure 9.4 shows the network of Twitter users who propagated the hashtag #ExpiredEunuchs. The propagators of the hashtag engaged the women's rights activists by using @mention ties. The Black Circle is @AuratMarch, which received a few inbound ties (@mention ties). Figure 10.5 shows the 2.0 Ego Network of @AuratMarch in the main network of #ExpiredEunuchs. The Black Circle is @AuratMarch, which the opponents targeted. The inward direction of the arrows reflects that the handle @AuratMarch was tagged in various tweets.

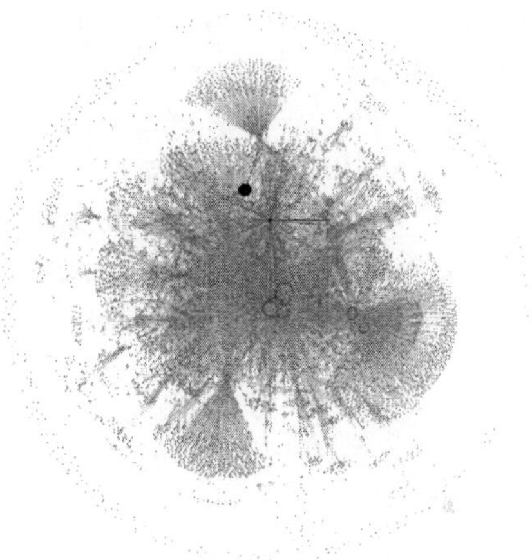

Figure 9.4: Network of #ExpiredEunuchs

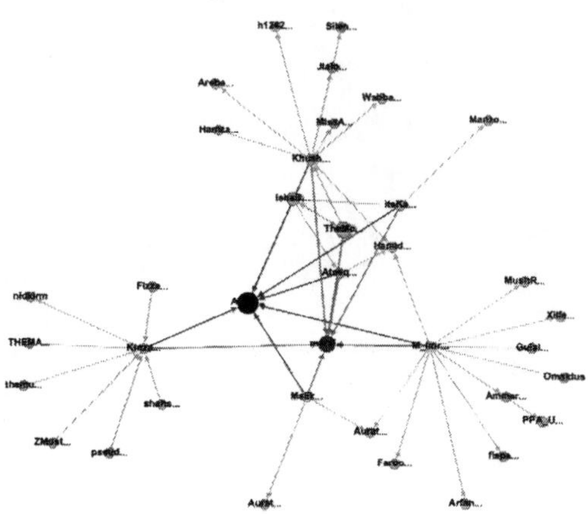

Figure 9.5: 2.0 Ego Network of @AuratMarch within the network of #ExpiredEunuchs

In 2021, like the previous year of 2020, the opponents of the women's march targeted women's rights activists. They propagated derogatory hashtags against the feminists who were protesting against patriarchy and oppression on Twitter. As mentioned earlier, the opponents got more organised every year. In 2020, they started tweeting with distinct hashtags, and the following year, they launched a propaganda campaign against one of the organisers. Based on the propaganda that the women's march organiser was running an NGO that was receiving illegal foreign funds, the hashtag #ForeignFnded march was propagated against women's rights activists. The following figure shows Ego Network 2.0 of @AuratMarch (the black circle). The percentage of nodes in the Ego Network was 4 per cent, and the ties' percentage was less than 10%. However, the figure shows the presence of different sub-networks within the main network, indicating various sub-communities participating in the hashtag conversations. Comparing @AuratMarch's Ego Networks in pro-women's march and anti-women march hashtags reveals how the hashtags were used as framing devices.

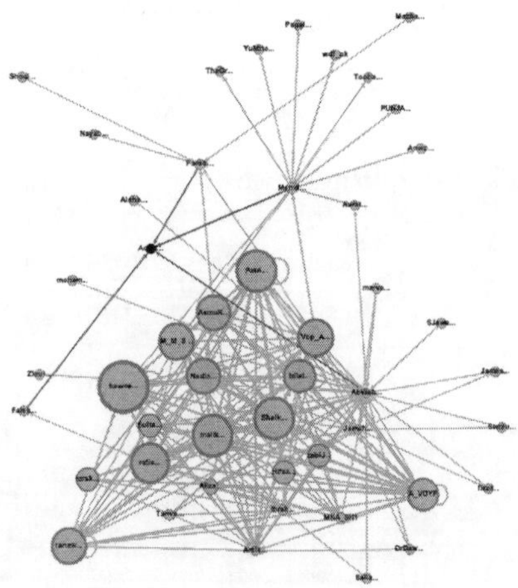

Figure 9.6: @AuratMarch 2.0 Ego Network within #ForeignFundedMarch Network

In 2022, the Ego Network 1.5 of @AuratMarch comprised 766 nodes and 4,259 ties (Figure 9.7). In percentages, the nodes in Ego Network 1.5 had 7 per cent of all the nodes, and the percentage of ties was 20 per cent.

The use of hashtags as framing devices on Twitter, particularly in the context of the #AuratMarch, highlights the evolving dynamics of online discourse and social network structures. Hashtags serve as organisational tools, shaping the narrative and fostering connectivity within the platform. The ease of producing and reproducing content on Twitter facilitates the propagation of these narratives, enabling users to align themselves and engage in discussions surrounding specific hashtags.

In the initial stages, the connectivity patterns surrounding #AuratMarch in 2019 were characterised by a central node (@AuratMarch) with female users forming close clusters, indicating support through retweets and quotes—men, predominantly opponents of the women's march, engaged with @AuratMarch or clustered around women users. The visual representation in Figure 9.1 illustrates the initial alignment of users around the central node.

The analysis of online social networks (as shown in the graphs) reveals that as the hashtag gained prominence, opponents organised themselves, creating separate hashtags against the women's march organisers. Supporters and opposers of the women's march started aligning themselves with their groups and reducing the interactions with different narratives, thus creating echo chambers. Secondly, the network structures changed from community clusters. The latter was a positive sign as people started discussing women's rights in smaller groups. However, the absence of connections across narratives indicates the polarisation with limited bridging connections.

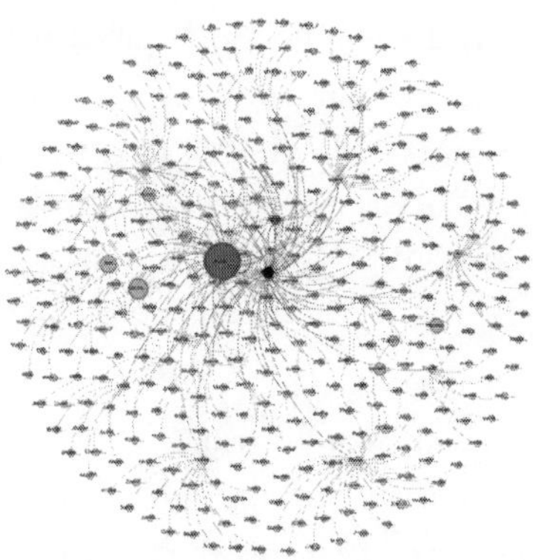

Figure 9.7: @AuratMarch 1.5 Ego Network 2022

Conclusion

Twitter is becoming a popular social media platform in Pakistan to discuss politics. Over the past decade, political parties and human rights activists have started using the platform to raise their voices. On the other hand, opponents of women's rights have also started propagating their opinions through hashtags. The platform has become a tug-of-war of hashtags. Every group intends to push their hashtag to the top trend panel on Twitter. For this purpose, Twitter's technological affordances of reproducibility of content, networked propagation and automated content generation have been used. Two cases have been discussed in detail to show the impact of Twitter's technological and social affordances on the country's digital politics.

Pakistan Tehreek-i-Insaf (PTI) used the platform to run hashtag campaigns that manifested their political resistance. PTI ran a hashtag, #ImportedGovernmentUnacceptable, which has become a symbol of political resistance on PTI's part. This hashtag was the biggest in the tweets sent with the #. However, the inorganic activity and the coordinated inauthentic behaviour indicate the manipulation of the platform to propagate the hashtag. At the same time, the emergence of the hashtag as a symbol of political resistance, even with a relatively smaller number of users using the hashtag, reflects the advantage that Twitter's technological and social affordances offer to propagate narratives.

Women's rights activists started using social media extensively in 2019 and propagated their political stance through the hashtag #AuratMarch, which has become a symbol of women's resistance. Every year, thousands of users use the hashtag to extend their support. The opponents of the women's rights movement initially (in 2019) used the same hashtag, #AuratMarch, to police the resistance. However, they have created and propagated distinct hashtags representing their political stance in recent years. The structures of online social networks revealed that pro- women's march hashtag networks contained higher modularity (which indicates stronger intra-community ties), lower average outdegree and broader network diameters than anti-women's march propagators.

The hashtagification process was helped by digital anonymity, decentralised information flow, easily reproducible content, and social accessibility. Political slogans were turned into news stories by hashtagification and shared through centralised web networks. These structured networks accelerated the hashtag's spread on Twitter. The investigation also showed that digital political activists gained leadership roles in 'information networks' as a result of their involvement online, indicating a rise in their social capital. These Twitter users eventually evolved into a crowdsourced political elite that has become central to the information flow on the platform.

References

Wasim Ahmed, Josep Vidal-Alaball, Joseph Downing and Francesc López Seguí. 2020. 'COVID-19 and the 5G Conspiracy Theory: Social Network Analysis of Twitter Data'. *Journal of Medical Internet Research* 22 (5): e19458. https://doi.org/10.2196/19458.

André Brock. 2012. 'From the Blackhand Side: Twitter as a Cultural Conversation'. *Journal of Broadcasting & Electronic Media* 56 (4): 529–549. https://doi.org/10.1080/08838151.2012.732147.

Chaudhry and Fahad. 2022. 'Imran Khan Loses No-Trust Vote, Prime Ministerial Term Comes to Unceremonious End'. Dawn.com 2022. Available at: https://www.dawn.com/news/1684168; 'Counting Characters', n.d. Available at: https://developer.x.com/en/docs/counting-characters (accessed 5 January 2024).

Nicole Ellison and Danah M. Boyd. 2013. 'Sociality Through Social Network Sites', in *The Oxford Handbook of Internet Studies*, edited by William H. Dutton, Oxford University Press. https://doi.org/10.1093/oxfordhb/9780199589074.013.0008.

Linton C. Freeman. 1977. 'A Set of Measures of Centrality Based on Betweenness'.*Sociometry* 40 (1): 35. https://doi.org/10.2307/3033543.

Naila Hamdy and Ehab H. Gomaa. 2012. 'Framing the Egyptian Uprising in Arabic Language Newspapers and Social Media'. *Journal of Communication* 62 (2): 195–211. https://doi.org/10.1111/j.1460-2466.2012.01637.x.

'Interior Ministry Complaint Alleging Nighat Dad's Misuse of Digital Rights Foundation Funds Is Misleading'. 2021. *Soch Fact Check* (blog). 7 January 2021. https://www.sochfactcheck.com/interior-ministry-complaint-alleging-nighat-dads-misuse-of-digital-rights-foundation-funds-is-misleading/.

Sam Irfan. n.d. 'Prime Minister of Pakistan Imran Khan Exclusive Interaction with YouTubers & Digital Publishers in Islamabad'. *Trendinginsocial.Com: Latest Entertainment, Fashion, Technology, Business, Travel & Sports News* (blog). Accessed 17 April 2023. https://www.trendinginsocial.com/prime-minister-of-pakistan-imran-khan-exclusive-interaction-with-youtubers-digital-publishers-in-islamabad/.

Sarah J. Jackson, Moya Bailey and Brooke Foucault Welles. 2020. *#HashtagActivism: Networks of Race and Gender Justice.* MIT Press.

Andreas M. Kaplan and Michael Haenlein. 2010. 'Users of the World, Unite! The Challenges and Opportunities of Social Media'. *Business Horizons* 53 (1): 59–68. https://doi.org/10.1016/j.bushor.2009.09.003.

'Khalil Ur Rehman, Please Sit - Comment - Images'. n.d. https://images.dawn.com/news/1184782 (accessed on 5 January 2024).

Haewoon Kwak, Changhyun Lee, Hosung Park and Sue Moon. 2010. 'What Is Twitter, a Social Network or a News Media?' In *Proceedings of the 19th International Conference on World Wide Web—WWW' 10*, 591. https://doi.org/10.1145/1772690.1772751.

Derek Moscato. 2016. 'Media Portrayals of Hashtag Activism: A Framing Analysis of Canada's #Idlenomore Movement'. *Media and Communication* 4 (2): 3–12.

Jie Qin. 2015. 'Hero on Twitter, Traitor on News: How Social Media and Legacy News Frame Snowden'. *The International Journal of Press/Politics* 20 (2): 166–84. https://doi.org/10.1177/1940161214566709.

Rizvan Saeed. 2021. 'Digital Autocratization of Pakistan', in *Routledge Handbook of Autocratization in South Asia.* Routledge.

———. 2023. 'Twitter and Development of Social Capital: A Gender Perspective'. *Telematics and Informatics Reports* 9 (March): 100037. https://doi.org/10.1016/j.teler.2022.100037.

Tweet Binder [@TweetBinder]. 2022. 'Now That @elonmusk Has Purchased Twitter, We Feel It's a Great Time to Share Twitter Stats about the Hashtag روظنمان_تموکح_ڈٹروپما# Maybe the Biggest Trend Ever Analyzed in Tweet Binder. 106,433,419 Tweets!! Https://T.Co/ppSGpb57Py'.Tweet. *Twitter*. https://twitter.com/TweetBinder/status/1518703397020577793.

Ben S.Wasike. 2013. 'Framing News in 140 Characters: How Social Media Editors Frame the News and Interact with Audiences via Twitter'. *Global Media Journal* 6 (1): 5–23.

10

e-Governance and Cybercrime in Sri Lanka

A Study of Legislations

Vishaka Suriyabandara, Vinsuka Kannangara and Sathya Gunawardana

Introduction

Cybercrimes are not just about targeting individuals nor do they relate simply to thefts. They have become more complicated than ordinary crimes in the age of the digital. In the contemporary period, cybercrime has spread to the organisational level including the governmental sectors which means that their effects cannot be disregarded. The Information and Communication Technology (ICT) sector is the fifth-largest revenue-earning industry in Sri Lanka. But at the same time, in Sri Lanka, the Sri Lanka Computer Emergency Readiness Team, Coordination Centre (Sri Lanka CERT-CC) reported receiving about 3,907 cybersecurity-related incidents in the year 2017, which was an increase from the numbers reported in the year 2010 (Sri Lanka CERT 2018).

When compared to the technologically advanced countries, Sri Lanka has not witnessed any major breach of security, cyber terrorism or cybercrime. However, we cannot discredit the fact that international cyber criminals might infiltrate government information systems for multiple reasons such as anarchy, training for hackers and others. Additionally, there is also a possibility that hackers may seek to expose information on critical agreements between the Sri Lankan government and other countries. In an interconnected digital world, this acquires significance. For instance, on several occasions, the WikiLeaks website disclosed sensitive information about the Sri Lankan government, using the means of intercepting cable messages (*The Guardian* 2010).

Over the past decade, Sri Lanka has seen rapid growth in technology infrastructure, internet availability and computer literacy. The number of households with internet access at home is estimated to be about 5.17 million in 2024 (Statista 2023). Similarly, the number of mobile internet users in Sri Lanka is estimated to rise to 7.11 million with the internet penetration rate estimated to be about 66.89 per cent in the year 2024 (Statista 2023). There is also a concentrated push in the field of digital development. Apart from such estimated growth, other developments include the establishment of the Information and Communication Technology Agency (ICTA) as the main ICT agency of the Sri Lankan government, and its subsidiary body, the Computer Emergency Response Team (CERT) which was specially enacted to combat cyber security threats in the country.

The ICTA acts as the apex ICT institution of the government. According to the Information and Communication Technology Act No. 27 of 2003 (ICT Act), as amended by Act No. 33 of 2008, it is responsible for all necessary measures to implement the government's policy as well as develop action plans related to ICT in Sri Lanka. Further, Section 6 of the ICT Act also requires ICTA to assist the government in formulating the 'National Policy' on ICT. ICTA is also mandated the implementation of the 'e-Sri Lanka Development Project' that was sponsored by the World Bank from the year 2004–2011. This project aimed to use ICT so as to develop the Sri Lankan economy, alleviate poverty and improve the overall quality of life for its citizens. In 2008, the ICTA was made into a permanent institution through an amendment.[1] Additionally, the country is also developing its digital policy seen in the draft 'National Digital Government/Governance Policy for Sri Lanka' which has identified nine key policy areas for debate and discussion. One of the thrusts of the policy is the development of digital laws to provide the necessary legal framework so as to usher in digital and technological development.

Thus, a comprehensive network of laws was enacted in Sri Lanka with the aim of addressing cybersecurity-related matters. Some of these laws include the Electronic Transactions Act No. 19 of 2006, Computer

Crimes Act No. 24 of 2007, Payment and Settlement Systems Act No. 28 of 2005, Payment Devices Frauds Act No. 30 of 2006 and the recently enacted Personal Data Protection Act No. 9 of 2022. However, although the field of information technology has grown rapidly, the aspects of implementation and enforcement still lag.

It has been observed that when it comes to cyber security, the governmental sector is heavily vulnerable to cyberattacks and most government employees have low levels of digital literacy. These vulnerabilities were displayed in the cyberattack which happened in 2016 where the president's official website was allegedly hacked by a 17-year-old (*The Guardian* 2016). On 11 September 2023, there was also a ransomware attack that affected Sri Lanka's government cloud system, that is, the Lanka Government Cloud (LGC). This incident led to the framing of the cybersecurity legislation introducing, for the first time, a cybersecurity national authority (Poireault 2023).

Based on the above discussion, the focus of this chapter is to analyse how cyberattacks would affect the governmental sectors along with suggesting measures to prevent them. According to a survey conducted by Sri Lanka CERT (SLCERT 2015) in 2015 with a sample of 347 respondents, it was observed that most of the respondents had commonsensical knowledge about cybersecurity, but about 35 per cent of them were unaware of the value of personal information in digital spaces. In total, 67 per cent of these respondents had been victims of computer viruses.

Scholars around the world have recommended increasing awareness and literacy of new media and modifications of the legal system as some of the ways to minimise cybercrimes. However, focus on awareness and legal measures may not be enough. As noted earlier, in Sri Lanka, the CERT which was established in 2006 is a subsidiary of ICTA whose main purpose is to combat cybersecurity threats in Sri Lanka. In 2018, CERT-CC (CERT-Coordination Centre) formulated the National Information and Cyber Security Strategy of Sri Lanka for the years 2019–2023, which focused on six strategic areas aimed at creating a robust cybersecurity ecosystem within the country. These included establishing a comprehensive governance framework together with a regulatory environment comprising relevant policies and legislation, strengthening the workforce, enhancing digital infrastructure, increasing civic awareness and encouraging the development of partnerships.

Even though Sri Lanka has a dedicated organisation to monitor cybercrimes, it has not been enough to minimise the cybercrimes which occur in Sri Lanka. The main reason was the lack of proper procedures to identify cybersecurity risks and prevention. In our study, it was observed that most governmental agencies have only basic websites without proper security, and most of the employees, including IT employees, lack knowledge of cyber security. Further, there was no established procedure to test the security of software systems that government agencies use—most of which were created by private software companies.

Though the study focuses on the government sector, private sector institutions are also equally affected. As private sector organisations are rapidly embracing cloud-based solutions and e-commerce businesses in Sri Lanka, these institutions are also required to protect their confidential data and business plans from unwanted intruders and other rival companies. Hence, a special focus of this chapter is to indicate how laws and ethics should be implicated in the discussion of cybercrimes and cybersecurity.

Apart from the lack of data, another huge issue faced when dealing with this theme and when creating the sample for this study is related to 'security issues'. In most of the interviews with the respondents, the banking sector companies and security field companies would not reveal any details regarding cybersecurity. The respondents also did not allow their employees to take part in such research and interviews due to fear of breach. Hence, in the studies, the sample was limited to the Sri Lanka Ports Authority where the employee count was over 9,600. It was also found that the Port Authority displayed computerisation to a high degree when compared to other governmental organisations, hence making the issue of cybercrime and/or threat significant. They had also put in place a number of 'e-systems' to aid the functioning of the port authority.[2]

The Question of Cybersecurity and Awareness

Saini, Rao and Panda (2012: 207) in their study indicate that a lack of cybercrime awareness is what leads to cybercrimes. It is their view that 'humans are the weakest link' in the larger scheme of digital security. Even though cybersecurity has improved with time, one of the biggest reasons cybercriminals are still thriving can be traced back to the lack of awareness of the users. It is still the network users who are often unknowingly inviting security breaches through carelessness and a lack of digital literacy. Further looking into what he said, there is a definite link between the awareness and carelessness of the users. This might be because even though users believe themselves to be aware of cybersecurity and cyber risks, they might lack the required technical knowledge. This fact is further emphasised by Panko (2004) by presenting a survey done by Cisco Systems which has revealed that users who work remotely, although they claim to have awareness of security risks, would still engage in actions that endanger the system security. Both lack of awareness and carelessness can also lead to negligence by the users. Scholars such as Kirwan and Power (2013) also note that in dealing with cybercrime and psychological behaviour, we must take into account not only the 'offender' but also the effects and consequences on the 'victims'. They argue for proportionate punishments and other preventative measures to respond to them. Kirwan and Power (2013) also suggest that the crimes themselves must lead to comparisons to similar offline offences that may be occurring elsewhere to generate results.

It is seen that social engineering is a concept where cyber criminals use deception and manipulation to gain confidential and sensitive information from unsuspecting users. These types of attacks have a direct link to the lack of awareness and can become a weakness in an organisation's security due to the characteristics and behaviours of the people (Metalidou, et al. 2014). Even trustworthy employees can cause problems to the organisation's information systems through human errors such as carelessness, failure to follow established protocols, poor training or omission by supervising personnel (Cho, Kim and Acquisti: 2012). Most companies have this issue, and the responsibility is to be shouldered by both the employees and the management. This is because companies inadvertently failed to train their employees in cybersecurity awareness and digital literacy programmes. LeVeque (2003) explains the need to implement an information security plan by strengthening the practices of management so as to establish the security of information as a core feature of the institution's strategic planning. Further, most organisations have their valuable information and services in the control of people who do not understand their value and the importance of maintaining their protection. They are also unaware of the consequences if the information were to be leaked or exposed.

Given these kinds of issues, the biggest problem faced by cybercrime law enforcement in the contemporary period is that many cybercrimes are carried out under the radar. There are several reasons for this. The main reason is that many victims are unaware they have been affected by cybercrimes. Some others are too embarrassed to report the crimes as it will most likely reveal their misjudgments, and some do not know to whom to report. Further, some of the victims even do not know whether the incident is a crime, or they falsely believe that law enforcement agencies cannot provide any relief to them. What we can understand by these reasons is that awareness is not limited to learning cybersecurity risks but also to understanding the steps to take in these kinds of events. Society is well aware of physical (or traditional) crimes, but cybercrimes are often not visible, and people are not aware of them apart from some scant reports in the media. It is here that scholars such as de Bruijn and Janssen (2017) argue for more evidence-based framing strategies in relation to building cybersecurity awareness among the people. However, it is found that even when people are aware of them, only a few types of cybercrimes like spam e-mails and cyberbullying are within their ambit of understanding. This simple but significant fact is further confirmed by the study conducted by Solaka and Topaloglua (2015), who explain that crimes such as child pornography and cyber fraud get the most attention while other types are disregarded or neglected most of the time in the media reports. They also found that there is still no certainty regarding the definition of cybercrime and behaviour determinations of those crimes in law and legal regimes. They noted that there was no 'significant difference between the legal and moral perspectives of the students' in relation to cybercrime (Solaka and Topaloglua 2015: 595).

Strawser and Joy (2015) in their study of cybersecurity and user responsibility revealed an aggravating fact where the victims of cybercrimes were further criticised and blamed by society. They gave examples of two incidents—one where incriminating photographs and videos of many Hollywood celebrities were released by hackers, and the second was the alleged North Korean cyberattack of Sony Pictures Entertainment. In both these cases, the public opinion was that victims should have taken measures to protect their valuables and they were to blame, if not fully, they were liable to at least share a part of the blame for the reasons behind the hackings. This kind of public opinion can cause many people to refrain from reporting cybercrimes due to fear of public discrimination and social embarrassment.

Simply put, people are afraid of the media attention garnered by cybercrimes (Böhme and Moore 2012). They also speculate that unwanted awareness and media attention can cause people to remain hesitant to participate in online activities. When online operations are instrumental in the development of a country, people limiting themselves in participation due to fear of cybercrimes caused by the lack of proper knowledge will certainly affect the country's technological development. Scholars such as Metalidou et al. (2014) agree that raising cybersecurity awareness is the key to reducing the security breaches created by human weaknesses. Bendovschi (2015) believes that the first thing to do to combat increasing crimes is worldwide awareness from an individual level to company perspectives about what lies in the cyber world. As he shows, nonprofit organisations such as the Secure Domain Foundation (SDF) or the International Association of Cyber-Crime Prevention (IACP) are trying to make companies and individuals aware of risks and attacks and also to find ways to defend themselves from these kinds of attacks. Raising awareness of cybercrimes can be divided into several different paths according to previous research papers. The government definitely has a bigger responsibility in this matter as Information Technology security and its knowledge should be thought about seriously in schools for all educational levels. It is therefore clear that schools should educate children on how to engage in online activities without becoming victims. This idea is also confirmed by scholars such as Lebek et al. (2014: 1050) who mention that security and countermeasures should target awareness and education of society regarding cybercrimes through Security Education, Training and Awareness (SETA) programmes. These measures will lead to a lower success rate of attacks.

The governmental structure has the authority to introduce such educational programmes to raise better awareness of cybercrimes in the future. Numerous scholars have already noted that manuals should be written and rewritten to prepare future generations to successfully respond to these challenges. A good example of government-funded awareness projects is Kenya, where they have national and sector-specific educational and professional training programmes to raise public awareness and promote cybersecurity courses at higher educational institutes and certifications of professionals by the national Computer Security Incident Response Team (Sambuli 2023).

Apart from government efforts, increasing the awareness of new media literacy is also needed to mitigate cybercrimes by many scholars. Lagazio, Sherif and Cushman (2014) also report that public and media pressures are also needed for better efforts in law enforcement. Another way to raise awareness is from an organisational level which targets their employees. Metalidou et al. (2014) argue that employee education about the importance of cybersecurity awareness should be a priority of the organisation. Bendovschi (2015) concludes that company-wide awareness is essential, considering most of the risks and vulnerabilities are created by companies' staff, whether it is intentional or not. That study also provides the idea of documenting the processes and the controls that are put in place. These enable a clear way to present information and enforce employee awareness and commitment which could be helpful to improve and maintain information security.

Even with the development of ICT and digital policy in many countries, many governments across the world including organisations lack even the basic tools to respond to digital disasters. For instance, Liao, Tsou and Huang (2011), who studied the internal control system of the state-owned commercial bank computer system in China found that the internal control design of the information system lacked 'hierarchy'. That study further revealed that each level of the information lacked the gear of control and specific control measures, which would be similar to the systems that are currently in place in a country like Sri Lanka. Most governmental organisation software systems are developed by the private sector. Unfortunately, the government does not have proper protocols to test these software systems to measure their security level. This weakness can and will be exploited by cybercriminals and is a major factor in targeting the government IT sector.

Many other authors have advised the use of cybersecurity frameworks to combat cybercrimes. One such framework is the National Institute of Standards and Technology (NIST) framework which is used in the private sector in the United States of America (USA) and helps prevent, detect and respond to cybercrimes. It can also be the basis for a new cybersecurity mechanism for improving current existing programmes. The Sri Lankan government sector can also make use of the existing framework and design it to be more suitable for its requirements. Countries like Sri Lanka are not able to afford and maintain expensive solutions, so governments tend to neglect the importance of technical measures to fight cybercrimes. Concerning this issue, Strawer and Joy (2015) suggest three rules for security solutions which are equally important for the government, the private sector and the community. These can be explained as follows:

- Security solutions should be proportionately affordable to what they are protecting;
- Security solutions should be reasonably easy to employ;
- Use, access and maintenance of security solutions should provide user convenience without sacrificing security. (Strawser and Joy 2015)

There are existing solutions that follow the rules noted above. It is ultimately the government's responsibility to conduct research and provide proper cybersecurity to the sectors and agencies because when computers and technology fail, it is the people who depend on the services provided by those infrastructures that suffer the consequences.

Legislations for the 'Digital' in Sri Lanka

Given the earlier discussions, it is clear that cybercrimes can have severe consequences for Sri Lanka's public sector, including financial losses, data breaches and damage to its security interests. As mentioned before in 2016, several hackers, including a seventeen-year-old schoolboy were arrested and charged with hacking the then Sri Lankan President Maithripala Sirisena's official website for two consecutive days. A couple of years ago, several government agencies, including the Sri Lankan Media Center for National Security, the Presidential Secretariat and 129 other government websites were also hacked and defaced, resulting in the theft of sensitive data, including the personal information of citizens. These incidents illustrate the vulnerability of Sri Lanka's public sector to cybercrime and the need for robust cybersecurity measures to protect against such attacks. Some of the existing laws can be discussed as follows:

- The Computer Crimes Act, No. 24 of 2007 (CCA), is the primary legislation governing cybercrime in Sri Lanka. It incorporates principles of the Budapest Convention on Cybercrime into domestic law. The process of identifying and incorporating computer or electronic-based crimes and evidence into Sri Lankan law started after the enactment of the Evidence Special Provisions Act, No. 14 of 1995 which allowed for the admission of audio and video recordings as evidence in courts of law.
- The CCA criminalises a wide range of cyber offences, including unauthorised access (Section 3 of the CCA), hacking, data theft, cyberstalking, attacks against national security, national economy and public order (Section 6 of the CCA), illegal interception of data (Section 8 of the CCA) and dealing with unlawfully obtained data (Section 7 of the CCA). Furthermore, attempting, abetting or conspiring to commit any of the above offences too, is an offence under the Act (Sections 11, 12 and 13 of the CCA).

However, the act has several limitations, including inadequate penalties for cybercrime and the lack of provisions for the investigation and prosecution of cybercrime cases. Moreover, there is a lack of awareness and capacity among law enforcement agencies and the judiciary regarding cybercrime, which further hampers the effective enforcement of the existing legal framework. Nevertheless, the CERT, in partnership with the ICTA, had attempted to address this problem by initiating a series of training sessions on cybercrime and electronic evidence. One of such important sector-based training initiatives was a series of workshops conducted for judges in Sri Lanka in collaboration with the Sri Lanka Judges' Institute (SLJI). This was undoubtedly a significant step taken towards strengthening law enforcement on cybercrimes.

- Subsequent enactments such as the Payment and Settlement Systems Act, Electronic Transactions Act and Payment Devices Frauds Act followed by the Computer Crimes Act and the Personal Data Protection Act are other applicable legislations relevant to cyber and electronic crimes in Sri Lanka. Out of these, the Payment Devices Frauds Act, No. 30 of 2006 was specifically enacted to prevent the use of illegal payment devices, which are in most cases stolen or fraudulent credit cards. The Act makes the ownership and use of such illegal payment devices a criminal offence subject to imprisonment and/or a fine.
- The Intellectual Property (IP) Act, No. 36 of 2003 also plays an important role in safeguarding IP rights against cybercrime violations. Sri Lankan IP Law recognises and protects numerous Intellectual Property rights such as patents, copyrights, trademarks, industrial designs, trade secrets and geographical indicators. With the development of technology, most of these IP rights were subject to infringement in cyberspace. The most common of these were through software piracy, trademark infringement or hacking of confidential information.
- As per the CCA, the procedure for investigating cybercrimes is the general investigative procedure set out under the Code of Criminal Procedure Act, No. 15 of 1979 (Section 15 of the CCA). However, notably, police officers conducting arrests under the CCA could be assisted by any 'expert' public officer having the required qualification & experience in electronic engineering/ software engineering technology as gazetted by the Minister (Section 17 of the CCA). Such experts have wide power under the Act including powers to enter upon any premises along with a police officer, to access any information system/computer/ computer system/any program/data/information, to require any

> person to disclose any traffic data or to orally examine any person. The CCA also provides for the search, seizure or interception of any hardware or electronic communication to aid investigations. Additionally, the Mutual Assistance in Criminal Matters Act, No. 25 of 2002, the Victim and Witnesses Protection Act, No. 4 of 2015, the Prevention of Money Laundering Act, No. 5 of 2006 (as amended by Act No. 40 of 2011) and the Financial Transactions Reporting Act No. 6 of 2006 also play a significant part in investigating and prosecuting cybercrimes. These laws help to form a legislative ecosystem which covers most aspects relating to cybercrimes.

However, the absence of a specified agency to conduct investigations into cybercrimes is a notable lacuna in Sri Lankan law. This is worsened given the lack of a robust cybersecurity law in Sri Lanka. The Cyber Security Bill, which aims to implement the national cybersecurity strategy and to prevent, mitigate and respond to cybersecurity threats, is still in the pipeline pending approval since 2019. Furthermore, though the CERTCC was established by the ICT Agency of Sri Lanka (ICTA) to protect against Sri Lanka's cyber threats (Fernando 2016), it is yet to be given the necessary powers and resources to conduct investigations on cybersecurity incidents.

Law enforcement in this area seems to predominantly be within the domain of the Sri Lanka police, which often lacks the required expertise or resources to conduct specified investigations into this area. In contrast, various other jurisdictions have specialised expert institutions to conduct quick and accurate investigations into cybercrimes and to ensure they are not repeated. The mere naming of an 'expert' in the technology field to assist the police in such criminal investigations is inadequate. The University of Colombo, School of Computing (UCSC) of Sri Lanka, has, since 2003, maintained a digital forensic laboratory (Center of Digital Forensic, CDF) which has been instrumental in assisting the police and the Criminal Investigation Department in gathering forensic evidence to prosecute cybercrime cases. It has been successful in employing several ad-hoc tools and forensic mechanisms to tackle challenging cybercrime issues. It is recommended that this unit be formally recognised as the National Investigation Centre for Computer Forensic Investigation (ISIF Asia 2010). Furthermore, it must be strengthened with additional funding and personnel in order to perform a more dominant role within the realm of cybercrime enforcement in Sri Lanka.

Conclusion

This chapter has provided a brief overview of cybercrimes and cybercrime legislation in Sri Lanka. It is observed that as far as the international efforts are concerned, Sri Lanka has completed a considerable number of actions including acceding to the Budapest Cybercrime Convention on 29 May 2015 and admitting to APCERT and FIRST (www.first.org) and carrying out APCERT Drill in 2011 (Fernando 2016). However, the Sri Lankan government still has a long way to go in this regard. Sri Lankan cybercrime laws need not only to increase their penalties but also to reinvigorate their enforcement measures to deter any future offenders. To do this, law enforcement agencies need to be provided with the necessary training and resources to effectively investigate and prosecute cybercrime cases. There is also a need to increase public awareness about cybercrime and its associated risks. This can be done through public education campaigns, digital literacy programmes and the dissemination of information through various media channels.

As noted earlier, another reason most cybercrimes go unnoticed in Sri Lanka is the lack of public awareness among the public about governing bodies on cyber security, which are mainly the CERT and the Computer Crime Investigation Division of the Sri Lankan Police. If Sri Lanka needs to prepare for the technologically advanced future, its citizens also need to be updated accordingly. This means new legislation should be introduced for cybercrimes which must be frequently amended and/or updated, and government agencies against cybercrimes should be more responsive to the needs of the larger society. Until these things are sorted out by the government, the country cannot expect development in the ICT sectors.

Notes

1 See https://www.icta.lk/who-we-are/our-role for more details (accessed on 30 January 2024).

2 See https://www.slpa.lk/ for more details (accessed on 30 January 2024).

References

Andreea Bendovschi. 2015. Cyber-attacks—Trends, Patterns and Security Countermeasures. *Procedia Economics and Finance*, 28: 24–31. Available at: https://www.sciencedirect.com/science/article/pii/S2212567115010771 (accessed on 29 December 2023).

R. Böhme and T.W. Moore. 2012. 'How Do Consumers React to Cybercrime? in *2012 eCrime Researchers Summit*, 1–12. Available at https://www.researchgate.net/publication/261038324_How_do_consumers_react_to_cybercrime (accessed on 23 December 2023).

D. Cho, S. Kim and A. Acquisti. 2012. 'Empirical Analysis of Online Anonymity and User Behaviors: The Impact of Real Name Policy', in *Proceedings of the 2012 45th Hawaii International Conference on System Sciences*, 3041–3050, Washington, DC, USA: IEEE Computer Society.

H. de Bruijn and M. Janssen. 2017. 'Building Cybersecurity Awareness: The Need for Evidence-based Framing Strategies'. *Government Information Quarterly*, 34(1): 1–7.

Jayantha Fernando. 2016. 'Cyber security & Cybercrime Strategies Sri Lankan Experience', ICTA: Sri Lanka. Available at: https://unctad.org/system/files/non-official-document/dtl_eweek2016_JFernando_en.pdf (accessed on 30 January 2024).

ISIF Asia. 2010. Cybercrime Legislation in the Asia Pacific Region. Available at: https://www.isif.asia/ (accessed on 26 December 2023).

G. Kirwan and A. Power. 2013. *Cybercrime: The Psychology of Online Offenders*. Cambridge University Press. https://doi.org/10.1017/CBO9780511843846.

M. Lagazio, N. Sherif and M. Cushman. 2014. 'A Multi-level Approach to Understanding the Impact of Cyber Crime on the Financial Sector'. *Computers and Security*, (45): 58–74. Available at: https://core.ac.uk/download/pdf/20543077.pdf (accessed on 30 January 2024).

Benedikt Lebek, Jörg Uffen, Markus Neumann, Bernd Hohler and Michael H. Breitner. 2014. 'Information Security Awareness and Behavior: A Theory-based Literature Review'. *Management Research Review*, 37 (12): 1049–1092. Available at: https://doi.org/10.1108/MRR-04-2013-0085.

Vincent LeVeque. 2006. *Information Security: A Strategic Approach*. New Jersey: Wiley.

C.H. Liao, C.W. Tsou and M.F. Huang. 2007. 'Factors Influencing the Usage of 3G Mobile Services in Taiwan'. *Online Information Review*, 31(6), 759–774. https://doi.org/10.1108/14684520710841757.

Efthymia Metalidou, Catherine Marinagi, Panagiotis Trivellas, Niclas Eberhagen, Christos Skourlas and Georgios Giannakopoulos. 2014. 'The Human Factor of Information Security: Unintentional Damage Perspective'. *Procedia - Social and Behavioral Sciences*, 147: 424–428. Available at: https://www.sciencedirect.com/science/article/pii/S1877042814040440 (accessed on 25 December 2023).

Raymond R. Panko. 2004. *Corporate Computer and Network Security*. Boston: Pearson.

K. Poireault. 2023. 'Ransomware Attack Wipes Out Sri Lankan Government Data'. Available at: https://www.infosecurity-magazine.com/news/ransomware-sri-lanka-government/ (accessed on 30 January 2024).

Hemraj Saini, Yerra Shankar Rao and T.C. Panda. 2012. 'Cyber-Crimes and Their Impacts: A Review'. *International Journal of Engineering Research and Applications*, 2 (2) Mar–Apr 2012: 202–209. Available at: https://citeseerx.ist.psu.edu/document?repid=rep1&type=pdf&doi=6b41f80de9a314af67b909b509d7119d0d29c787 (accessed on 23 December 2023).

Nanjira Sambuli. 2023. 'When the Rubber Meets the Road: Cybersecurity and Kenya's Digital Superhighway', Carnegie Endowment. Available at: https://carnegieendowment.org/2023/10/12/when-rubber-meets-road-cybersecurity-and-kenya-s-digital-superhighway-pub-90766 (accessed on 30 January 2024).

SLCERT. 2015. Cybersecurity Awareness Survey Report 2015. Available at: https://www.slcert.gov.lk/cybersecurity-awareness-survey-report-2015/ (accessed on 25 December 2023).

Duygu Solaka and Murat Topaloglua. 2015. 'The Perception Analysis of Cyber Crimes in View of Computer Science Students'. *Procedia—Social and Behavioral Sciences*, 182: 590–595.

Sri Lanka CERT. 2018. *Information and Cyber Security Strategy of Sri Lanka, 2018–2023*. Available at: https://sherloc.unodc.org/cld/uploads/res//treaties/strategies/sri_lanka/lka0001s_html/Information_and_Cyber_Security_Strategy_of_Sri_Lanka_20182023.pdf (accessed on 30 December 2023).

Statista. 2023. Internet-Sri Lanka. Available at: https://www.statista.com/outlook/co/digital-connectivity-indicators/internet/sri-lanka (accessed on 25 January 2024).

Bradley J. Strawser and Donald J. Joy. 2015. 'Cyber Security and User Responsibility: Surprising Normative Differences'. *Procedia Manufacturing*, 3: 1101–1108.

The Guardian. 2010. 'WikiLeaks Cables: Sri Lankan President Responsible for Massacre of Tamils'. Available at https://www.theguardian.com/world/2010/dec/01/wikileaks-sri-lanka-mahinda-rajapaksa (accessed on 23 December 2023).

The Guardian. 2016. 'Sri Lankan Teenager Hacks President's Website to Try to Get Exams Delayed'. Available at: https://www.theguardian.com/world/2016/aug/30/sri-lankan-teenager-hacks-presidents-website-to-try-and-get-exams-delayed (accessed on 23 December 2023).

About the Editors and Contributors

The Editors

Dipankar Sinha is Professor of Political Science and Director, Centre for Social Sciences and Humanities, University of Calcutta. He is also Honorary Associate of the Centre for Media History, Macquarie University and Nominated Member, Association of Global Studies (formerly Association of Third World Studies), USA. Sinha has been engaged in postgraduate teaching and research for the last three decades. He also acts as advisor in various academic, governmental, and semi non-governmental, corporate and civil society organisations. Sinha has authored several volumes and a number of articles on the interface of development, communication and media. His books include *The Information Game in Democracy* (Routledge 2018), *The Social Sciences in a Global Age: Decoding Knowledge Politics* (Routledge 2021) and *Pandemic, Governance and Communication: The Curious Case of COVID-19* (Routledge 2022).

Samir Sharma is Head and Assistant Professor in the Department of Political Science at St. Joseph's College, North Point, Darjeeling, India. He was awarded the Order of Merit by the University of Calcutta in 2007 for graduating first-class-first from St. Xavier's College. He has a PhD from the Centre for Political Studies (CPS) at Jawaharlal Nehru University, New Delhi, and a post-graduate diploma from the Institute of Federalism at the University of Fribourg, Switzerland. Samir is also Associate Fellow at the Centre for Multilevel Federalism (CMF), Institute of Social Sciences, Delhi. Previously, he has worked with the Institute of Chinese Studies (ICS), Delhi and was a member of the 'Indian Think-Tank Delegation' to the China Foreign Affairs University (CFAU), Fudan and Sichuan universities on themes that included regional security international economy and finance. Apart from his interest in digital and virtual landscapes, his research area covers China Studies and federalism.

The Contributors

Bishal Rai is Head and Assistant Professor in the Department of Economics, St. Joseph's College, North Point, Darjeeling, India. His teaching and research interests focus on development economics, regional economics, education and health, human capital and econometric analysis. He has published papers in journals and various edited volumes. His most recent publication is titled 'A Critique of Gender Inequality: Study of Education and Health in the North Bengal Region' (Emerald Publishing 2023).

Jigme Yeshe Lama is Assistant Professor at the University of Calcutta, India, in the Department of Political Science. He has a PhD from the Centre for East Asian Studies, School for International Studies (SIS), Jawaharlal Nehru University, Delhi, and has participated in the '2012 Taiwan Study Camp for Future Leaders from South Asia'organised by the Ministry of Foreign Affairs, Republic of China (Taiwan). In 2015, he was awarded the Mira Sinha Bhattachejea Award for best paper by the Institute of Chinese Studies (ICS), New Delhi, India. He also edited the book *Changes on the Roof of the World: Reflection on Tibet* (Pentagon Press) in 2016. His research interest covers culture in theories of international relations, Himalayan studies, Chinese domestic politics, Tibet and postcolonial studies.

Kaustubh Deka teaches at the Department of Political Science, Dibrugarh University, Assam. He was formerly at the Centre for North East Studies and Policy Research, Jamia Milia Islamia, New Delhi. He holds a PhD from the Centre for Political Studies, School of Social Science, Jawaharlal Nehru University, New Delhi. He has also been a fellow at the Hindu Centre for Politics and Public Policy, Chennai, where he researched the issues of youth activism and political participation in the context of India's Northeast. His academic interests cover aspects of borderland studies, ecological politics in Northeast India, as well as trends in youth activism and new forms of politics in the northeast region. His recent publications include 'Youth activism' in the *Routledge Companion to Northeast India*, edited by J.J.P. Wouters and T.B. Subba (Routledge, 2023).

Nischal Regmi is faculty and the Head of the Department of Computer and IT Engineering, Everest Engineering College, Nepal. He has been working in the engineering education sector for more than a decade and a half and as a researcher in the NGO sector for six years. He has a Masters in Computer Science from Tribhuvan University, Nepal. As an academic, he has a broad interest in understanding how society and technology interact with each other. In his research, Regmi mostly resorts to the techniques of computational sciences for explicating patterns from complex data along with tackling diverse themes like social media use by non-profits, digital inequality, internet policies and energy demand of ICT infrastructure.

Nisha Tamang is Assistant Professor of Geography at Darjeeling Government College, Darjeeling, India and life member of The Geographical Society of India, Kolkata. She has a keen interest in studying demography, urban and environmental issues that manifestin her research papers. She has published papers on environmental issues especially related to urban solid waste. Her work, 'Societal Perception and Attitudes towards Domestic Solid Waste Practices in Darjeeling Municipality, West Bengal', was published in June 2021 in the *Journal of Oriental Research Madras*. She has recently participated at the International Conference on Emerging Issues in Environment, Livelihood and Development: A Future Roadmap towards Sustainable Future organized at the University of North Bengal and sponsored by the Ministry of Earth Sciences, Government of India in January 2024.

Preeksha Malhotra is an independent media researcher and journalist based in India. She holds a key interest in the themes of media governance, media culture and mis/disinformation in South Asia. She works towards understanding how we can build a more trustworthy media ecosystem to encourage communication across stakeholders to garner greater participation of citizens in a democracy.

Rahul Ganguly is a doctoral student at the Department of Humanities and Social Science, Indian Institute of Technology Delhi. He is working on the relationship between urbanism, ethnic identity and development in Darjeeling and Kalimpong (India). His research interests include urban sociology, political sociology and ethnicity. His chapter on land and belonging in urban Darjeeling is forthcoming in the Eastern Himalayan Series (Rachana, 2024).

Ratan Kumar Roy, PhD, is Assistant Professor of the School of General Education at BRAC University, Dhaka, Bangladesh. He worked as a Research Fellow at the Centre for Culture, Media & Governance, Jamia Millia Islamia (JMI), New Delhi, India. He was trained in Anthropology and Sociology at the University of Dhaka and the South Asian University and has worked as a television journalist in Bangladesh. His major publications include *Television in Bangladesh—News and Audiences* (Routledge 2021), *Korean Wave in South Asia—Transcultural Flow, Fandom and Identity* (Palgrave MacMillan 2022), *Seeing South Asia: Visuals Beyond Borders* (co-editor, Routledge 2022) and *Television Publics in South Asia* (Routledge 2023). He is the Director of the International Research Center at SIMEC Institute of Technology, Dhaka.

Rizvan Saeed is a communication scholar and development consultant currently pursuing a Ph.D. in Health Communication from Ohio University, USA. He has worked with the United Nations Population Fund (UNFPA) as an advisor on gender mainstreaming in Punjab, Pakistan. His research interests include digital communication, stigma, health communication and masculinities.

Sathya Gunawardana is an LLM Candidate at the George Washington University Law School at Washington DC (USA). Her current areas of specialisation include Corporate and Business law and financial regulation. Previously she worked as an Assistant Lecturer attached to the Faculty of Management Studies and Commerce, University of Sri Jayawardenepura, Sri Lanka and as a Research Officer attached to the Supreme Court of Sri Lanka. Sathya has completed her Bachelor of Law from the University of Colombo, and is a member of the Bar Association of Sri Lanka.

Shailesh B. Pandey is Professor of Computer Engineering and Head, Research Management Cell, at Everest Engineering College (EEC), Kathmandu, Nepal. He received his PhD in computer science with an emphasis on natural language processing from the University of York, UK. His research interests lie in the broad areas of artificial intelligence, natural language processing and technology and society. He joined EEC after spending six years working at Martin Chautari, a leading research institute in Nepal. There, he was primarily responsible for conceiving, designing and executing two multi-year Ford Foundation-supported projects on key aspects related to the potential of internet and internet-based technologies in Nepal. He also works as a consultant/researcher for artificial intelligence and engineering-related projects in the technology companies in Nepal.

Tshumila Lama is Assistant Professor of Political Science at Raja Rammohun Roy Mahavidyalaya, Hooghly district, West Bengal (India). She completed her Bachelor (Honours) in Political Science in 2018 from St Joseph's College, Darjeeling, and Masters in Political Science in 2020 from the University of North Bengal. She cleared UGC-NET in December 2018 and UGC NET-JRF in December 2019 and is currently pursuing her PhD in Political Science from the University of North Bengal. Her research interests include electoral studies, political parties, regional politics and religion and politics.

Vinsuka Kannangara is a law scholar at the University of West London and is also an ambassador for UK and US firms. He is also PR manager at the Scholars Guild, Sri Lanka.

Vishaka Suriyabandara is a Professor in the Department of Political Science at the University of Sri Jayewardenapura, Sri Lanka and an attorney-at-law. She has written on themes of cyberbullying and domestic violence in Sri Lanka.

Index